The Classical Upaniṣads

GUIDES TO SACRED TEXTS

THE DAODE JING: A GUIDE
Livia Kohn

THE RIGVEDA: A GUIDE
Stephanie Jamison and Joel Brereton

THE BOOK OF COMMON PRAYER: A GUIDE
Charles Hefling

THE ANNALECTS: A GUIDE
Erin M. Cline

THE NEW TESTAMENT: A GUIDE
Donald Senior, C.P.

THE YIJING: A GUIDE
Joseph Adler

THE BUDDHIST TANTRAS: A GUIDE
David B. Gray

THE CLASSICAL UPANIṢADS: A GUIDE
Signe Cohen

The Classical Upaniṣads

A Guide

SIGNE COHEN

OXFORD
UNIVERSITY PRESS

OXFORD
UNIVERSITY PRESS

Oxford University Press is a department of the University of Oxford. It furthers the University's objective of excellence in research, scholarship, and education by publishing worldwide. Oxford is a registered trade mark of Oxford University Press in the UK and certain other countries.

Published in the United States of America by Oxford University Press
198 Madison Avenue, New York, NY 10016, United States of America.

© Oxford University Press 2024

All rights reserved. No part of this publication may be reproduced, stored in a retrieval system, or transmitted, in any form or by any means, without the prior permission in writing of Oxford University Press, or as expressly permitted by law, by license, or under terms agreed with the appropriate reproduction rights organization. Inquiries concerning reproduction outside the scope of the above should be sent to the Rights Department, Oxford University Press, at the address above.

You must not circulate this work in any other form
and you must impose this same condition on any acquirer.

Library of Congress Cataloging-in-Publication Data
Names: Cohen, Signe, author.
Title: The classical Upaniṣads : a guide / Signe Cohen.
Description: 1. | New York : Oxford University Press, 2024. |
Series: Guides to sacred texts | Includes bibliographical references and index.
Identifiers: LCCN 2023040830 (print) | LCCN 2023040831 (ebook) |
ISBN 9780197654163 (paperback) | ISBN 9780197654156 (hardback) |
ISBN 9780197654187 (epub)
Subjects: LCSH: Upanishads—Criticism, interpretation, etc.
Classification: LCC BL1124.56 .C66 2024 (print) | LCC BL1124.56 (ebook) |
DDC 294.5/9218—dc23/eng/20231023
LC record available at https://lccn.loc.gov/2023040830
LC ebook record available at https://lccn.loc.gov/2023040831

DOI: 10.1093/oso/9780197654156.001.0001

Paperback printed by Marquis Book Printing, Canada
Hardback printed by Bridgeport National Bindery, Inc., United States of America

MIX
Paper from responsible sources
FSC® C103567
FSC www.fsc.org

*This book is dedicated with gratitude to my Sanskrit teachers,
Georg von Simson, Jens Braarvig, Ludo Rocher, Wilhelm Halbfass,
and George Cardona, as well as to my own Sanskrit students,
past, present, and future.*

Contents

Guides to Sacred Texts

What is a sacred text? The *Oxford English Dictionary* offers a definition of "sacred" as "Set apart for or dedicated to some religious purpose, and hence entitled to veneration or religious respect." The definition is necessarily vague. What does it mean to be "set apart?" What constitutes a "religious purpose?" How formal is "veneration?" Does minimal "religious respect" qualify? The sphere of meanings surrounding the word "sacred" will depend on the religion involved. For that reason, "sacred texts" in this series is a term conceived broadly. All of the texts covered by this series have held special regard—they have been "set apart"—in a religion either ancient or modern. Such texts are generally accorded more serious attention than other religious documents. In some cases the texts may be believed to be the words of a deity. In other cases the texts may be part of an atheistic religion. This breadth of application indicates the rationale behind Guides to Sacred Texts.

This series offers brief, accessible introductions to sacred texts, written by experts upon them. While allowing for the individuality of each text, the series follows a basic format of introducing the text in terms of its dates of composition, traditions of authorship and assessment of those traditions, the extent of the text, and the issues raised by the text. For scripture that continues to be utilized, those issues will likely continue to generate controversy and discussion among adherents to the text. For texts from religions no longer practiced, the issues may well continue to address concerns of the present day, despite the antiquity of the scripture. These volumes are useful for introducing sacred writings from around the world to readers wanting to learn what these sacred texts are.

A Guide to Pronouncing Sanskrit

This book uses the International Alphabet of Sanskrit Transliteration (IAST), a commonly used system for rendering Sanskrit words into English.

Vowels

a – like the vowel in English "cup"
ā – like **a**, but twice as long
i – like the vowel in English "stick"
ī – like **i**, but twice as long
u – like the vowel in English "shook"
ū – pronounced like u, but twice as long
ṛ – the letter r functioning as a vowel. It was likely pronounced like a Spanish r in classical Sanskrit, but is today often pronounced "ri"
e – like the vowel in English "send" but twice as long
ai – like the vowel in English "hike"
o – like the vowel in English "hot" but twice as long
au – like the second vowel in English "about"

Consonants

k – like English k
kh – like English k with a strong breath sound following it ("bric**k h**ouse")
g – like English g in "goat"
gh – like English g in "goat" with a strong breath sound following it ("lo**g h**ouse")
ṅ – like "ng" in English "sing"

c – like "ch" in English "chicken"

ch – like "ch" in English "chicken" with a strong breath sound following it ("tha**tch h**ouse")

j – like English j in "joker"

jh – like English j in "joker" with a strong breath sound following it ("lo**dge h**ouse")

ñ – like English "ny" in "canyon"

ṭ – like English t, but with the tongue curled back farther toward the roof of the mouth

ṭh – like English t, but with the tongue curled back farther toward the roof of the mouth with a strong breath sound following it

ḍ – like English d, but with the tongue curled back farther toward the roof of the mouth

ḍh – like English d, but with the tongue curled back farther toward the roof of the mouth with a strong breath sound following it

ṇ – like English n, but with the tongue curled back farther toward the roof of the mouth

t – like English t

th – like English t with a strong breath sound following it (like "po**th**ole," not like "th" in "both")

d – like English d

dh – like English d with a strong breath sound following it ("hea**dh**unter")

n – like English n

p – like English p

ph – like English p with a strong breath sound following it (like "cu**ph**older," not like "ph" in "photo")

b – like English b

bh – like English b with a strong breath sound following it ("a**bh**or")

m – like English m

y – like English y in "yellow"

r – like Spanish r

l – like English l

v – pronounced halfway between English v and English w

ś – like English "sh"

ṣ – like English "sh" but with the tongue curled back farther toward the roof of the mouth

s – like English s

h – like English h

ṃ – either like English m or like a nasalization of the preceding vowel (like the "n" in French "bon")

ḥ – like English h

1
Introduction

What Are the Upaniṣads?

The Upaniṣads are philosophical and religious texts, composed in Sanskrit from the eighth century BCE onward, that focus on the identify between a person's inner self, *ātman*, and a cosmic divine force, *brahman*. According to the Upaniṣads, the knowledge of this mystical identity can lead to immortality and liberation from rebirth.

There are several hundred texts called "Upaniṣads." The late medieval *Muktikā Upaniṣad* contains a list of 108 Upaniṣads (including the *Muktikā* itself), while a 1657 translation of the Upaniṣads into Persian contains 48 Upaniṣads (as well as two older Sanskrit texts that are not Upaniṣads at all). But there are also other many other texts called Upaniṣads not included in these collections, such as the seventeenth-century *Allah Upaniṣad* that identifies the inner self, *ātman*, with the God of Islam (Allah), and the late *Khristopaniṣad*, which identifies *ātman* with Christ. Other Upaniṣads identify *ātman/brahman* with the gods (Viṣṇu and Śiva and various forms of the Goddess). In total, over 200 texts called *Upaniṣad* are known to us today.

The focus of this book will be the thirteen "Classical Upaniṣads" generally regarded as the oldest ones: *Bṛhadāraṇyaka*, *Chāndogya*, *Taittirīya*, *Aitareya*, *Īśā*, *Kena*, *Kaṭha*, *Muṇḍaka*, *Śvetāśvatara*, *Māṇḍūkya*, *Praśna*, *Kauṣītaki*, and *Maitrī Upaniṣad*. These texts are many centuries older than the other Upaniṣads, and many ideas expressed in these texts are central to much of later Indian thought. This does not mean, however, that these Upaniṣads contain a unified

The Classical Upaniṣads. Signe Cohen, Oxford University Press. © Oxford University Press 2024.
DOI: 10.1093/oso/9780197654156.003.0001

system of thought; rather, they are varied explorations into the nature of reality. There is no cohesive "philosophy of the Upaniṣads"; the texts are teeming with colorful characters who make many and often contradictory observations on the nature of the self and the world. Not only does each Upaniṣad contain ideas at odds with those of other texts; parts of a text may contain ideas at odds with other passages in the same text. Although later commentators attempted to build coherent philosophical systems on these texts, the older Upaniṣads themselves are not systematic; rather, they are exuberant wanderings through varied ideas and images, drawing on the languages of metaphor and myth.

What does the word *upaniṣad* mean? *Upaniṣad* is a feminine noun in Sanskrit, derived from the verb *sad*, which means "to sit," with the preverbs *upa-* ("near") and *ni-* ("down"). *Upaniṣad* is therefore often translated as "sitting down near (the feet of a teacher)" and thought to be related to the ancient Indian practice of a student sitting at the teacher's feet to receive their wisdom. The transmission of teachings from teachers to students is central in the texts called Upaniṣads. But teachers and students also play significant parts in many other ancient Sanskrit texts, so it is not clear why these particular late Vedic texts would be characterized as the teachings received while sitting at a teacher's feet. Some scholars have proposed alternative explanations for the term *upaniṣad*, such as "secret doctrine" (Deussen 1919, 15), "hidden connection" (Olivelle 1998), "two things being placed in relation to each other" (Gren-Eklund 1984, 117), "effective power" (Falk 1986, 80–97), or "formula of magical equivalence" (Witzel 2004, xliii).

The word *upaniṣad* first occurs in the late Vedic ritual text *Śatapatha Brāhmaṇa* (10.4.5.1) in the sense of a "secret teaching," here referring to the esoteric teaching about the deeper meaning of the complex fire ritual called *agnicayana*. In this context, it is clear that *upaniṣad* is not yet a literary genre, but rather an esoteric doctrine. This meaning of *upaniṣad* as "secret doctrine" is also reflected in the oldest text given the title Upaniṣad, the *Bṛhadāraṇyaka*

Upaniṣad (2.1.20), where the term *upaniṣad* is explained as *satyasya satya*, "the real behind the real," a gloss that recalls the meaning of the term in the *Śatapatha Brāhmaṇa*. This interpretation of *upaniṣad* as a secret teaching is also reflected in the subtitle of the first translation of the Upaniṣads into a European language. The French scholar Abraham Hyacinthe Anquetil-Duperron (1731–1805), who translated the Upaniṣads into Latin from Persian, gave his book the subtitle *Secretum tegendum* (Latin for "a protected secret"), which was his translation of the term *upaniṣad* itself.

It is possible to interpret the term *upaniṣad* quite literally as "that which lies beneath," which may be connected to the texts' preoccupation with discovering the deepest, ultimate reality that lies beneath all the shifting forms of the visible world. While the texts called Upaniṣads introduce many new and groundbreaking ideas into the Indian intellectual tradition, such as *karma*, reincarnation, and liberation through knowledge, they also contain traces of earlier ritual ways of thinking about the world. But while earlier texts, such as the ritual Brāhmaṇas, were concerned with knowing the most minute detail of how to perform a sacrifice, the oldest Upaniṣads turn their attention toward the inner meaning of sacrificial action, the deeper truths underneath the surface.

The Upaniṣads as a Genre

Who composed the Upaniṣads? The texts are in all likelihood the literary products of scholarly collectives, rather than individual authors. The oldest Upaniṣads, like the older Vedic texts before them, were transmitted orally within closed groups of Brahman priests who were trained religious specialists. These schools of transmission are called *śākhās*, "branches" or "schools." Each *śākhā* is responsible for the accurate oral transmission of one of the Vedas, the oldest textual collections of India (originally the *Ṛgveda*, *Yajurveda*, and the *Sāmaveda*; later *Atharvaveda śākhās* also sprung up; see chapter 2). The late Vedic *Caraṇavyūha* by Śaunaka lists all the known *śākhās* at the time. This list includes five schools of the *Ṛgveda*, forty-four schools of the *Yajurveda*, twelve of the *Sāmaveda*, and nine of the *Atharvaveda*. Many of these schools are now only known by name, while others have become extinct. A few still exist today; the *Mādhyaṃdina* school of the *White Yajurveda* is still popular in North India, the *Kāṇva* school of the *White Yajurveda* is kept alive by Kannada-speaking Brahmans in Karnataka in southwestern India, the *Taittirīya* school of the *Black Yajurveda* is present in South India, and the *Jaiminīya* school of the *Sāmaveda* is found among Nambudiri Brahmans in Tamilnadu in South India.

Over time, each *śākhā* began adding different texts to the oldest textual collection (*Saṃhitā*) that they transmitted: ritual texts called Brāhmaṇas, Āraṇyakas devoted to particularly dangerous or esoteric rites, and eventually Upaniṣads that explained the connection between a person's inner self (*ātman*) and the cosmic force (*brahman*). Many Upaniṣads are formally affiliated with a particular Veda, such as the *Ṛgveda* or the *Black Yajurveda*. This is not merely an arbitrary classification, but a statement of origin: the Upaniṣad originated within the scholarly and priestly communities that were responsible for transmitting that particular Veda. The Upaniṣads emerged as the intellectual products, not of individuals, but of schools of intellectuals who had specialized in one particular ancient Vedic textual collection. Thus, the *Aitareya* and *Kauṣītaki Upaniṣad* were composed by priests who specialized in the transmission of the *Ṛgveda*, the *Taittirīya*, *Kaṭha*, and *Śvetāśvatara Upaniṣad* by specialists in the *Black Yajurveda* (a version of the text that includes commentary), the *Bṛhadāraṇyaka* and *Īśā Upaniṣad* by specialists in the *White Yajurveda* (the version without embedded commentary), the *Chāndogya* and *Kena Upaniṣad* by specialists in the *Sāmaveda*, and the *Muṇḍaka*, *Praśna*, and *Māṇḍūkya Upaniṣad* by priests trained in the tradition of the *Atharvaveda*.

Each *śākhā* must have regarded the texts they transmitted and composed as their own collective property, as indicated by the frequent warnings in the Upaniṣads against teaching the text to someone who is not one's son or student:

> So a father should teach this formulation of truth only to his oldest son or to a worthy student, and never to anybody else, even if he were to offer him this whole earth surrounded by waters and full of wealth, for this formulation is greater than all those things! (*Chāndogya Upaniṣad* 3.11.5)

> This highest secret was proclaimed in a former age in the Vedānta. One would not reveal it to someone who does not have a calm disposition, or to one who is not one's son or student. (*Śvetāśvatara Upaniṣad* 6.22)

Over time, however, Upaniṣads were gradually detached from their Vedic *śākhās* and began to assume a life of their own. By the time Śaṅkara composed his commentaries to ten (or eleven, if we accept his commentary on the *Śvetāśvatara* as genuine) of the oldest Upaniṣads in the eighth century, the *śākhā* affiliation of an Upaniṣad had become a mere formality, an archaic remnant from a former age.

Later Upaniṣads, such as the medieval Upaniṣads devoted to gods like Śiva, Viṣṇu, or the Goddess or to the practice of Yoga or the renunciation of all worldly goods, still claim *śākhā* affiliations, but at this point, these associations with particular Vedas no longer tell us anything about the texts' authorship. Instead, these later Upaniṣads were composed by people who felt a strong affection for a particular deity, or by groups who embraced a specific lifestyle. Interestingly enough, even the later Upaniṣads are still anonymous. The ideas they promote are far more important than their authorship.

In the oldest Upaniṣads, the concerns of the *śākhā* that composed it still resonate throughout the texts. The *Ṛgveda Saṃhitā* consists of hymns to the various Vedic deities, the *Sāmaveda Saṃhitā* of chants to be sung during the Vedic rituals, and the *Yajurveda Saṃhitā* of sacrificial formulas and specific instructions for how to perform the elaborate Vedic rites. The *hotṛ*, or *Ṛgveda* priest, was in charge of invoking the gods during the Vedic ritual; the *udgātr*, or *Sāmaveda* priest would chant; the *adhvaryu* or *Yajurveda* priest was responsible for any ritual actions—and later a fourth priest, the *brahman*, associated with the *Atharvaveda*, was in charge of supervising the ritual as a whole. This ritual specialization is reflected in the texts each type of priest transmitted in his *śākhā*, including the Upaniṣads composed within that school. The Upaniṣads of the *Ṛgveda* include more references to Vedic gods and to the creation of the world than the Upaniṣads of other *śākhās*, while the Upaniṣads of the *Sāmaveda* are preoccupied with songs and chants and sacred sounds, the Upaniṣads of the *Yajurveda* deal with actions (*karma*) and their results, and the Upaniṣads of the *Atharveveda* dwell on understanding the mysterious *brahman*. These *śākhā*-specific concerns can be seen in all the oldest Upaniṣads but are largely absent from the later Vaiṣṇava, Śaiva, Śākta, Yoga, or Saṃnyāsa Upaniṣads. These later Upaniṣads are still formally affiliated with particular *śākhās*, but the Vedic associations are no longer any indications of the text's themes; they seem to be more claims to ancient Vedic authority than anything else.

The oldest Upaniṣads are still deeply rooted in the older Vedic worldview. Although the Upaniṣads introduce significant new ideas (*ātman*, *brahman*, salvation through knowledge, *karma*, reincarnation) that are not found in the Vedas, many Vedic ideas and references to the old Vedic gods and sacrificial rituals still linger in the oldest Upaniṣads.

What are some of the characteristics of the Upaniṣads as a genre? In addition to their thematic preoccupation with *ātman* and *brahman*, there are also other features that characterize the texts that came to be identified as Upaniṣads and make them stand out from other religious and philosophical texts composed by Brahmans in ancient India.

The Upaniṣads are anonymous literature. Only one of the classical Upaniṣads, the *Śvetāśvatara Upaniṣad*, is attributed to an individual author, and even this attribution is often taken as a pious fiction. In general, the Upaniṣads are believed to be collective compositions, formulated by schools of Vedic recitation (*śākhās*), who have compiled the texts over centuries, rather than by individual authors. This form of authorship often results, as we will see, in texts that are more loosely structured than philosophical treatises authored by individuals.

The Upaniṣads often present philosophical and abstract ideas through dialogues. The dialogue partners may be teachers and students, fathers and sons, husbands and wives, kings and sages, or rival wisdom teachers. By presenting specific ideas relating to *ātman* and *brahman*, not just as abstract ideas, but as the teachings of particular authoritative teachers, the Upaniṣads illustrate an essential feature of oral societies: texts and ideas cannot exist separately from people, and new ideas are introduced by named teachers who speak them out loud, rather than by texts that are read.

The Upaniṣads are composed in late Vedic Sanskrit, a rich and grammatically complex language that is often challenging to render adequately into modern English. To complicate matters, the Upaniṣadic authors also introduce many puns and others forms of wordplay that are impossible to recreate in English; the best a modern translator can do is usually to put a lengthy footnote to explain the double meaning in the Sanskrit word or expression. But these puns are not used to add whimsy or humor to the Sanskrit text; rather, they hint at "hidden connection" between two things designated by similar terms. In previous generations, Western scholars have often complained that there is a large number of "false etymologies" in the Upaniṣads. The texts often "explain" one word in terms of another. The name of the Vedic god Indra is explained in the following way in the *Aitareya Upaniṣad*, for example: "He saw this person, the all-pervading *brahman*, and he said: 'I have seen this (*idam adarśam*).' Therefore, he is called Idandra. Idandra is his name. But cryptically, they call him who is called Idandra, *Indra*. For the gods are fond of the cryptic" (1.13–14). From the perspective of modern linguistic scholarship, the text's etymology of *Indra* is incorrect; the name is not at all derived from "this" (*idam*) and some form of the verb "to see" (*dṛś*). But the Upaniṣadic authors were not composing a treatise on etymology; they were composing a religious text. Ancient Indian grammar and etymology were highly developed fields, and learned authors certainly knew that the name Indra was not derived from the verb "to see." But the point of this textual passage is not to make a claim about the historical etymology of a divine name, but rather to express a significant truth about the Vedic god Indra himself. Indra is often regarded as a paradigmatic wisdom seeker in the Upaniṣads, and connecting his name to the perception of the highest reality of *brahman* therefore makes perfect theological sense. While it is not accurate that "Indra" is derived from the verb "to see," it is nevertheless true, from an Upaniṣadic perspective, that Indra is connected with perception of the highest reality.

How Many Upaniṣads Are There?

The medieval *Muktikā Upaniṣad* lists 108 Upaniṣads, broken down into several categories:

(1) "Principal" (*mukhya*) Upaniṣads: *Īśā*, *Bṛhadāraṇyaka*, *Kaṭha*, *Taittirīya*, *Śvetāśvatara*, *Praśna*, *Muṇḍaka*, *Māṇḍūkya*, *Kena*, *Chāndogya*, *Maitrāyaṇī* (=*Maitrī*), *Kauṣītaki*, and *Aitareya*.

(2) "General" (*sāmānya*) Upaniṣads: *Subāla*, *Māntrika*, *Nirālamba*, *Paiṅgala*, *Adhyātmā*, *Muktikā*, *Sarvasāra*, *Śukarahasya*, *Skanda*, *Śārīraka*, *Garbha*, *Ekākṣara*, *Akṣi*,

Prāṇāgnihotra, *Sūrya*, *Ātmā*, *Vajrasūcī*, *Mahā*, *Sāvitrī*, *Ātmabodha*, and *Mudgala*.

(3) "Ascetic" (*Saṃnyāsa*) Upaniṣads: *Jābāla*, *Paramahaṃsa*, *Advayatāraka*, *Bhikṣuka*, *Turīyātīta*, *Yājñavalkya*, *Śāṭyāyanīya*, *Brahma*, *Tejobindu*, *Avadhūta*, *Kaṭharudra*, *Nāradaparivrājaka*, *Parivrājaka*, *Parabrahma*, *Āruṇeya*, *Maitreya*, *Saṃnyāsa*, *Kuṇḍikā*, *and Nirvāṇa*.

(4) Yoga Upaniṣads: *Haṃsa*, *Triśikhi*, *Maṇḍalabrāhmaṇa*, *Amṛtabindu*, *Amṛtanāda*, *Kṣurikā*, *Dhyānabindu*, *Brahmavidyā*, *Yogatattva*, *Yogaśikhā*, *Yogakuṇḍalinī*, *Varāha*, *Śāṇḍilya*, *Pāśupata*, *Mahāvākya*, *Yogacūḍāmaṇi*, *Darśana*, and *Nādabindu*.

(5) Upaniṣads devoted to the Goddess (*Śākta Upaniṣads*): *Sarasvatīrahasya*, *Sītā*, *Annapūrṇā*, *Devī*, *Tripurātāpinī*, *Bhāvanā*, *Tripurā*, *Saubhāgyalakṣmī*, and *Bahvṛca*.

(6) Viṣṇu Upaniṣads (*Vaiṣṇava* Upaniṣads): *Tārasāra*, *Nārāyaṇa*, *Kalisantaraṇa*, *Nṛsiṃhatāpanī*, *Mahānārāyaṇa*, *Rāmarahasya*, *Rāmatāpanīya*, *Gopālatāpanīya*, *Kṛṣṇa*, *Hayagrīva*, *Dattātreya*, *Gāruḍa*, *Vāsudeva*, and *Avyakta*.

(7) Śiva Upaniṣads (*Śaiva* Upaniṣads): *Kaivalya*, *Kālāgnirudra*, *Dakṣiṇāmūrti*, *Rudrahṛdaya*, *Pañcabrahma*, *Atharvaśikhā*, *Bṛhajjābāla*, *Śarabha*, *Bhasma*, *Gaṇapati*, *Rudrākṣa*, *Jābāla*, and *Akṣamālikā*.

The "principal" Upaniṣads in the *Muktikā Upaniṣad* are, with two exceptions (*Maitrāyaṇī* and *Kauṣītaki*), texts to which the famous eighth-century commentator Śaṅkara composed commentaries. These "principal" Upaniṣads are often regarded as the oldest ones, and for many Hindus, these are the Upaniṣads that define the genre. There are many more texts called "Upaniṣad" than the 108 named in the *Muktikā Upaniṣad*, but it is likely that precisely 108 texts were listed because the number is sacred in India. What all these texts have in common is a preoccupation with the mystical identity between *ātman* and *brahman*. In 1965, the Indian Christian theologian Dhanjibhai Fakirbhai even published his own text under the name *Kristopanishad* ("The Upaniṣad of Christ"). While this is hardly an Upaniṣad in the traditional sense, it blends Upaniṣadic ideas with Christian theology. Fakirbhai describes the Christian God in the same way as the classical Upaniṣads characterize *ātman/brahman*, as *saccidānanda*, "being," "consciousness," and "bliss" (Fakirbhai 1965). The invocation of the genre name Upaniṣad in the title of the *Kristopanishad* and the use of Upaniṣadic rhetoric become an assertion of ancient authority.

New Types of Upaniṣads

While the earliest Upaniṣads contain little hints of theism here and there, a systematic identification of the cosmic force *brahman* or the inner *ātman* with a personal god is not encountered until the *Śvetāśvatara Upaniṣad*. In identifying the *ātman* with the god Śiva, the *Śvetāśvatara Upaniṣad* marks the beginning of a theistic trend in the Upaniṣads that continued for many centuries.

Śaiva Upaniṣads, or Upaniṣads devoted to the god Śiva, began to flourish after the composition of the *Śvetāśvatara Upaniṣad*. These Upaniṣads identify *ātman* and *brahman* with Śiva himself, or extol one of Śiva's two sons, Skanda or Gaṇeśa, as the highest reality. These Śaiva Upaniṣads, composed during a time period that began shortly after the composition of the *Śvetāśvatara Upaniṣad* and concludes around the sixteenth or seventeenth century of the Common Era, are a testament to the gradual rise of Śiva worship in India, as well as to the enduring presence of Upaniṣadic ideas.

In this time period, we also see a gradual rise of Vaiṣṇava Upaniṣads, texts that identify *ātman/brahman* with the god Viṣṇu or with one of Viṣṇu's *avatāras* (incarnations). The worship of Viṣṇu has ancient roots in Indian religion, and there are three hymns in the *Ṛgveda* (ca. 1500 BCE) devoted to Viṣṇu. In the *Ṛgveda*, Viṣṇu is depicted as a benevolent figure, possibly a sun god. He is a friend and ally of the thunder god Indra and helps him slay the chaos monster Vṛtra. Even though Viṣṇu is a minor figure in the Vedas, he becomes one of the most central gods in later Hinduism. In classical Hinduism, Viṣṇu is a cosmic protector, and he helps maintain the world through a series of *avatāras*. Mythological texts often list ten or twenty-two *avatāras* of Viṣṇu. Some of Viṣṇu's best-known and most popular incarnations include Kṛṣṇa, the warrior prince Rāma, and the Man-Lion (Nṛsiṃha). Kṛṣṇa is one of the main characters in the *Bhagavadgītā* ("The Song of the Lord," ca. third–second century BCE), perhaps the best-known Hindu text today. In the *Bhagavadgītā*, which is a part of the larger *Mahābhārata* ("Great Story of India") epic, Kṛṣṇa gives advice to the anguished warrior Arjuna on the eve of a great battle. The other great epic Sanskrit poem, the *Rāmāyaṇa* (ca. third century BCE), tells the story of Rāma's heroic struggle to rescue his kidnapped wife and slay a ten-headed demon. There are also numerous other mythological texts detailing the deeds of Viṣṇu and his incarnations. The medieval *Muktikā Upaniṣad* lists fourteen Vaiṣṇava Upaniṣads, devoted either to Viṣṇu himself or to one of his incarnations. In these texts, Viṣṇu is identified with the cosmic *brahman* and/or the inner *ātman*.

From around the twelfth century of the Common Era, a new kind of Upaniṣad began to flourish. These texts, often called Śākta Upaniṣads ("Upaniṣads of Power") or *Devī Upaniṣads* ("goddess Upaniṣads"), were devoted to goddesses, who were seen as manifestations of the cosmic power, *śakti*, and identified with *brahman* itself. There is no authoritative list of Upaniṣads that have been designated as Śākta or Devī Upaniṣads, but some of the most commonly mentioned ones include the *Sītā Upaniṣad*, the *Devī Upaniṣad*, the *Tripurā Upaniṣad*, the *Tripurātāpinī Upaniṣad*, the *Bhāvanopaniṣad*, the *Bahvṛcopaniṣad*, and the *Saubhāgyalakṣmī Upaniṣad*.

Many of the Śākta Upaniṣads contain Tantric ideas. Hindu Tantra is an esoteric tradition that focuses on the cosmic power (*śakti*) and its ritual channeling, goddess worship, *mantras* (sacred utterances), *maṇḍalas* (sacred diagrams), and occasionally transgressive ritual actions. Goddess worship, *mantras*, and *maṇḍalas* all play a significant role in the Śākta Upaniṣads. Significantly, by *calling* these texts "Upaniṣads," the authors of these texts align them with the older Upaniṣads, which are again grounded in the Vedic tradition. This appeal to the orthodox tradition serves to establish the goddess worship these texts argue for within the established and respected tradition of the classical Upaniṣads.

There are about twenty Upaniṣads that can collectively be designated as Saṃnyāsa Upaniṣads, or "Upaniṣads of Renunciation." These texts explore the idea that abandoning certain aspects of ordinary life, such as marriage, sex, having children, and living in a permanent abode, will help the renouncer is the quest for religious liberation. As Patrick Olivelle points out, however, "Saṃnyāsa Upaniṣads" is not a native Indian category, unlike such classifications as "Śaiva Upaniṣads" or "Śākta Upaniṣads," which originate in the Sanskrit tradition itself (Olivelle 1992, 5). The term "Saṃnyāsa Upaniṣad" is first used by the German Sanskrit scholar Paul Deussen in his German Upaniṣad translation from 1897. Olivelle includes an English translation of all twenty of these texts in his definitive work on the Saṃnyāsa Upaniṣads (Olivelle 1992).

The idea of renouncing the world is quite alien to the earliest Vedic religion, which instead emphasizes the importance of having many children, especially sons, and on amassing wealth through one's own efforts and the generosity of the gods. In the Vedic worldview, immortality means living on through one's children and grandchildren. The Upaniṣads' shift away from the ritual worship of the gods toward inner contemplation and knowledge is accompanied by ideas of a different form of ideal of immortality. This immortality is defined as escape from the cycle of death and rebirth (*saṃsāra*) and can be achieved through the knowledge that one's inner self (*ātman*) is identical with the cosmic divine force (*brahman*). Having a family is not at all necessary to achieve this knowledge; in fact, several of the older Upaniṣads suggest that it is better to rise above the desire to have children and lead the life of a renunciant in order to achieve liberation.

By the time of the composition of the *Dharmasūtras* ("Aphorisms on Law"), composed a few centuries after the very oldest Upaniṣads, the tension between having children to ensure one's immortality and renouncing family life to devote oneself to a quest for the ultimate truth was resolved through a compromise: the four stages of life (*puruṣārthas*). According to this doctrine, a man would pass through four different life stages after his childhood. The *Dharmasūtras* are male-centered and invariably present the default human person as male, although some of these stages could also apply to women. First, the man would be a chaste student (*brahmacārin*), devoting himself to his studies of the sacred texts. Next, he would become a married householder (*gṛhastha*), and during this stage, he would have sex with his wife and become the father of children. When the children are grown, he would move into the forest with his wife and become a forest hermit (*vanaprastha*), living a simpler life with fewer possessions, but not yet abandoning all worldly ties. The fourth and final stage is *saṃnyāsa*, or renunciation. If he reaches this stage, a man will leave his family and all his possessions behind and become a homeless beggar, devoting himself exclusively to his spiritual pursuits. Thus, a man can have a family at one point in his life, and still become a full-time ascetic later on when his family obligations have been completed.

The Saṃnyāsa Upaniṣads focus on this final life stage and describe the life of an ascetic in great detail. The date of the Saṃnyāsa Upaniṣads is difficult to determine. Sprockhoff dates the older prose Saṃnyāsa Upaniṣads to the last few centuries before the Common Era and the later verse Saṃnyāsa Upaniṣads to the medieval period. Olivelle, however, argues that even the oldest Saṃnyāsa Upaniṣads may be as late as the first centuries of the Common Era (Olivelle 1992, 5).

The *Muktikā Upaniṣad* classifies twenty texts as Yoga Upaniṣads. These texts are considerably later than the classical Upaniṣads to which Śaṅkara wrote his commentaries, and most of them appear to have been composed in the Middle Ages. While the union of *ātman* and *brahman* is still a central theme in these Upaniṣads, they also incorporate a great deal of material concerning the philosophy and practice of Yoga.

According to the system of Yoga elaborated in Patañjali's *Yogasūtras* (second–fifth century CE?), there are two eternal principles in the world, *puruṣa* and *prakṛti*. *Puruṣa* ("the person") is pure consciousness, while *prakṛti* ("nature") encompasses everything, physical and psychological, that is different from *puruṣa*. The elements that make up the physical world are parts of *prakṛti*, as are psychological factors such as a sense of self, thought, and intellect. The goal of Yoga is the liberation of *puruṣa*, which takes place when a person realizes the absolute difference between *puruṣa* and *prakṛti*. The closely affiliated Sāṃkhya school of philosophy teaches that this liberating insight can be obtained without any external aids, through knowledge (*jñāna*) alone, while the Yoga school maintains that a rigorous system of breath control, physical postures, and meditation is necessary in order to truly grasp the fundamental difference between *puruṣa* and *prakṛti*. Additionally, Yoga differs from the atheistic Sāṃkhya school in postulating that there exists an eternally liberated *puruṣa*, *Īśvara* ("The Lord"), who can play a part in the liberation of the individual. In the Yoga Upaniṣads, this deity is often identified with other popular deities, such as Viṣṇu or Śiva.

Early proto-Sāmkhya and Yoga concepts can be traced back to some of the classical Upaniṣads, such as the *Śvetāśvatara Upaniṣad*. It is even possible that Yoga itself grew out of Upaniṣadic ideas. The classical Upaniṣads do not, however, contain any sort of systematic presentation of Yoga or Sāmkhya ideas. The Yoga Upaniṣads, on the other hand, include a great deal of information that must have been derived from the *Yogasūtras*, as well as other related speculation. They represent an interesting stage in the historical development of the Upaniṣads; we can see in these texts an expansion of the genre to include new ideas and systems of thought that move far beyond the original focus on the identity of *ātman* and *brahman*. The Yoga Upaniṣads are also a valuable resource for those who want to understand the historical development of Yoga.

The Yoga Upaniṣads are, unfortunately, very difficult to date with any precision. They are composed in classical Sanskrit, without any Vedic grammatical or metrical variants, and linguistically, they can be dated to almost any time after the fifth century of the Common Era.

2
The Historical Context of the Upaniṣads

The oldest Upaniṣads were composed in India between 800 BCE and the first few centuries of the Common Era. These centuries were a time of great social and intellectual change in India. The sacred texts of the earlier Vedic period (ca. 1500–800 BCE) describe a pastoral society preoccupied with ritual veneration of deities, the herding and protection of animals, and occasional conflicts with enemy clans or cattle raiders. By the time of the Upaniṣads, however, Indian society had become more urban, trade flourished, and goods and ideas circulated over longer distances.

In the earlier Vedic society, arcane ritual knowledge had been paramount. Highly specialized Brahman priests had been the caretakers of a vast body of esoteric knowledge that was considered essential for the welfare of society and individuals. But in the period when the Upaniṣads were composed, people were beginning to ask questions about the deeper meaning behind these rituals, and about life itself. We can see in the Upaniṣads an intellectual shift away from the mastery of ritual arcana toward abstract thought and philosophy. As the old rituals were declining in importance, it became particularly important to redefine what it meant to be a Brahman priest. No longer a mere ritual specialist, a Brahman is now defined in terms of knowledge of the highest reality, the divine principle of *brahman*. As the *Muṇḍaka Upaniṣad* expresses it:

> When he sees the world as built with rituals
> A Brahman should be disgusted.

The Classical Upaniṣads. Signe Cohen, Oxford University Press. © Oxford University Press 2024.
DOI: 10.1093/oso/9780197654156.003.0002

"What's created can't create that which is uncreated."
To understand, he must go with firewood in his hands
to a teacher who knows the Vedas and is focused on *brahman*.
(1.2.12)

As we will see in this chapter, the Upaniṣads do not represent a radical rupture with earlier Vedic thought, but rather a shift in emphasis, away from the practical details of the sacrificial rituals and toward more abstract philosophical interpretations of the world.

The Vedic Background

While humans have lived on the Indian subcontinent for at least 10,000 years, the oldest preserved religious texts from India, the four Vedas, date to around 1500–1000 BCE. The people who composed the Vedas called themselves *Āryas* ("noble ones"). Although the issue of the settlement of Northern India is hotly debated (see Bryant 2004), many scholars agree that these earliest Sanskrit speakers were likely nomadic pastoralists who arrived in Northern India in the second millennium BCE from the Iranian plateau.

These speakers of Vedic Sanskrit must have come into contact with non-Sanskrit speakers in India quite early on, as evidenced by the loan words from other languages (including Old Dravidian) in Vedic Sanskrit (Bryant 2004, 86–87). Early Sanskrit texts refer to non-Sanskrit speakers as *mlecchas*, or "barbarians." The term is derived from a verb *mlech*, which means to "speak unclearly," which suggests that the Sanskrit-speakers found the language of the *mlecchas* incomprehensible. But the oldest texts do not dwell on the *mlecchas*. Rather, the culture that produced the earliest Sanskrit texts is intensely Sanskrit-centered, and there is relatively little recognition of other lands, cultures, and languages. The very term "Sanskrit" means "polished" or "refined," and the Sanskrit language itself is seen as the mark of civilization. This doesn't mean that the world described in the earliest Indian texts is a narrow one, but Sanskrit culture is always described as part of cosmic, rather than a global, context. The human world is one of several realms; the Vedic texts describe the realms of earth, atmosphere, and highest heaven, and those realms are inhabited by deities and spirits of different kinds. Many of them speak Sanskrit, although there is one example of demons (*asuras*) speaking like *mlecchas* (barbarians) because they lack the ability to pronounce Sanskrit correctly. The late Vedic text *Śatapatha Brāhmaṇa* (3.2.1.23) gives an example of the speech of the demons; while they speak sort-of-Sanskrit, they appear to speak a non-standard dialect that substitutes l for r. The authors of the text suggest that this happened because the goddess Vāc, who is the Sanskrit language personified, had abandoned the demons in favor of the gods. By implication, then, Sanskrit is a divine language, while other dialects and languages are not—and therefore much less interesting to the Sanskrit authors.

Vedic hymns also use the terms *Dāsa* and *Dāsyu* to describe the (non-Sanskrit-speaking) enemies of the Sanskrit-speaking people. The Vedic people appear to have fought battles against the *Dāsa* and *Dāsyu*, and both sides were engaged in stealing cows from one another. While several scholars have attempted to identify the *Dāsa* and *Dāsyu* with specific tribes or groups of people, they seem to represent chaos, disorder, and irreligion in general, as seen in this passage where the poet prays to the Vedic war god Indra to smash them:

> The Dasyu of non-deeds, of non-thought, the non-man whose commandments are other, is against us. You smasher of non-allies, humble the weapon of this Dāsa. (*Ṛgveda* 10.22.8, Jamison and Brereton 2014)

While many passages suggest that the *Dāsa* and *Dāsyu* were human enemies, other Vedic hymns make them out to be superhuman monsters: "Just he, the household lord, subdued the mightily roaring Dāsa, with his six eyes and three heads" (*Ṛgveda* 10.99.6, Jamison and Brereton 2014). Overall, in the Vedic hymns, the *Dāsa* and *Dāsyu* are characterized as representing everything that is antithetical to the Vedic way of life. They are "non-men" compared to the manly heroes of extolled in the Vedas, and their deeds are "non-deeds," which imply both that their actions are insignificant and that they are inappropriate. The *Dāsa* and *Dāsyu*, while they may represent actual tribes known to the Vedic people, function in the texts mainly as foils to civilized Sanskrit speakers. We know little about their culture and language; they are merely defined in the texts in opposition to the Vedic people.

The language in which the Vedas are composed is an archaic form of Sanskrit (Vedic Sanskrit) that is closely related to the language of the Iranian *Avesta*, the ancient sacred text of Zoroastrianism (ca. 1000 BCE). There are striking parallels in the names of Vedic and Avestan deities, and the Vedas and the *Avesta* even contain some of the same poetic metaphors and turns of phrase. The origins of both Vedic and Avestan language and culture can be traced back to the proto-Indo-Iranian period, perhaps some five hundred years before the composition of their oldest texts. The sacred fire (*Agni* in India, *Atar* in Iran) was central to rituals in both cultures, and both the Indians and the Iranians revered a sacred plant used in rituals (*Soma* in India, *Haoma* in Iran).

The four Vedas (*Ṛgveda*, *Yajurveda*, *Sāmaveda*, and *Atharvaveda*) are the oldest preserved texts composed in Sanskrit. The Sanskrit word *veda* means "knowledge" or "wisdom." The oldest collection of Vedic texts is the *Ṛgveda* ("the wisdom of the verses"), a little more than a thousand hymns addressed to various gods and goddesses, most of them representing aspects of nature, such as thunder, wind, sun, moon, waters, fire, and the sacred plant Soma.

The poems of the *Ṛgveda* were composed by poets called *ṛṣis*. The names of the *ṛṣis* associated with each hymn of the *Ṛgveda* are listed in the late Vedic text *Sarvānukramaṇī* (ca. fourth century BCE). Most of the listed names of Vedic poets are male, but there are also a few female names among these poets. Most of these female names are designations for abstract concepts that happen to be grammatically feminine in Sanskrit, such as Vāc ("speech") or Śraddhā "faith" (see Witzel 2009). It is therefore debated whether these feminine *ṛṣi* names refer to female poets or simply to grammatically feminine concepts that are thematically significant in the hymns in question.

The *Ṛgveda Saṃhitā* is divided into ten *maṇḍalas* ("circles"), usually referred to as "books" in English. Books 2–7 are generally regarded on linguistic grounds as the oldest core of the text. These books are often referred to as the "family books" since their poems are ascribed to specific families of *ṛṣis*. These six books are arranged in order from the shortest (book 2) to the longest (book 7). Within each *maṇḍala*, the hymns are arranged according to the deity invoked. Hymns to the fire god Agni come first, followed by hymns to the thunder god Indra, and then hymns to other deities. Within the collection of hymns to each deity, the poems are arranged from longest to shortest. The eighth book of the *Ṛgveda Saṃhitā* contains mostly hymns associated with two families of poets, the Kāṇvas and the Āṅgirasas. The ninth book consists exclusively of hymns to the sacred plant Soma, while the rest of the books of the *Ṛgveda* contain hymns to various Vedic gods and goddesses. Books 1 and 10 are generally regarded as later additions to the oldest core of the text.

After the *Ṛgveda Saṃhitā* follow the *Saṃhitās* of the three other Vedas, the *Yajurveda* ("the wisdom of the sacrificial formulas"), the *Sāmaveda* ("the wisdom of the songs"), and the *Atharvaveda* ("the wisdom of the Atharvan priests"). The *Yajurveda* is preserved in two branches, the *Kṛṣṇa* (Black) *Yajurveda* and the *Śukla* (White) *Yajurveda*. The *Kṛṣṇa Yajurveda* contains both verses and prose commentary mixed together, while the *Śukla Yajurveda* contains the verse text separately from the commentary. The *Kṛṣṇa Yajurveda* text is preserved in three versions: The *Taittirīya Saṃhitā*, the *Maitrāyaṇī Saṃhitā*, and the *Kāṭhaka Saṃhitā*. The *Śukla Yajurveda*'s text *Vājasaneyī Saṃhitā* is in turn preserved in two different recensions, *Mādhyaṃdina* and *Kāṇva*. The *Sāmaveda* is a collection of chants (*sāman*), consisting mainly of poems already found in the *Ṛgveda* but meant to be chanted rather than recited. The *Atharvaveda* is preserved in two different versions, the *Śaunaka* and the *Paippalāda* recensions. The *Atharvaveda* contains incantations for healing, attracting a lover, and so on, as well as some marriage and funeral hymns. The *Atharvaveda* is generally regarded as later than the other three Vedas, although it does contain some genuinely archaic material as well.

These four Vedas were not written down but transmitted orally from teachers to students over the generations. The earliest evidence of writing in India (except for the undeciphered writing system of the Indus Civilization, ca. 2500–1800 BCE) comes from the reign of the Buddhist king Aśoka (third century BCE). But even after the introduction of writing in India, the oral tradition flourished and was often regarded as more reliable than writing. The Vedas were not committed to writing until the twelfth century CE, since these texts were long regarded as too sacred to write down. Writing was considered a polluting activity, and the *Mahābhārata* epic (ca. 400 BCE–400 CE) even states that "those who write the Vedas go to hell" (13.24.70). The accuracy of the oral transmission of the Vedas was ensured by sophisticated memorization techniques. Each Vedic text was recited in multiple ways to ensure that it was free of errors: forward, backward, and in complex patterns of repeated syllables.

But while the Upaniṣads grow out of the earlier Vedic tradition, they also represent a new form of knowledge. *Chāndogya Upaniṣad* 7 describes a student, Nārada, who approaches the learned Sanatkumāra and asks him to be his teacher. Nārada outlines the education he has already received, which includes studying all the four Vedas, but he is still ignorant of the true nature of the self and in need of further instruction. Here, the text makes quite clear that traditional Vedic education, including memorizing the four Vedas, is ultimately insufficient compared to the insights of the Upaniṣadic teachers.

We do not know a lot about daily life in Vedic times except for what can be deduced from the Vedic texts. Religious hymns and prayers to the gods do not necessarily provide us with a great deal of information about the daily life of the people who worshipped those deities. Since the extant Vedic texts are largely composed by educated male priests, it is particularly difficult to deduce based on these sources what everyday life may have looked like for non-elite men, women, or children.

There is much we do not know about the society that produced the Vedas, but we can tell from the texts that the Vedic people were pastoral and raised cattle, sheep, goats, and horses. They also practiced some agriculture, and barley is mentioned in the texts. Vedic texts frequently mention rulers called *rājan* ("king"), although some scholars have preferred to translate the term as "chieftain." Vedic society was divided into *viś*, which may be translated "clan," and a king appears to have ruled over several clans. There are no references to permanent cities or houses in the Vedic texts, and bricks are only mentioned in the context of building non-permanent fire altars, which are demolished again at the ritual's end.

Many Vedic poems mention cows, and cattle must have been an essential part of Vedic life. Humans prayed to the gods for cows, and they compared milk to life-giving rain and butter to gold. Cattle raids seem to have been frequent, and the Vedic poets were concerned with cattle theft and finding missing cows. Horses are also often mentioned in the Vedic poems. Horses are highly valued, important for transportation—and also a good source of entertainment; betting on racing horses is mentioned several times. While poets, warriors, cow herders, and kings are mentioned most frequently in the Vedas, other professions like carpentry, chariot making, metalwork, and herbalism are mentioned as well.

Vedic society was patriarchal. The Vedic poets pray for long life, cows, and many sons, and the relationship between fathers and sons is often emphasized in the Vedic hymns. The god of fire, Agni, is compared to a benevolent father, protecting his children.

Women are mentioned less often in the Vedic poems. But we do not get the impression that women had no voice at all in Vedic society; one memorable Vedic poem (*Ṛgveda* 10.34) describes a man addicted to playing dice. Because he can't quit his gambling addiction, his wife leaves him, and his mother-in-law declares that he is as useless as an old horse. This hymn makes it quite clear that the gambler's wife has agency and makes her own life choices, and that the mother-in-law's opinions matter to the poor gambler.

One particularly interesting genre of Vedic poetry is the dialogue hymns of the *Ṛgveda*. These hymns feature two speakers who debate complex social and religious issues without coming to agreement. Some scholars have suggested that these dialogue hymns may have inspired the creation of Indian theater. One of the dialogue hymns, *Ṛgveda* 1.179, is a heated debate between a sage, Agastya, and his wife, Lopāmudrā. Agastya is engrossed in his religious practice, and as a result, he has neglected his sexual relationship with his wife. In the hymn, Lopāmudrā pleads with Agastya to give up his ascetic practices and have sex with her. Agastya argues that his religious duties must come first but suggests that Lopāmudrā too has a role to play in the religious ritual. Lopāmudrā does, however, succeed in seducing her husband. This hymn suggests that a tension between religion and family life may have played a part in Vedic society. Another tense relationship between a male and a female speaker can be seen in the dialogue hymn in *Ṛgveda* 10.95. In this dialogue, a mortal man, Purūravas, addresses his lover, the immortal Urvaśī. She is an *apsaras*, a celestial nymph, and she is about to leave him, perhaps because a human man is not the natural partner for an immortal woman, and she is going to return to her own kind. He pleads with her to stay with him, but she responds:

> What shall I do with this speech of yours? I have marched forth, like the foremost of dawns. Purūravas—go off home again. I am as hard to attain as the wind. (2)

After many unsuccessful pleas, Purūravas eventually threatens self-harm: "And if the gods' pet should fly away today, never to return, to go to the most distant distance. . . . Then he might lie in the lap of Dissolution. Then again the ravening wolves might eat him" (14), which softens her heart: "O Purūravas, don't die. Don't fly away. Don't let the unkindly wolves eat you" (15). But although a permanent relationship between the two seems impossible due to the difference in their nature, the hymn ends on a semi-hopeful note: While Purūravas must remain mortal, their son will stay with him, and he can reach a different form of immortality in heaven through ritual: "Your progeny will sacrifice to the gods with an oblation, but you will also rejoice in heaven" (18). This hymn is a lovely poetic exploration of human mortality. Could a human being ever reach the immortality represented here by the female figure of the heavenly *apsaras*? Perhaps, the poem suggests, but only in a religious and ritual sense.

In post-Vedic Brahmanical religion, society is divided into *varṇas* ("classes"): the priestly class of Brahmans, the military and ruling class called Kṣatriyas, the merchant and farmer class called Vaiśyas, and the servants called Śūdras. Although these four *varṇas* are mentioned in the creation hymn in *Ṛgveda* 10.90, there is no evidence that these groups were understood as rigid hierarchical categories in the Vedic period. The stunning creation myth in *Ṛgveda* 10.90 describes a cosmic giant, Puruṣa ("The Person"), from whose body the entire world is created, including the Brahmans, Kṣatriyas (here called *Rājanyà*, "ruler"), Vaiśyas, and Śūdras: "The Brahmin was his mouth. The ruler was made his two arms. As for his thighs—that is what the freeman was. From his two feet the servant was born" (*Ṛgveda* 10.90.12, Jamison and Brereton 2014). But even though these four main *varṇas* of later Brahmanical religion are mentioned in the Vedas and underpin the social world depicted in the Upaniṣads, several texts imply that being, say, a Brahman by birth is not enough; one must also have the correct education and knowledge to be a true Brahman (see discussion in Lindquist 2017).

A person's identity is closely related to education. Becoming an initiated student is compared to a second birth (*Atharvaveda* 11.5.3; *Śatapatha Brāhmaṇa* 11.5.4.16.). The study of the Vedas defines a man's identity: after the *upanayana* ceremony, in which a boy receives a sacred thread upon coming of age, he is allowed to study the sacred Vedas and is seen as a full social person. This initiation ritual is symbolically equated with a second birth, and he is now referred to as *dvija*, or twice-born (*Atharvaveda* 11.5; *Śatapatha Brāhmaṇa* 11.3.3, 11.5.4). This religious identity is more important than the identity bestowed upon a person at birth; it is an existential, as opposed to a biological birth.

Vedic Religion

The religion of the Vedic period recognizes multiple deities. The Vedic pantheon is particularly rich in deities associated with various aspects of nature, such as the thunder god Indra, the fire god Agni, the sacred plant Soma, the storm god Rudra, the sun god Sūrya and his female counterpart Sūryā, the wind god Vāyu, the dawn goddess Uṣas, and her sister Rātrī, the night. Many of the Vedic deities are simply named after the natural phenomenon they represent; Sūrya is the Sanskrit word for "sun," while Uṣas means "dawn" and Agni "fire." But there are also some more abstract deities among the Vedic gods: Varuṇa is the guardian of cosmic order (*ṛta*), Mitra is the god of friendships and contracts, and Vāc is the goddess of language.

The most prominent deity in the Vedic pantheon is Indra, the god of thunder and war. His weapon, the *vájra*, is frequently described in the *Ṛgveda*. In the earliest period, the *vájra* appears to have been a physical weapon such as a mace or a hammer, but later it is identified with a thunderbolt. Many hymns of the *Ṛgveda* allude to a great battle fought between Indra and his archenemy, the serpentine Vṛtra. Indra slays Vṛtra with his *vájra*, and by doing so he releases both waters and cows that have been trapped inside a mountain.

The fire god Agni also has a central place in the *Ṛgveda*. As an embodiment of the sacrificial fire, Agni is an intermediary between gods and humans. He is compared to a priest bringing the gods to earth.

There has been a great deal of speculation about the precise identity of the hallucinogenic plant called Soma. Soma is both a god and a plant in the *Ṛgveda*, as well as the name for the juice that is extracted from the plant. The Soma plant was gathered, soaked in water, and pressed, and the resulting juice was mixed with water or milk. Soma is described as invigorating and exhilarating, and it inspires poets and gives strength to warriors in battle. It also seems to have a hallucinogenic effect. There have been many different theories proposed about the precise botanical identity of the plant; suggestions have ranged from the plausible (ephedra, cannabis, mushroom, rue) to the unlikely (rhubarb). In later time periods, other non-hallucinogenic plants were substituted for Soma in ritual, and it is quite likely that the original plant was no longer available at that point.

The twin male deities called the Aśvins ("horsemen") are also prominent in the *Ṛgveda*. They are not identified by individual names, but always appear together in Vedic texts. They are both said to be the husbands of Sūryā, the sun maiden. They are benevolent deities who help people in need, including those who are drowning. They are also credited with giving a prosthetic leg made of metal to an injured mare.

One interesting group of Rigvedic deities are the Ādityas, or the sons of the goddess Aditi ("the boundless"). This group includes deities like Varuṇa, Mitra, and Aryaman, the god of hospitality, but also minor deities like Dakṣa (skill), Bhaga (good fortune), and

Aṃśa (share). Heaven (Dyaus) and Earth (Pṛthivī) are invoked as a divine father and mother in the *Ṛgveda*, but they are occasionally also called "mothers" or "sisters" as well. Although they are sometimes said to be the parents of all the gods, they do not play a very large part in the *Ṛgveda*. The Ṛbhus are a group of divine craftsmen, credited with miraculously transforming a single cup into four, with creating a chariot for the Aśvins and horses for Indra, creating a cow from scratch, and making their own aging parents young again. They are closely associated with the Soma sacrifice, and their transformation of one cup into four is tied to the Soma offerings.

Rudra, whose name means "Howler," is a minor storm god in the *Ṛgveda*. Rudra is a dangerous god who can bring disaster and disease, but he is also capable of healing those who are afflicted with illness. The Vedic poets beg Rudra not to hurt their families and children, but they also praise him as "kind" (*śiva*). Under the name Śiva, Rudra later becomes one of the main gods in the post-Vedic period. Part of Rudra's transition from an obscure and dangerous storm god to a benevolent omnipotent deity is reflected in the *Śvetāśvatara Upaniṣad*.

Another Vedic god who becomes far more prominent in the later period is the sun god Viṣṇu. Viṣṇu is only addressed in a few hymns in the *Ṛgveda*, often together with Indra. Viṣṇu's three strides are mentioned; he takes three steps that cover the entire earth, the atmosphere, and the highest heaven. This Ṛgvedic motif of the three strides, which likely represent the positions of the sun in the sky, is echoed in the later myth about Viṣṇu's incarnation as a dwarf who turns into a giant to take three steps and reclaim the universe from a demon. Like Rudra/Śiva, Viṣṇu is one of the major Hindu deities worshipped today.

The *Ṛgveda* contains mainly hymns of praise to the different Vedic deities, above all Indra, Agni, and Soma. Goddesses are less prevalent than male gods in the extant Vedic texts, but both Uṣas and Vāc are significant female figures in the Vedic pantheon. Uṣas is the dawn personified. She is described as a lovely young woman who dispels darkness and brings light and inspiration to poets.

While the Vedic gods become marginal in the Upaniṣads, they are still mentioned in some passages. Intriguingly, Indra is the Vedic god who most often makes an appearance in the Upaniṣads. But he is no longer associated with war or thunder; instead, he becomes an exemplary wisdom seeker, a student searching for the truth about *ātman* and *brahman*.

Religious rituals were a central part of life in the Vedic period. While the *mantras* of the *Ṛgveda*, *Yajurveda*, *Sāmaveda*, and *Atharvaveda* were used in rituals, we do not have a great deal of information about the ritual context. The Vedic rituals are described in far greater detail in the Brāhmaṇa texts, the prose commentaries that are attached to the Saṃhitā texts. Vedic religion did not involve temples or other permanent structures. Instead, the rites were performed on a demarcated sacrificial ground, consecrated anew for each sacrifice. The gods were not represented by images of any kind.

The most important ritual in the *Ṛgveda* is the Soma sacrifice. The simplest form of the Soma sacrifice was the rite called *agniṣṭoma* ("praise of Agni"), which was performed in a single day, but other solemn Soma sacrifices took multiple days. After initial consecration ceremonies and offerings, the Soma plant was ritually purchased from a designated "Soma seller," and the altar (*vedi*) was constructed. During the main and final day of the Soma sacrifice, Soma is pressed and offered three times, in the morning, at midday, and in the evening.

The sacred fire is central to Vedic ritual. Almost all Vedic rituals involve offering something in the fire. The *agnihotra* ("Fire Offering") ritual was a simple ceremony performed twice a day that involved pouring milk or melted butter into the fire.

Vedic rituals are divided *gṛhya* (domestic) and *śrauta* (solemn) rituals. Technically, the criterion that distinguishes a *gṛhya* ritual from a *śrauta* one is the number of fires that must be lit for the ritual. A *gṛhya* ritual only requires a single fire, while a *śrauta* ritual needs at least three (and sometimes more). The three fires required for a *śrauta* ritual are called *gārhapatya* ("belonging to the householder"), *āhavanīya* ("to be offered into"), and *dakṣiṇāgni* ("the southern fire"). All *śrauta* rituals must be preceded by a ritual lighting of these three fires, *agnyādheya* ("establishing the fires"). The more complex Vedic rituals, the *agnicayana* and the *aśvamedha* rituals, took many days to complete and demanded a full staff of ritual specialists. The *agnicayana* ("piling the fire altar") ritual involved the construction of brick altars, while the *aśvamedha* (horse sacrifice) ritual involved the ritual killing of a horse to ensure the continued power and well-being of a king. This elaborate ritual involved releasing a horse that would wander around the kingdom for a year accompanied by the king's men, followed by a month of complex rituals back at the royal court, and the final sacrifice of the horse. The entire ritual involved hundreds of people and animals and was extremely expensive. Although horse sacrifices were very rare, Vedic rituals did include other forms of animal sacrifice as well. The sacrificial animal was tied to an offering pole (*yūpa*) and then either beheaded or strangled.

While a simple *agnihotra* ritual may have been performed by a single priest, the more complex rituals required several trained professionals. The person who needed the sacrifice to be performed, called the *yajāmāna*, would pay priests to perform the ritual on his behalf. Normally, there would be at least one priest representing each of the three oldest Vedas: the *hotṛ* priest of the *Ṛgveda* would invoke the gods, the *adhvaryu* priest of the *Yajurveda* would tend to the practical details of the sacrifice, and the *udgātṛ* priest of the *Sāmaveda* would chant. There was also a fourth priest participating in the *śrauta* rituals, the *brahman*, whose responsibility it was to oversee the entire ritual and ensure that everything was done correctly. Later, the *brahman* priest came to be associated with the fourth Veda, the *Atharvaveda*, but this association seems to be secondary.

What did people in the Vedic period pray for when they addressed the gods? The focus of the Vedic hymns is on this life and this world, and the blessings the gods can give humans here and now, such as sons, grandsons, cows, and long life. Although there are a few hints of afterlife beliefs in the Vedic texts, there is no fully developed soteriology (doctrine of salvation) in these texts. Some hymns mention a legendary figure, Yama, who was the first man to die. As the first mortal, he was appointed lord of the dead, and he knows the path that others must follow to get safely to the afterlife when they die (*Ṛgveda* 10.14.2). Other hymns mention deceased ancestors, who will partake in the offerings their descendants put out for them, which suggests the existence of an ancestor cult in Vedic religion (*Ṛgveda* 10.15). The funeral fire is said to carry a dead person to the ancestors (*Ṛgveda* 10.16). But the afterlife is not described in any detail in the Vedas. The Vedic poets see death as inevitable but focus on the blessings of this life.

Vedic Philosophy

While the Vedas are mostly centered on deities and rituals, there are also some interesting philosophical speculations in them that lay the groundwork for the intellectual world of the Upaniṣads. *Ṛgveda* 10.129, a cosmogonical hymn, speculates about the creation of the world but does so by invoking abstract ontological concepts. The opening line of this hymn describes an initial undifferentiated reality beyond both being and non-being: "There was neither being nor non-being then." The second stanza suggests that this primordial state was not associated with death or time: "There was neither death not immortality then. There was no sign of night nor of day." This notion of an undifferentiated oneness recurs in the Upaniṣads, but here it is the goal rather than the starting point; *ātman/brahman* lies beyond all dualities. *Ṛgveda* 10.129 further introduces the idea that there may be truths that even the gods do not know (stanzas 6–7):

> Who truly knows it? Who shall here proclaim it? From where was it born, from where came this creation? The gods came after the creation of the world. So, who then knows from here it came? This creation, where it came from, whether it was made or not, only he knows it, who watches over the world in the highest heaven. Or maybe he doesn't know? (Jamison and Brereton 2014)

The idea that there is a limit to the knowledge of the gods themselves will be encountered again in the Upaniṣads.

A central concept in the Vedas is *ṛta* (order, truth), which is an important precursor to the concept of *dharma* in later Hinduism. *Ṛta* is both the physical and moral order of the universe; it is what makes days, nights, the seasons appear in the right order and upholds the cosmos, but it is also a moral law for humans to live by. The god Varuṇa is the guardian of *ṛta*, and as such, he punishes sinners for their transgressions. As an abstract force beyond even the gods themselves, *ṛta* also foreshadows the idea of *brahman* as a cosmic principle in the Upaniṣads.

The notion of a unifying reality between all the shifting forms of the world, so prominent in the Upaniṣads, is also foreshadowed in the Vedas. The very last hymn in the *Ṛgveda*, 10.191, is a praise to unity, suggesting that the ancient gods sit down together with their minds united as one. The idea that the gods are united into one presages the Upaniṣadic idea of *brahman* as the one divine principle beyond all the individual gods.

The most common term for time in the *Ṛgveda* is *ṛtu*, a word that is closely associated with the correct time for ritual performance. *Kāla*, which is the most commonly used term for time in the Upaniṣads, occurs only once in the *Ṛgveda*, in 10.42.9, where it also carries the sense of the correct moment for an action. Although time and ritual are often intertwined in the oldest Vedic texts, there are also passages in Vedic texts that hint at other, more complex notions of time, apart from the rhythms of the ritual calendar. When *Ṛgveda* 10.90.2 states that Puruṣa, the primordial man, is "both what has been and what will be," this suggests the existence of a higher principle that encompasses all of time, an idea that will be further developed in the Upaniṣads. While the notion of abstract time as a cosmic principle is already present in the remarkable hymns to time (*kāla*) in the *Atharvaveda* (19.53–54), which present time as the creator of all things, this idea becomes more pervasive in the Upaniṣads as well. The *Atharvaveda* also hints at the existence of two forms of time, one associated with this world and one with the highest heaven (19.53.3). The *Jaiminīya Brāhmaṇa* 1.11 similarly contrasts "whatever is on this side of the sun, night and day" with "immortality," which is located beyond the sun, which seems to imply a contrast between temporality and a different, atemporal state. For the most part, however, time in earlier Vedic literature is closely tied to the rhythms of the natural world and the performance of rituals. While these ideas are still found in the oldest Upaniṣads, several later Upaniṣadic texts elaborate on the ideas—present in germinal form in Vedic literature—of time as an abstract, cosmic power.

Macrocosmos and Microcosmos

The Upaniṣadic authors, like those of the preceding Saṃhitā and Brāhmaṇa texts, are deeply interested in the mystical connections between the cosmic/divine realm, the human realm, and the realm of ritual, which mediates between the divine and the human world (see discussion in Witzel 1997). The late Vedic *Śāṅkhāyanagṛhya sūtra* (I 1.2.3–5) states that *śruti* ("the heard" sacred text) is both *adhidaivam* (pertaining to the divine), *athādhyātmam* ("pertaining to the self"), and *adhiyajñam* ("pertaining to the sacrifice") (see discussion in Smith 2019). The Upaniṣads also frequently discuss and analyze the homologies between the macrocosm of the divine realm and the microcosm of the human body, and like the older Vedic texts, they also see both elements of the human body and elements of the larger cosmos reflected in the ritual realm as well.

From the perspective of the Vedic and Upaniṣadic authors, these three spheres of reality—the cosmic, the ritual, and the human—mirror each other, and elements of each realm have counterparts in the other two. The human body belongs to the earthly realm, but the human eye also corresponds to the fire of the ritual realm and the sun of the cosmic/divine realm. These correspondences may not be obvious to the casual observer, but when someone truly grasps the deeper structure of these three interwoven realms, they will be able to both understand and control the realms of ritual and cosmos as well as their own lived reality. Discovering these hidden connections between elements of the three realms gives a person power over all three realms, and this knowledge will aid a person in winning power, wealth, and ultimately immortality (Olivelle 1998, 24).

Such a connection between the world of the humans and the ritual and cosmic reality is called *bandhu* ("bond" or "relative"). The underlying idea is that the central elements of the human experience, such as the parts of our body, have their "relatives" in the ritual and cosmic spheres, and that these relationships, once grasped, helps us understand all of reality.

As mentioned previously in this chapter, the hymn to the cosmic person (Puruṣa) in *Ṛgveda* 10.90 describes both the cosmos and the social classes of human society as emerging from the body of a primordial human being. Similar point-by-point comparisons and identifications between parts of the body and parts of the larger universe are found in several of the classical Upaniṣads. In the opening passage of the *Bṛhadāraṇyaka Upaniṣad* (1.1), for example, the world is compared to a body, although it is here an animal, rather than a human body. Referring to the ancient horse sacrifice called *aśvamedha*, the Upaniṣad declares: "The head of the sacrificial horse is the dawn, its sight is the sun, its breath is the wind, and its open mouth is the fire common to all." But not only is this horse identified with elements of the physical world; its parts are also equated with space and time itself: the body of the sacrificial horse is equated with the year, its back with the sky, its belly with the intermediate region, its underbelly with the earth, its flanks with the quarters, its ribs with the intermediate quarters, its limbs with the seasons, its joints with the months and fortnights, and its feet with days and nights. This striking image of the universal horse, which fuses the microcosm of the animal's body with the macrocosm of space and time, sets the tone both for the *Bṛhadāraṇyaka Upaniṣad* and the other older Upaniṣads as they provide us with glimpses of the universe in the human body and of the sun in the ritual fire.

The *Bṛhadāraṇyaka Upaniṣad* ties together the larger cosmos, the world of human experience, sacred texts, different classes of beings, and social structure in 1.5.4–7. The text identifies human speech with the earth, with the verses of the *Ṛgveda*, with the gods, and with fathers. The human mind is identified with the intermediate world between heaven and earth, the formulas of the *Yajurveda*, the ancestors, and mothers. Human breath is identified with the heavenly world, the chants of the *Sāmaveda*, the humans, and children. *Bṛhadāraṇyaka Upaniṣad* 3.1.3–6 identifies the *hotṛ* priest of the *Ṛgveda* with fire and with speech, the *adhvaryu* priest of the *Yajurveda* with the sun and with sight, the *udgātṛ* priest of the *Sāmaveda* with wind and with breath, and the Brahman priest (of the *Atharvaveda*) with the moon and with the mind. But this is not just a series of poetic metaphors; in one intriguing passage, the *Bṛhadāraṇyaka Upaniṣad* describes the person's dissolution and absorption into the cosmic sphere upon death:

> When a man dies, his speech goes into the fire, his breath into the wind, his sight into the sun, his mind to the moon, his hearing to the quarters, his body to the earth, his *ātman* to space, the body hair into plants, the hair into trees, his blood and semen into water. (3.2.13)

The *Chāndogya Upaniṣad* is particularly concerned with the High Chant of the Vedic ritual, but this chant is not just a component of the ritual; it is also identified with the sun and with human breath (1.2.1–12). In this way, the entire cosmos and all human life is sacralized; every breath a human being takes is, for someone who knows correctly, both a powerful ritual chant and mystically connected with the life-giving sun.

The Taittirīya Upaniṣad identifies the fourfold mystical utterance of ritual, *bhūr*, *bhuvas*, *suvar*, and *mahas*, with the earth, the intermediate region, the heavenly world, and the sun, as well as with the fire, the wind, the sun, and the moon. But these four utterances are also equated with the verses of the *Ṛgveda*, the chants of the *Sāmaveda*, the sacrificial formulas of the *Yajurveda*, and *brahman* itself, as well as with the human outbreath, inbreath, interior breath, and food (1.5). While the details of these mystical connections vary from text to text, and even within the same text, the underlying idea that humans are closely related to the cosmos is articulated again and again in the Upaniṣads.

The knowledge of the mystical connections between the elements of the three realms is not only of theoretical interest for the curious philosopher; it is a transformative knowledge. According to *Bṛhadāraṇyaka Upaniṣad* 1.5.14, the creator god Prajāpati "is the year in sixteen parts. Fifteen parts of him are the nights, while the sixteenth part is constant. . . . A man who knows this is also the year; he is Prajāpati in sixteen parts." The knowledge of Prajāpati's mystical identification with the year, and by extension, with time itself, allows the person who possesses this knowledge to become both Prajāpati and time as well.

The Upaniṣads' View of the Vedas

How did the Upaniṣadic authors view the older Vedic texts? There is no single simple answer to this question. The oldest Upaniṣads grew out of the textual traditions of the Vedic *śākhās* and are in many way extensions of Vedic thought. But the Upaniṣads also represent a shift in orientation in the history of ideas in India, a turn away from external ritual toward internal exploration.

Several of the older Upaniṣads invoke the Vedas sources of authority. Some Upaniṣadic texts mention three Vedas (*Ṛgveda*, *Yajurveda*, *Sāmaveda*), while others add the *Atharvaveda* and refer to four Vedas. It should be noted, however, that the Upaniṣadic authors may not be referring to the canonical texts as we know them today, but rather to more loosely structured collections of verbal utterances classified as *ṛc* (verse), *yajus* (sacrificial formula), and *sāman* (chant) respectively.

But whereas the older Upaniṣads frequently challenge the authority of the Vedas, the later classical Upaniṣads regard the Vedas as a source of authority but find creative ways of redefining what the Vedas are. The *Chāndogya Upaniṣad* 1.4.2–3 relates how the gods themselves abandon the Vedas in favor of a better refuge:

> The gods were afraid of death, and they took refuge in the three Vedas. They covered (*chad*) themselves with meters. Because they covered themselves with them, the meters are called *chandas*. But Death saw them there, in the Ṛg, in the Sāman, and in the Yajus, just as one might see a fish in the water. When they [the gods] discovered this, they rose out of the Ṛg, out of the Sāman, and out of the Yajus, and they took refuge in sound. The text of the *Chāndogya Upaniṣad* then goes on to describe how the sound *oṃ* becomes the new refuge of the gods.

In the *Muṇḍaka Upaniṣad*, knowledge of the four Vedas is defined as a "lower" kind of knowledge compared to the knowledge of the imperishable syllable *oṃ* described in the Upaṇiṣads:

> He said to him: "There are two kinds of knowledge, so those who know *brahman* tell us: the higher and the lower. Of these, the

> lower is *Ṛgveda*, *Yajurveda*, *Sāmaveda*, *Atharvaveda*, phonetics, ritual, grammar, etymology, and astrology. The higher is that through which one understands the imperishable." (*Muṇḍaka Upaniṣad* 1.1.4–5)

The critique of the authority of the Vedas culminates in the late *Āruṇeya Upaniṣad*, which claims that out of all the Vedas, one should recite just the Āraṇyakas and the Upaniṣads (2). Here, the Upaniṣads have themselves become a part of the Vedic canon, more valuable than the older part.

A somewhat different view of the relationship between Vedas and Upaniṣads is encountered in *Śvetāśvatara Upaniṣad*, which suggests that the cosmic principle *brahman* is "hidden in the secret Upaniṣads of the Veda" (5.6), perhaps an echo of the passage from the *Chāndogya Upaniṣad* cited above referring to the gods hiding in the Vedas. The *Śvetāśvatara Upaniṣad* suggests that while the ultimate truth can only be found in the Upaniṣads, the Upaniṣads themselves are contained with the Vedas, constituting the "secret" part. The *Śvetāśvatara Upaniṣad* does not seek to challenge the authority of the Vedas in the same way as the *Bṛhadāraṇyaka* and *Muṇḍaka Upaniṣad* do; instead, it suggests that the Upaniṣads are the esoteric essence of the Vedas:

> The syllable (*akṣara*) of the Ṛg, that all the gods are seated on in the highest heaven—
> When one does not know that, what use is a Ṛg?
> Seated here together are those who know it. (4.8)

Here, the syllable *oṃ*, the *akṣara* of the Upaniṣads, is, as in the *Chāndogya Upaniṣad*, the ultimate space inhabited by the gods. But in the *Śvetāśvatara Upaniṣad*, *oṃ* is not the alternative textual universe the gods inhabit after they abandon the Vedas; rather *oṃ* is identified as contained within the *Ṛgveda* itself. The *Śvetāśvatara Upaniṣad* does not attempt to establish *oṃ* as a new source of authority that supersedes the Vedas, but rather as the hidden, esoteric secret already present in the Vedas themselves. In the next stanza, the words of the Vedas and the Vedic rituals become part of the material stuff from which the universe is created:

> The meters, sacrifices, rituals, observances, the past, the future, and what the Vedas say—from that the illusionist creates the whole universe. (4.9)

By regarding the Vedas as part of the primordial matter, the *Śvetāśvatara Upaniṣad* simultaneously re-establishes the authority of the Vedas challenged by earlier Upaniṣads and allows that authority to be surpassed by that of the Upaniṣads. Since the Vedas represent the first stage of creation, it is implied that a more developed form of the Vedic texts can exist. The Vedas are therefore not replaced by the Upaniṣads; they are transformed into the Upaniṣads.

The *Praśna Upaniṣad* further elaborates on the idea of *oṃ* as the distillation of all the Vedas into a single sound. The syllable *oṃ* is traditionally divided into three individual components, the sounds *a*, *u*, and *m*. The sound *a* is identified with the *Ṛgveda*, *u* with the *Yajurveda*, and *m* with the *Sāmaveda*. Together, therefore, the three Vedas form the sacred syllable *oṃ*.

> The three sounds lead to immortality when they are combined, joined together and not separated. . . . With the Ṛg verses, one obtains this world, with Yajus formulas the intermediate regions, and with Sāman chants that place which the poets describe. But with *oṃ* alone as a support will the man who knows it obtain that which is serene, the supreme which lies beyond old age and death, free from fear. (5.6–5.7)

Here, the Vedas are not inferior to the Upaniṣads; they are merely incomplete. Only when the Vedas are combined and compressed into the single syllable *oṃ* do they serve their full purpose in the process of liberation.

The idea of the Upaniṣads as the essence of the Vedas is further elaborated in the later *Muktikā Upaniṣad.* In this Vaiṣṇava Upaniṣad, the god Viṣṇu in his incarnation as the human prince Rāma explains to his devotee Hanuman that he is the creator of all the Vedas. Rāma then goes on to explain the relationship between the Vedas and the Upaniṣads: "Like oil in sesame seeds is Vedānta [the Upaniṣads] present in the Veda" (1.9).

The term *Vedānta* (literally "the end of the Vedas") is used in the later classical Upaniṣads to refer to the Upaniṣadic texts themselves. This self-referential name places the Upaniṣads themselves at the end of the Vedic tradition, suggesting that the Upaniṣads are (chronologically) the conclusion to the Vedas. But since the term *anta* can mean "essence" as well as "end," *Vedānta* also implies that the Upaniṣads are also a completion of the Vedas in a deeper sense; they are the essence and the fulfillment of the Vedas. As we will see later in this volume, the name Vedānta is also later given to a rich complex of interrelated philosophical traditions whose teachings are based on the Upaniṣads.

The Upaniṣads and Buddhism

To fully understand the historical and cultural context of the classical Upaniṣads, it is also necessary to pay attention to two religious movements that flourished in North India during the time period when some of the older Upaniṣads were likely composed: Buddhism and Jainism.

Buddhism originated around the fifth century BCE. Siddhattha Gotama, the man who later came to be called the Buddha, was born as a prince in Lumbini in what is today southern Nepal. As a young man, he left his palace life behind and became a wandering ascetic. After several years, he reached enlightenment, and was from then on known as the Buddha ("The Awakened One"). The Buddha encapsulated his spiritual insights into four simple theses, which he called "The Four Noble Truths":

(1) All this is suffering
(2) The root of suffering is desire
(3) Suffering is extinguished when desire is extinguished
(4) This is accomplished by following the eight-fold path

The eight-fold path to the extinction of suffering includes right understanding, right thought, right speech, right action, right livelihood, right effort, right mindfulness, and right concentration. An essential part of this eight-fold path, right understanding, is grasping the impermanence of all things: everything that exists will eventually cease to exist. According to the Buddha's teachings, there is nothing eternal in this world, and therefore also no such thing as an eternal self or soul. This lack of self is immensely difficult for humans to accept; we yearn for eternity and permanence and delude ourselves into thinking that we have an eternal soul, but this delusion is ultimately just another cause of suffering. Freedom from suffering can only be reached once humans realize that all things are fleeting and without any eternal substance.

Like the Upaniṣads, Buddhism claims that living beings are trapped in a cycle of death and rebirth due to their ignorance and their *karma*, and that salvation is liberation from this cycle. Unlike the Upaniṣads, however, Buddhism denies the existence of an eternal *ātman* (self) that reaches liberation; instead, the final liberation (*nirvāṇa*) in Buddhism is an experience without an experiencer.

While the Upaniṣads were composed in Sanskrit, the earliest Buddhist texts are composed in the Middle Indic dialect Pāli. While Pāli is ultimately derived from Sanskrit, its grammar and phonology are simpler, and Pāli was likely much more comprehensible than Sanskrit to ordinary people in North India at the time of the Buddha.

Geographically, the Upaniṣads must have been composed in an area not too far from where Buddhism first arose. The Buddha lived in Magadha, not too far from the Videha region where the legendary Upaniṣadic sage Yājñavalkya is said to have taught. The Buddha's first sermon took place right outside Kāśī (modern-day Varanasi), a city also mentioned in the Upaniṣads.

Scholars have often assumed that the classical Upaniṣads can be divided chronologically into two groups, pre-Buddhist and post-Buddhist. The *Bṛhadāraṇyaka* and *Chāndogya Upaniṣads* are generally considered pre-Buddhist, and the *Maitrī* post-Buddhist (but note the divergent opinion on the dating of these texts in Bronkhorst 2007). But where is the dividing line, and how would one determine the relative age of the other Upaniṣads and the earliest Buddhist texts?

The ideas of *karma* and reincarnation are taken for granted in the teachings of the Buddha, while they are presented as new and esoteric teachings in the Upaniṣads. Buddhist texts and the Upaniṣads agree that earthly existence is unsatisfying, and that human beings must seek something beyond it. But are these shared ideas evidence of direct mutual influence, or merely part of a larger shared cultural treasury of ideas that flourished in northern India in the period? Johannes Bronkhorst's study (2007) of the local culture of the Greater Magadha region, where both Buddhism and Jainism originated, suggests that some of the ideas that the Upaniṣads and Buddhism have in common originated in the local culture of the Greater Magadha region.

While they have some commonalities, the Upaniṣads and Buddhism also teach ideas that are completely at odds with one another. The idea of an eternal self, *ātman*, is central in the Upaniṣads, while the Buddha teaches that there is no such thing as an eternal self. One could even interpret Buddhism's rejection of the idea of *ātman* as a refutation of the Upaniṣads, which would suggest familiarity with Upaniṣadic teachings. The Buddha's rejection of the levels of the self in the *Dīgha Nikāya* 1.186–187 may be read as a refutation of the *Taittirīya Upaniṣad*'s doctrine of the five layers of the self. The *Dīgha Nikāya* describes "a recluse or Brahman" teaching three erroneous conceptions of the self, a self made of food, a self made of mind, and a self made of understanding, concepts that correspond exactly to three of the five forms of *ātman* described in the *Taittirīya Upaniṣad:* the self made of food, the self made of breath, the self made of mind, the self made of understanding, and the self made of bliss. Although this passage from the *Dīgha Nikāya* also shows a familiarity with other notions of self, such as a purely material one made up of the physical elements, the parallels with the *Taittirīya Upaniṣad* are nevertheless intriguing. It is possible, in spite of the Buddha's rejection of the doctrine of *ātman*, that the notion of the five-fold self in the *Taittirīya Upaniṣad* influenced the Buddhist notion of the five aggregates (*skandha/khandha)* that make up a human being: Form, sensation, sensory perception, mental formations, and consciousness. Although these five *khandhas* do not make up a self according to Buddhist doctrine, they do function together as a pseudo-*ātman* in that they make up a living being, albeit temporarily.

While some scholars have argued that the earliest Buddhism may not have been directly familiar with the Upaniṣads (see Horsch 1968), there does seem to be some evidence that the authors of the earliest Buddhist texts were influenced by the Upaniṣads, even if they did not agree with the Upaniṣadic ideas.

The parable of the chariot in the *Kaṭha Upaniṣad* 3, for example, has a parallel in the Buddhist text *Mahānāradakassapa Jātaka*, where the body is also compared to a chariot and the mind to a charioteer. There is also a parallel passage in the Pāli *Dhammapada* 17.2. The fourth century CE Buddhist text *Abhidharmamahāvibhāṣāśāstra*, which belongs to the Sarvāstivāda school of Buddhism, quotes a passage that is found in both *Śvetāśvatara Upaniṣad* 3.13 and *Kaṭha Upaniṣad* 6.17: "The inner *ātman* is in the heart of creatures, and is the size of a thumb. It is full of splendor." The *Abhidharmamahāvibhāṣāśāstra* also paraphrases *Śvetāśvatara Upaniṣad* 3.8: "We must know this person, and then we can pass beyond birth, decay, sickness, and death. There is no other path for going there."

Some of the Upaniṣadic characters reappear in the Jātaka tales of the Pāli Buddhist canon, which are narratives about the previous lives of the Buddha. The learned Uddālaka in the *Uddālaka Jātaka* may very well be based on Uddālaka Āruṇi of the Upaniṣads, while his son Śvetaketu becomes the main character of the Buddhist *Setaketu Jātaka*. While the names are different, there is also a strong resemblance between the conversation between Yājñavalkya and King Janaka in *Bṛhadāraṇyaka Upaniṣad* 4 and the conversation between the Buddha and King Ajātasattu in the Buddhist *Sāmaññaphalasutta*.

It is even possible to read the focus on awakening in Buddhism (*Buddha* means "the awakened one," and *bodhi*, one of the terms for enlightenment in Buddhism, literally means "awakening") as a mildly sarcastic response to *Māṇḍūkya Upaniṣad*'s idea of the fourth state of the self, deeper than dreamless sleep.

But Buddhism may also have influenced some of the later classical Upaniṣads; one can see some traces of Buddhist thought in the *Maitrī Upaniṣad*, for example. *Maitrī Upaniṣad* 2.4 refers to the supreme being as *nirātman* ("without a self"), a curious statement in an Upaniṣad that otherwise explains the nature of the self in detail. The use of the significant Buddhist term *śūnya* ("empty") in the same passage suggests a familiarity with Buddhist vocabulary, although the teachings of the *Maitrī Upaniṣad* are otherwise not Buddhist. There seems to be ample evidence, therefore, of some mutual interchange of ideas between the middle Upaniṣads and Buddhism. But while early Buddhist texts depict numerous debates between Buddhists and Brahmans (in which the Buddhists emerge victorious), there are no similar encounters with Buddhists described in early Brahmanical texts, including the Upaniṣads.

The Upaniṣads and Jainism

While the Jain teacher Mahāvīra is assumed to have been a slightly older contemporary of the Buddha, Jains themselves do not regard him as the founder of their religion. According to Jainism, the path to liberation from the cycle of death and rebirth has been taught by *tīrthaṅkaras* ("ford makers") or *jinas* ("conquerors"), who are omniscient teachers, since times immemorial. The twenty-fourth *jina* of this world age, Mahāvīra (literally "Great Hero"; his original given name was Vardhamāna), lived in the fifth century BCE and is usually regarded as a slightly older contemporary of the Buddha. Like the Buddha, Mahāvīra was born a prince but left his royal life behind and chose to become a wandering ascetic before attaining enlightenment. Mahāvīra is not, however, regarded as the originator of the Jain teachings, but just the last in a long line of spiritual teachers who have conveyed the same message about the path to salvation. Like the Upaniṣads and Buddhism, Jainism teaches that living beings are trapped in an endless cycle of death and rebirth, and that it is their ignorance and their accumulated *karma* that keep them in the cycle.

Jainism is divided into two major groups, Digāmbara ("dressed in the sky," i.e., naked) and Śvetāmbara ("dressed in white"). The theological differences between the two schools mainly concern the details of Mahāvīra's life story, whether women can reach liberation in this lifetime, whether monks should wear clothes or be naked, and which texts are canonical.

One of the most central religious tenets of Jainism is nonviolence, *ahiṃsā*, toward all living beings, which is defined as refraining from actions that cause unnecessary suffering to living beings. For Jain mendicants, the practice of *ahiṃsā* translates into strict vegetarianism as well as prohibitions against harming even the tiniest insect. For laypeople, there is some more leeway in this regard, as it is not always possible in the course of ordinary life to avoid harming simple, one-sensed life-forms. But even for laypeople, it is a goal to avoid harming complex life-forms such as animals and humans, and vegetarianism is the religious norm. But *ahiṃsā* is not just abstaining from physical violence toward others; hatred and a desire to harm are also contrary to the ideal of *ahiṃsā*.

Jainism teaches that all living beings have an eternal soul, called *jīva* (literally "life") or *jīvātman* ("life-self"), and that this soul is reborn until it reaches liberation, which is defined as a state of eternal bliss. The *jīva* is similar to the *ātman* of the Upaniṣads in that it is eternal and capable of reaching liberation, but a main difference between the two concepts is that there is no suggestion in Jainism (unlike some of the Upaniṣads) that all souls are ultimately one. The *jīvas* of Jainism are very much unique entities that must seek liberation for themselves, not parts of a greater cosmic whole. There are two types of *jīvas*, those that move (including humans and animals) and those that do not (including plants). The *jīva* consists of pure consciousness and is by nature both blissful and omniscient, but both the bliss and the omniscience have become obscured by *karma* and need to be recovered through the annihilation of *karma*.

A *jīva* is in Jain philosophy classified as a substance (*dravya*), and it may possess qualities such as knowledge, energy, and bliss, in varying degrees. The Jain view of life is far more expansive than what we find in other religious traditions; humans, animals, and plants are all classified as living beings, but so are rocks, raindrops, gusts of wind, and sparks of fire. Living beings are divided into four categories called *gatis*: gods, hell-beings, humans, and plants/animals. The plant and animal category is further subdivided into beings that are stationary (*sthāvara*) and those that are moving (*trasa*).

Like the Upaniṣads, Jainism teaches that ignorance is a basic problem of existence. The souls of living beings are trapped in an endless cycle of reincarnation, fueled by *karma*, and must strive for liberation from the cycle. As in the Upaniṣads, wise teachers are needed to point the way to liberation.

Intriguingly, the fifth–fourth century BCE canonical Jain text *Isibhāsiyāiṃ*, which lists wise sayings attributed to various sages, mentions several figures from the Upaniṣads. The twelfth chapter of the text lists several verses ascribed to Yājñavalkya (Jaṇṇavakka in the Middle Indic Ardhamāgadhī language of the *Isibhāsiyāiṃ*). These verses address issues such as overcoming greed and anger, and the importance of living the life of a mendicant, ideas that are very much in accordance with those of Yājñavalkya in the *Bṛhadāraṇyaka Upaniṣad* (4.4.22).

Other Upaniṣadic philosophers mentioned in the *Isibhāsiyāiṃ* include Uddālaka (Addālaa), Yama (Jama), and Nārada. While the verses ascribed to them do not correspond exactly to anything these characters utter in the Upaniṣads, their teachings about knowledge and liberation are not incompatible with Upaniṣadic ideas.

A passage from the fourth–third century BCE Śvetāmbara Jain canonical text *Sūyadaḍaṃga* (1.1.1.9) seems to be inspired by the *Chāndogya Upaniṣad*: "In the same way as one lump of clay appears in different shapes, so consciousness takes on different forms and appears as the entire world." The corresponding passage in *Chāndogya Upaniṣad* 6.1.4 is "By means of one lump of clay one can know everything made from clay, for the transformation is just an appellation and a name, but the reality is that it is just clay." It seems, therefore, that early Jainism was familiar with both characters and ideas from the older classical Upaniṣads.

3

Dating and Authorship

Dating of the Upaniṣads

Most scholarly estimates of the date of composition for the classical Upaniṣads range from around 800 BCE to 100 CE. These dates are far from certain, but simply represent best estimates based on linguistic, literary, and historical evidence. Like the older Vedic texts that preceded them, the Upaniṣads were transmitted orally from teachers to students. How can one possibly determine the date of orally transmitted texts that were only committed to writing at least a millennium after their initial composition?

First, we may look at the relationship of the Upaniṣads to other texts from ancient India. It is very clear, based on metric and linguistic evidence, the development of ideas, as well as explicit statements in the texts themselves, that the oldest Sanskrit texts are the Saṃhitās of the four Vedas (the *Ṛgveda*, *Yajurveda*, *Sāmaveda*, and *Atharvaveda*), followed by the ritual texts of the Brāhmaṇas, the esoteric Āraṇyakas, and the older Upaniṣads. But while this relative chronology between the texts is well established, an absolute chronology with fixed dates for each text is much more difficult to determine.

It is reasonable to assume, based on the development of language, metrical forms, and ideas, that the oldest Upaniṣads are at least 500 years younger than the *Ṛgveda Saṃhitā*. But the date of the *Ṛgveda Saṃhitā* itself is far from certain. The most tangible, but also most bewildering, piece of evidence for the date of the *Ṛgveda* comes from outside the Indian subcontinent. The Mitanni Treaty,

The Classical Upaniṣads. Signe Cohen, Oxford University Press. © Oxford University Press 2024.
DOI: 10.1093/oso/9780197654156.003.0003

a written military agreement between two fourteenth-century BCE kings in ancient Anatolia (today's Turkey/Syria), the Hittite king Suppiluliuma and the Mitanni king Sattiwaza, invokes several Vedic gods, including Mitra, Varuṇa, Indra, and the Nāsatyas (Aśvins). Additionally, the Hittite horse training manual of Kikkuli (also fourteenth century BCE) contains numerous early Sanskrit words relating to horses, as well as some Sanskrit numerals. In both these texts, the Indian words appear in an archaic form of Sanskrit, either slightly older than or contemporaneous with the language of the *Ṛgveda*. Although the precise historical circumstances that led to Vedic Sanskrit being used in Anatolia are far from clear, this evidence suggests a probable date of the composition of the *Ṛgveda Saṃhitā* in its current linguistic form around 1500–1200 BCE.

As mentioned in the previous chapter, the language of the *Ṛgveda* is closely related to that of the oldest attested text from Iran, the *Avesta*. Linguists assume, therefore, that the language of the Veda and that of the *Avesta* must have evolved from a common Indo-Iranian ancestor language, and that the Veda and the *Avesta* may have been composed within a few centuries of each other. But how old is the *Avesta*? That is unfortunately also a difficult question to answer with absolute precision, although the *Avesta* was written down much earlier than the Vedas. Scholarly estimates for the date of the *Avesta* vary between 1400 and 600 BCE, although more scholars favor the middle of the date range, around 1000 BCE.

Some scholars have used references to metals in the Vedas to attempt to date the texts. All four Vedas mention gold, bronze, and copper, while references to iron are only found in the *Atharvaveda*. Iron is attested in the archaeological record from India from around 1200–1000 BCE, and one could therefore speculate that the *Atharvaveda* was composed around 1000 BCE, and that the *Ṛgveda* is some centuries older. This evidence is of course merely suggestive but not conclusive in any way; it is perfectly possible for poets who are familiar with iron to compose hymns that make no mention of the metal.

In short, it seems reasonable to assume that the Vedas in their current linguistic form may date to around 1500–1000 BCE, the Brāhmaṇas and Āraṇyakas to around 900–800 BCE, and the Upaniṣads to around 800 BCE onward, but these dates are far from certain and could be off by several centuries. There is some supporting evidence for the dating of the Upaniṣads in the frequent references in these texts to kings and their courts, and to fixed dwellings. The older Upaniṣads mention the kingdoms of Kuru and Pañcāla in northeast India quite frequently. These regions correspond well to the geographical locations associated with the archaeological Northern Black Polished Ware Culture (named after a particular type of pottery), which flourished from around 700–300 BCE and is associated with growing urbanization and trade, which is quite consistent with the society described in the classical Upaniṣads.

As discussed in the previous chapter, some scholars have argued that the oldest Upaniṣads, such as the *Bṛhadāraṇyaka* and *Chāndogya*, were composed prior to the formation of Buddhism, while the *Maitrī Upaniṣad*, which seems to be one of the latest classical Upaniṣads on linguistic and conceptual grounds, seems to be familiar with Buddhism. Although the precise dating of the historical Buddha is also surrounded by controversy, most scholars accept a date of around the fifth century BCE for the beginnings of Buddhism. Buddhist sources all agree that the Buddha lived to the age of eighty, but they disagree on precisely when he lived. The so-called Ceylonese Long Chronology based on chronicles from Sri Lanka places the Buddha's life from 624 to 544 BCE. The Corrected Long Chronology uses the dates 567–487 BCE, while the Indian Short Chronology based on Indian sources as well as Tibetan and Chinese translations use the dates 448–368 BCE. The Modern Chronology has adjusted the dates of the Buddha to 563–483 BCE. How did these sources arrive at these dates for the lifetime of the Buddha? The chronicles from Sri Lanka state that the Buddha died 218 years before the consecration of the emperor Aśoka, which they date to 326 BCE. The Corrected Long Chronology accepts that 218 years passed between the death of the Buddha and the consecration of Aśoka, but notes that the Aśokan inscriptions themselves mention several contemporary Greek rulers, which would imply that the correct date for his consecration would be around 268 BCE—and that the dates of the Buddha would therefore also be later. The Indian Short Chronology, on the other hand, is based on *Vinaya* (monastic discipline) texts that place the Buddhist Council of Vaiśālī as well as Aśoka's consecration a mere 100 or 110 years after the Buddha's death. The Modern Chronology, accepted by many (but not all) modern scholars of Buddhism, is based on a slight adjustment of the Corrected Long Chronology, considering that some sources suggest that three years passed between Aśoka's ascent to power and his consecration ceremony. In other words, although the dates of the Buddha cannot be fixed with any absolute certainty, there is scholarly consensus that he likely lived around the sixth–fourth centuries BCE. The presence of some possible Buddhist-adjacent terms and ideas in the *Maitrī Upaniṣad*, which appears on linguistic grounds to be later than the *Kaṭha* or *Śvetāśvatara Upaniṣads*, may suggest a date of composition for some of the later classical Upaniṣads around the fourth–second centuries BCE. As we saw in the previous chapter, the mention of several Upaniṣadic teachers in the fifth–fourth century BCE canonical Jaina text *Isibhāsiyāiṃ* confirms that the oldest classical Upaniṣads likely originated before the fifth century BCE.

Mention must be made, however, of the alternative dating of the Upaniṣads proposed by Johannes Bronkhorst in his important and controversial book *Greater Magadha* (Bronkhorst 2007). Bronkhorst argues that there must have existed a distinct local culture in the Greater Magadha area that was separate from Vedic culture, and that Buddhism, Jainism, and Upaniṣadic thought arose out of this local Greater Magadha culture. Bronkhorst rejects the idea that the oldest Upaniṣads must have been composed prior to the beginning of Buddhism and dates the composition of the

Bṛhadāraṇyaka Upaniṣad to around 200 BCE (2007, 258–259). He proposes that the Yājñavalkya Kāṇḍa of the *Bṛhadāraṇyaka Upaniṣad* originated as an independent text, separate from the rest of the Upaniṣad. According to Bronkhorst's reading, the commentators Kātyāyana and Patañjali regard the statements of Yājñavalkya (but not Yājñavalkya himself) as contemporaneous with the grammarian Pāṇini, and Bronkhorst concludes that Kātyāyana (and Patañjali after him) must have known the Yājñavalkya Kāṇḍa of the *Bṛhadāraṇyaka Upaniṣad* as a recently composed work (2007, 238). Intriguing as this theory is, a linguistic and metrical analysis of the *Bṛhadāraṇyaka Upaniṣad* suggests a much earlier date of composition for the entire text, including the Yājñavalkya Kāṇḍa. The *Bṛhadāraṇyaka Upaniṣad* still contains significant traces of Vedic grammar (subjunctive forms, locatives without endings) and Vedic metrical variations in the verses included in the text, and these archaisms are evenly distributed throughout the text.

What is the internal chronology of the classical Upaniṣads themselves? Based on linguistic and metrical evidence, the classical Upaniṣads can be listed in roughly chronological order as follows:

(1) The *Mādhyaṃdina* recension of the *Bṛhadāraṇyaka Upaniṣad*
(2) *Chāndogya Upaniṣad*
(3) *Aitareya Upaniṣad*
(4) *Kauṣītaki Upaniṣad*
(5) The *Kāṇva* recension of the *Bṛhadāraṇyaka Upaniṣad*
(6) *Taittirīya Upaniṣad*
(7) *Īśā Upaniṣad*
(8) *Praśna Upaniṣad*
(9) *Muṇḍaka Upaniṣad*
(10) *Kaṭha Upaniṣad*
(11) *Śvetāśvatara Upaniṣad*
(12) *Kena Upaniṣad*
(13) *Maitrī Upaniṣad*

But even a relative chronology based on linguistic criteria can be flawed. As we can see from the fact that one of the two recensions of the *Bṛhadāraṇyaka Upaniṣad* appears linguistically older than the other, texts can be edited and modernized over time. It is only possible to establish a relative chronology of the Upaniṣadic texts *in the form that we now have them*, but each text may have a long history of transmission and change before it reached that form. Another complicating factor is geographical diversity. Certain linguistic phenomena, such as feminine nouns ending in -ā or -ī showing the more "modern" genitive/ablative forms in -ai, rather than the older ending -āḥ, were innovations that originated in one region and then spread to neighboring regions over the next centuries. In the case of these feminine nouns, for example, the more "modern" ending shows up in the texts of the *Taittirīya* school several centuries before their occurrence in the texts of other Vedic schools. Similarly, we know that the use of perfect tense rather than imperfect for narration is often a sign of later composition, except when the text (like the *Chāndogya Upaniṣad*) originated in the Central Eastern area. It is certainly possible to use linguistic criteria to date a particular text or textual passage, but this needs to be done with caution and with awareness of the regional and *śākhā*-specific variations in late Vedic language.

The question of dating is further complicated by the possibility that each individual Upaniṣad may not be a unified composition but may contain pieces of earlier and later text side by side. It is likely, for example, that the first chapter of the *Aitareya Upaniṣad* is older than the other two, and that the first chapter of the *Taittirīya Upaniṣad* is older than the rest of the text. Among the verse Upaniṣads, the *Muṇḍaka Upaniṣad* and the *Śvetāśvatara Upaniṣad* appear to have an older core of text composed in the 11–12-syllable *triṣṭubh-jagatī* meter, while the stanzas in the 8-syllable *anuṣṭubh-śloka* meter are likely later additions to the text. The situation is a little different for the *Kaṭha Upaniṣad*, however; in this text, both *triṣṭubh-jagatī* and *anuṣṭubh-śloka* stanzas are found side by side, but the metrical variants in the *anuṣṭubh-śloka* stanzas are more archaic and appear to be part of the oldest layer of the text along with the *triṣṭubh-jagatī* sections.

The Transmission of the Upaniṣads

The Upaniṣads were originally composed and transmitted within schools of Vedic recitation called *śākhās* (literally: "branches"; see the previous chapter).

Among the classical Upaniṣads, the *Aitareya* and *Kauṣītaki Upaniṣads* are affiliated with the *Ṛgveda*, the *Taittirīya*, *Śvetāśvatara*, and *Kaṭha Upaniṣads* with the *Black Yajurveda*, the *Bṛhadāraṇyaka* and *Īśā Upaniṣads* with the *White Yajurveda*, the *Chāndogya* and *Kena Upaniṣads* with the *Sāmaveda*, and the *Muṇḍaka*, *Praśna*, and *Māṇḍūkya Upaniṣads* with the *Atharvaveda*. The *Maitrī Upaniṣad* is usually classified as an Upaniṣad of the *Black Yajurveda*, although the late medieval *Muktikā Upaniṣad* affiliates the *Maitrī* Upaniṣad with the *Sāmaveda*, perhaps because the text contains many quotations from the *Chāndogya Upaniṣad.*

Some of the oldest Upaniṣads are still deeply embedded within older Vedic texts. The *Bṛhadāraṇyaka Upaniṣad* forms the last part of the *Śatapatha Brāhmaṇa*, while the *Chāndogya Upaniṣad* makes up the last eight of the ten chapters of the *Chāndogya Brāhmaṇa*. The *Aitareya Upaniṣad* is part of the second chapter of the *Aitareya Āraṇyaka*, the *Īśā Upaniṣad* is chapter 40 of the *Vājasaneyī Saṃhitā*, the *Kena Upaniṣad* is part of the *Jaiminīya Upaniṣad Brāhmaṇa*, and the *Taittirīya Upaniṣad* comprises the last three chapters of the *Taittirīya Āraṇyaka*. The slightly later classical Upaniṣads, such as the *Kaṭha*, *Muṇḍaka*, and *Śvetāśvatara*, are not embedded in older Vedic texts in the same way but are free-standing compositions. This gives us some insight into how the Upaniṣads likely arose as a genre: originally, Upaniṣads must have been the later, more speculative parts of the corpus transmitted by Vedic *śākhās*, but over time, these types of texts, containing teachings about the ultimate nature of reality, became an independent textual genre of their own.

Although many post-classical Upaniṣads are formally classified as texts of the *Atharvaveda* by default even if they have no connection to the *Atharvaveda* or its transmission, the affiliation of the *Muṇḍaka* and *Praśna Upaniṣads* with the *Atharvaveda* is more than a mere formality. The *Muṇḍaka Upaniṣad* ascribes knowledge of the highest *brahman* to Atharvan himself, the mythical founder of the *Atharvaveda*, while the *Praśna Upaniṣads* features Pippalāda, the legendary founder of the Paippalāda school of the *Atharvaveda*.

Upaniṣads often quote other Upaniṣads, and the intricate system of cross-referencing between Upaniṣadic texts is also informed by *śākhā* affiliations. An Upaniṣad is far more likely to quote from other texts belonging to the same *śākhā* than from those of other schools. The *Īśā Upaniṣad* quotes from the *Bṛhadāraṇyaka Upaniṣad*, another text affiliated with the *White Yajurveda*, while the *Maitrī Upaniṣad* cites from two other texts affiliated with the *Black Yajurveda*, the *Kaṭha* and the *Śvetāśvatara Upaniṣads*.

Some of the post-classical Upaniṣads, composed a millennium or more after the others discussed here, also claim Vedic affiliation, but in those cases, those *śākhā* affiliations seem to be claims to authority, rather than markers of any actual association with a Vedic *śākhā*.

Secrecy in the Upaniṣads

"The gods," declares the *Bṛhadāraṇyaka Upaniṣad* (4.2.3), "adore the cryptic and despise the overt." But this fascination with the cryptic is not limited to the gods. The Upaniṣadic texts themselves are rich in cryptic utterances, arcane *mantras*, puzzling riddles, and strict admonitions to keep the sacred knowledge of the cosmic *brahman* confidential.

Notions of secrecy, confidentiality, and concealment are central in the Upaniṣads, and these texts articulate a form of secrecy that serves to create and uphold social boundaries. Particularly interesting is what we may call the *performance of secrecy* in the Upaniṣads, or public claims that there exists a body of knowledge whose content can only be revealed to those who have authorized access. This discourse of secrecy creates closed spaces of power and authority that are inaccessible, but still visible, to the larger public.

Secrecy has occupied a central space in the Brahmanical tradition since Vedic times. The solemn Vedic *aśvamedha* (horse sacrifice) rite included a ritualized riddling contest (*brahmodya*), where contestants demonstrated their mastery of obscure knowledge by answering questions like "What is the furthest limit of the earth?" However, the winner of the *brahmodya* was always the *brahman* priest, who would kept silent, since he had knowledge of that which could not be spoken. This notion of a truth that cannot be uttered in public takes center stage in the late Vedic Upaniṣads.

A reflection of the preoccupation with secrecy in the Upaniṣads can be seen in the very name of these ancient texts. As noted in chapter 1, among the proposed meanings of the term *upaniṣad* itself is "secret doctrine." Olivelle, in his standard edition and translation of the Upaniṣads, translates the term *upaniṣad* as "hidden connection" (Olivelle 1998a). Very literally, *upaniṣad* can be translated as "that which lies beneath," a meaning that is not too far removed from the proposed idea of a "secret doctrine" or "hidden connection." Since the Upaniṣadic texts are intensely occupied with uncovering the truth about the ultimate reality that underlies all visible things, the genre name itself may reflect precisely this attentiveness to that which is hidden or secret. The Indian commentarial tradition seems to concur, as many ancient commentators on the Upaniṣads gloss the term *upaniṣad* itself as *rahasya*, or "secret."

On occasion, the word *upaniṣad* is used in the Upaniṣads themselves to refer to a secret teaching:

> Those who know this and those who do not know both perform the rituals using this syllable [*oṃ*]. But knowledge and ignorance are different. Only that which is performed with knowledge, with faith, and with an awareness of the hidden *upaniṣad* becomes truly potent. (*Chāndogya Upaniṣad* 1.1.10)

> When a man knows these hidden *upaniṣads* of the Sāman chants, speech will give him the milk which is the very milk of speech, and he will come to own and eat his own food. (*Chāndogya Upaniṣad* 1.13.4)

The Upaniṣads themselves dwell on this notion of confidential transmission of teachings, restricted to those who are granted privileged access to the sacred knowledge. When his student Ārtabhāga asks him in a public setting about what happens after death, Yājñavalkya insists on taking him aside and answering the question in private (*Bṛhadāraṇyaka Upaniṣad* 3.2.13). By pulling Ārtabhāga aside, Yājñavalkya, who is not otherwise shy about announcing his opinions on a wide range of metaphysical questions in public settings, seems to imply here that there is a certain kind of knowledge that can only be shared with a student in a private setting, rather than in the public sphere.

A similar confidential guru-disciple relationship develops between Yama, the Lord of the Dead, and the young Brahman boy Naciketas in the *Kaṭha Upaniṣad.* Yama does not initially want to reveal the mysteries of death to the young boy, but when he finally agrees to do grant his request, he speaks like a teacher addressing a student:

> Come, I will tell you this secret (*guhyam*) and eternal *brahman*, and what happens to the *ātman* when it reaches death. (*Kaṭha Upaniṣad* 5.6)

The whole story of Naciketas' encounter with Yama is itself presented in this Upaniṣad as a secret that can only be told in the right setting:

> The wise man who hears or tells
> this tale of Naciketas,
> an old tale told by Death,
> will rejoice in the world of *brahman.*
>
> If a man, pure and faithful, proclaims this highest secret (*guhyam*)
> in a gathering of Brahmans
> or at a meal for the dead (*śrāddha*),
> it will lead him to eternal life. (*Kaṭha Upaniṣad* 3.16–17)

Here, the very telling of the secret is a means to salvation, provided that the audience and the occasion are right. It should be noted that the guests present at the ritual meal for the dead (*śrāddha*) would likely consist of ritually pure Brahman males, as later described by the Sanskrit law books. The esoteric teachings Death imparts to Naciketas are not to be kept concealed from everyone, but are restricted to a worthy Brahman audience.

Other Upaniṣads suggests that the Upaniṣadic texts themselves are secrets that should only be communicated to sons and students:

> One should not disclose this to anyone who is not a son or a student. (*Bṛhadāraṇyaka Upaniṣad* 6.3.12)

> So a father should teach this formulation of truth only to his oldest son or to a worthy student, and never to anybody else, even if he were to offer him this whole earth surrounded by waters and full of wealth, for this formulation is greater than all those things! (*Chāndogya Upaniṣad* 3.11.5)

> This highest secret was proclaimed in a former age in the Vedānta. One should not reveal it to someone who does not have a calm disposition, or to one who is not one's son or student. (*Śvetāśvatara Upaniṣad* 6.22)

> Here is the truth that the seer Aṅgiras proclaimed of old. A man who has not performed the vow may not learn it. (*Muṇḍaka Upaniṣad* 3.2.11)

> This most mysterious secret shall be imparted to no one who is not a son or a student, or who has not yet attained tranquility. (*Maitrī Upaniṣad* 6.29)

> But if a woman or a *śūdra* learns the *Savitṛ* formula, the *Lakṣmī* formula, or the *Praṇava*, they all go downward [i.e., to hell] after death. Therefore, let these never be communicated to such people! If anyone communicates these to them, they and their teachers will all go downward after death. (*Nṛsiṃha Upaniṣad* 1.3)

Passages like the ones cited above suggest that the Upaniṣadic texts and their ideas were regarded as the property of the *śākhās* that transmitted them, and that the texts should not be made accessible to outsiders. In spite of these references to the Upaniṣadic doctrines as secret, there is plenty of evidence, such as quotations that wander across *śākhā* boundaries, that the Upaniṣads were known outside the traditions of recitation that transmitted the texts orally from teachers to students. Since individual Upaniṣads frequently refute the ideas of texts that belong to rival schools of transmission, we must assume that the Upaniṣadic authors also had some familiarity with the teachings of other schools. This implies that the Upaniṣadic teachings were probably kept much less secret than some of the passages quoted above would suggest. The admonitions to secrecy are, perhaps, better read as claims to ownership and authority over the texts and their teachings, rather than historical evidence for the absolute inaccessibility of the texts to anyone outside a privileged group. I would argue that the Upaniṣads are less about specific secrets than about secrecy itself. Secrecy creates boundaries; knowledge is only accessible to those within the group. Secrecy is therefore an important factor in the creation of social identity and in maintaining a group's prestige. Secrecy draws its power precisely from deliberately calling attention to itself, and separating those who know the secret from those who do not.

As we know from the study of religious groups that invoke secrecy, such as Greek mystery religions and the Freemasons, the function of a code of secrecy is not merely to keep certain ideas away from the public eye, but also to create a sense of community between the initiates and to elevate the social status of the initiated ("those in the know") in the eyes of others. Through secrecy a sense of community is imparted to the members of the *śākhā* that transmits an Upaniṣadic text, and a sense of the authority of the tradition is communicated to those who are not members.

True knowledge is only accessible to a select few who are worthy of seeing the mysteries, and imagery of concealment reinforces the inaccessible nature of that elusive secret:

> The Ancient One [the *ātman*, or Self] who is difficult to see,
> wrapped in secrecy (*gūḍha*), hidden in a cave (*guhā*),
> residing within impenetrable depth. (*Kaṭha Upaniṣad* 2.12)

The vocabulary of secrecy and concealment in the Upaniṣads involves a playful exploration of the many Sanskrit words derived from the verbal root *guh* ("to hide, to keep secret"), as we can see in the stanza cited above. Not only is the word for "secrecy" (*gūḍha*) formed from this root, but so is the word for "cave" (*gūha*). "Cave" is often used in Sanskrit to designate a hiding place in general, but this word is also frequently used metaphorically for the (secret) heart of a human being in the Upaniṣads:

> Know that it lies hidden
> in the cave of the heart. (*Kaṭha Upaniṣad* 1.14)
>
> They call these two *Shadow* and *Light*,
> the two who have entered.
> One into the cave of the heart,
> and the other into the highest realm beyond. (*Kaṭha Upaniṣad* 3.1)
>
> He who was born before the Heat,
> before the Waters were born,
> he who has seen through living beings—
> entering the cave of the heart
> one sees him abiding there. (*Kaṭha Upaniṣad* 4.6)
>
> One who knows this, my dear, hidden within the cave of the heart,
> cuts the knot of ignorance in this world. (*Muṇḍaka Upaniṣad* 2.1.10)
>
> It is vast, heavenly, of inconceivable form,
> and yet it appears smaller than the small.
> It is farther than the farthest,
> and yet it is right here.
> It is right here inside those who see,
> hidden within the cave of the heart. (*Muṇḍaka Upaniṣad* 3.1.7)

In the Upaniṣads, the body itself becomes the locus of secrecy, a place where secrets are concealed and revealed. The cave of the heart is the ultimate hiding place, accessible only to the person who inhabits that body. This mapping of secrecy onto the individual's body mirrors the Upaniṣadic revelation about the cosmic divine force, *brahman*: it is one with the *ātman*, the human self, and must be sought within, rather than in the world outside. The interiority of the ultimate reality suggests that the "cave of the heart" hides deeper truths than those that can be displayed publicly.

But "secrecy" in the Upaniṣads is not just as the possession of secret knowledge, inaccessible to outsiders, but more significantly the assertion of correct *way* of knowing. One of the most frequently repeated phrases in the Upaniṣads is "*ya evaṃ veda* . . ."—"He who knows thus. . . ." To know *correctly* is crucial in the Upaniṣads, and to know wrongly potentially fatal.

The boundaries between those who know and those who do not know are illustrated by the dramatic Upaniṣadic metaphor of the shattered head. Knowledge of the highest sacred reality may be a dangerous thing in the wrong hands, as evidenced by late Vedic and Upaniṣadic stories of people whose heads shatter when they venture into areas of secret knowledge that are beyond their mental and spiritual capacity to handle (Witzel 1987b and Insler 1989–1990). Secrets are dangerous; they can tear apart flesh and bone. Heads tend to shatter in the Upaniṣads not only when people grapple with philosophical issues beyond their mental powers, but also when issues of textual confidentiality are at stake, and especially when people outside the boundaries of a *śākhā* challenge those on the inside.

In the famous public contest scene at King Janaka's court in *Bṛhadāraṇyaka Upaniṣad* 3, Yājñavalkya warns the female philosopher Gārgī not to ask too much, or her head will split apart. While Gārgī does listen to his warning and keep her head, another one of Yājñavalkya's challenger fails to heed the warning and comes to a terrible end:

> "I ask you [says Yājñavalkya] about that person who is the *upaniṣad*, who carries the other persons away, who brings them back, and who rises above them. If you will not tell me who that is, your head will shatter."

Śākalya did not know him, and his head did indeed shatter. (*Bṛhadāraṇyaka Upaniṣad* 3.9.26)

Śākalya's shattered head is not only indicative of the power of knowledge and the dangers of ignorance but also reflects the authority of Yājñavalkya in the *Bṛhadāraṇyaka Upaniṣad*. Shattered heads in the Upaniṣads not only represent a general lack of knowledge but also, significantly, lack of authorized access within a text. Gārgī's head remains intact because she recognizes Yājñavalkya's authority, retracts her question and becomes silent. She realizes that she is inquiring into mysteries to which she has no access, and she steps back. Śākalya's head shatters because he challenges Yājñavalkya without possessing the latter's knowledge about *ātman*. He was a mere pretender, but did not truly possess the secret knowledge to which he had laid claim. As Insler has pointed out in his study of exploding heads in ancient Indian literature (Insler 1989–1990), threats of heads shattering are often made during theological debates. The threats are only averted when the defeated party recognizes the authority of the other: "If you had not admitted this, your head would have flown apart" (*Śatapatha Brāhmaṇa* 11.5.3.13).

Many religious traditions that value secrecy warn of dire theological consequences for those that access the secrets without proper spiritual preparation. The seventeenth-century German alchemical text *Occulta Philosophia* warns, for example, that access to the secrets of the Philosopher's Stone might lead those who are not spiritually advanced to abandon their earnest search for God in favor of a more facile path to immortality, which will lead them to perdition (see the Senior-Adolphus dialogue of the 1613 *Occulta Philosophia, Gesprech von der heimlichen Goldtblum*, quoted from Ebeling 2001, 69.) The Upaniṣads, however, depict the destructive potential of accessing knowledge beyond what one is prepared for in a more bodily and visceral way; the body of the uninitiated is simply too fragile a vessel to hold the powerful secret. Tales of heads shattered by mysteries too profound for one's intellect are tales of perforated boundaries and social transgressions; they suggest to both "insiders" and "outsiders" that maintaining the boundaries between those who know and those who do not know is necessary for the outsiders' safety. In the Brahmanical tradition, the rhetoric of secrecy affirms priestly and masculine mastery over the deepest mysteries of the universe. But the *existence* of secrets that can only be possessed by a small number of worthy men must be communicated to those who lack access as well. The existence of a secret is perpetually revealed, while the content of the secret is concealed. Secrecy can signify religious and social power, but only if those excluded from the secret are aware of their own exclusion and place value on that from which they are excluded.

The secrets in the Upaniṣads are not kept completely hidden from "outsiders"; even those to whom the secrets cannot be revealed (lest their heads shatter) are entitled to *know* that there are secrets to which they have no access. The existence of secrets must be communicated; secrecy is a discursive activity that marks boundaries and structures power relationships.

The main secret revealed by the Upaniṣads is the mystical unity between the individual self (*ātman*) and the cosmic force (*brahman*). But the secrecy so frequently proclaimed in the Upaniṣads was not particularly effective in keeping the texts' ideas away from the public eye in real life, as evidenced by the multitude of near-contemporary Buddhist and Jain authors who display an easy familiarity with many of the Upaniṣadic secrets. The *Bhagavadgītā*, a text roughly contemporaneous with the *Kaṭha Upaniṣad* and the *Śvetāśvatara Upaniṣad*, likewise cites both of these texts extensively, in spite of the admonitions to secrecy contained in each of these Upaniṣadic texts. The purported Upaniṣadic secret-keeping appears not to have been particularly effective, if it was even attempted. As we have noted, the doctrine of *karma* is presented as a secret in *Bṛhadāraṇyaka Upaniṣad* 3.2.13, but it was hardly a well-kept secret. *Karma* is mentioned frequently in the very oldest Buddhist and Jain texts, but the authors see no need to even explain what *karma* is; they take it for granted that their audience already knows what *karma* is and how it functions. One of the deepest "secrets" of the Upaniṣads is now so well known as to require no particular explanation or justification. I argue, however, that the admonitions to secrecy in the Upaniṣads are not mere failed attempts at concealment, but rather discursive (and possibly successful) strategies for creating religious boundaries and zones of power.

It is necessary to problematize the received wisdom that the Upaniṣads and other ancient sacred Hindu texts were indeed transmitted in absolute secrecy from Brahman teachers to initiated students as the texts themselves suggest. This secrecy proclaimed by the texts should probably be understood as a performance of religious authority rather than an accurate depiction of historical reality. Formulations of secrecy validate and authorize the social and religious power of a learned elite; they separate upper-class men who "know" from the women and lower class men who, per definition, "do not know."

I would argue that the function of secrecy in the Upaniṣads is, perhaps paradoxically, not to keep something hidden, but rather to call attention to the hiding itself in order to mark that which is kept secret as extraordinary and powerful. Secrecy is a discursive validation of both the secrets and the secret-keepers, those who keep the ultimate truth hidden "in the cave of the heart." Secrecy insists that there is something *more*, something deeper, something beyond that which can be publicly known. The *Bṛhadāraṇyaka Upaniṣad* claims that the gods themselves despise the overt, perhaps because the overt does not signify or point to anything beyond itself. Secrecy, on the other hand, alludes to something *other*, a greater mystery, something as yet unknown. Perhaps this is why the Upaniṣads insist, then, that "the gods adore the cryptic."

The Authors of the Upaniṣads

While many of the hymns of the *Ṛgveda* are ascribed to named poets, either in the hymns themselves or in the late Vedic *Sarvāṇukramaṇī*, most of the literature that followed the Vedas is anonymous. This holds true of the Upaniṣads as well. With the possible exception of the *Śvetāśvatara Upaniṣad*, the classical Upaniṣads are not ascribed to named authors, and it is very unlikely that they represent the work of single individuals. The texts are the products of Vedic *śākhās*, or traditions of transmission, rather than individual authors. For this reason, several Upaniṣads are named after the schools that composed and transmitted them, such as the *Aitareya Upaniṣad*, named after a *śākhā* of the *Ṛgveda*, and the *Taittirīya* and *Kaṭha Upaniṣads*, named after the *Taittirīya* and the *Kaṭha śākhās* of the *Black Yajurveda*.

This is not to say that we do not encounter ideas traced back to individuals in the Upaniṣads; on the contrary, the Upaniṣads abound in charismatic teachers who propound novel ideas. But the Upaniṣadic teachers are literary characters. While it is not impossible that some of the teachers mentioned in the Upaniṣadic texts may once have lived and taught in India, we cannot conclude anything about their historicity or lack thereof based on these texts. The Sanskrit scholar Walter Ruben attempted to draw a portrait of each individual "philosopher" of the Upaniṣads in his book *Die Philosophen der Upanishaden* (Ruben 1947). He chose to treat each teacher mentioned in the Upaniṣads as a historical figure whose ideas were captured in these texts. But as Lindquist (2011a, 2011b, 2011c) points out, Upaniṣadic teachers serve literary functions, and they have different functions in different texts. Yājñavalkya, the main character in the *Bṛhadāraṇyaka Upaniṣad*, is also featured in an older text from the same *White Yajurvedaśākhā*, the *Śatapatha Brāhmaṇa*. In both texts, Yājñavalkya is demonstrating his vast knowledge in front of King Janaka of Videha. But while the Yājñavalkya of the *Bṛhadāraṇyaka Upaniṣad* is only interested in the *ātman* and does not care about ritual minutiae, the Yājñavalkya of the *Śatapatha Brāhmaṇa* demonstrates his detailed knowledge of the *agnihotra* sacrifice. Their teachings are entirely different, but both Yājñavalkyas speak with great knowledge and authority. It is difficult to conclude that both these texts refer to a particular historical teacher; rather, both texts use the *literary character* of Yājñavalkya to embody a particular kind of authoritative wisdom to be admired even by kings.

It is interesting to note that some of the great teachers of the Upaniṣads are not Brahmans, but rather kings: Ajātaśatru in the *Bṛhadāraṇyaka Upaniṣad*, Aśvapati Kaikeya in the *Chāndogya Upaniṣad*, and Pravāhaṇa Jaivali in the *Chāndogya Upaniṣad*. Some scholars have therefore suggested that the Upaniṣads, with their many new and radical ideas, may have been composed by Kṣatriyas (the second-highest or warrior class, to which kings belong), rather than by Brahmans. Since these texts were transmitted by schools of Brahmans, however, it is unlikely that the Upaniṣads were composed outside Brahmanical circles. When read in context, each of the episodes where kings are shown to be wiser than Brahmans does not appear to imply that *all* kings are wiser than *all* Brahmans, but rather that some wise kings know more than some misguided Brahmans (particularly those associated with rival schools). Several of the older Upaniṣads are suggesting that a person does not automatically possess full knowledge of the true nature of reality just by virtue of being a Brahman and being trained as a ritual expert, but that is of course not proof that Brahmans did not compose the texts.

The authors of the Upaniṣads were likely the scholarly collectives (*śākhās*) that transmitted the Saṃhitās of the Vedas as well as their Brāhmaṇas and Āraṇyakas. Why did these *śākhās* not attach the names of individual teachers to these innovative Upaniṣadic texts? First, because the texts were likely the product of collaboration lasting several generations, rather than the work of individuals working by themselves. And second, because these texts were the property of the *śākhā*, rather than of any individuals who may have contributed to them.

One of the final stanzas of the *Śvetāśvatara Upaniṣad* (6.21) reads: "By the power of his austerities and by the grace of God, the wise Śvetāśvatara first came to know *brahman* and proclaimed it." Although the text presents itself as the work of a single person, the sage Śvetāśvatara, and credits his insights both to his own efforts and divine grace, it is not clear whether such a person as Śvetāśvatara ever existed, or if he is merely a literary device in the text, part of the Upaniṣad's claim to authority for its novel teachings. It is not uncommon for ancient Sanskrit texts to be attributed to mythical sages or poets; the vast *Mahābhārata* epic is said to be the work of the sage Vyāsa, for example, even if most scholars today would agree that the sprawling epic is not likely to be the work of a single person, but rather an oral text composed over many generations.

An intriguing clue to the mystery of Śvetāśvatara may be found in the alternative title of the text, *Śvetāśvatarāṇām Mantropaniṣad* ("The *Mantra-Upaniṣad* of the Śvetāśvataras"). The plural form of "Śvetāśvatara" used here suggests that the text may not be the composition of an individual sage Śvetāśvatara, but rather the product of a school of transmission (*śākhā*) called *Śvetāśvatara*. A school by that name is mentioned in the late Vedic text *Caraṇavyūha*. It is possible, therefore, that the text has its origins in an otherwise lost Śvetāśvatara *śākhā* of the *Yajurveda*, and that the *Śvetāśvatara Upaniṣad*, much like the other Upaniṣadic texts, was a collective, rather than an individual creation.

4
The Classical Upaniṣads

Synopsis of the Classical Upaniṣads

It is not easy to give a brief synopsis of each of the classical Upaniṣads, since these texts contain such a wealth of material, including narratives, dialogues, philosophical musings, ritual speculations, cosmology, poetry, and etymology. Each Upaniṣadic text presents a series of intriguing assertions about the human condition, the meaning of life, and the path to spiritual liberation, but the texts do not unfold as a series of logical arguments or coherent narratives. This does not mean, however, that the Upaniṣads are incoherent or illogical, but rather that they have their own way of presenting ideas. These are texts that demand a great deal of their readers. In the following, I have summarized what I perceive to be the most important ideas in each of the classical Upaniṣads; no doubt others could have chosen to emphasize different ideas. But for readers seeking to orient themselves in these rich and challenging texts, the following should at least present a rough road map, with a few sightseeing stops along the way at particularly striking vistas.

Dialogues are an important part of the Upaniṣads. Many of the main ideas in these texts are presented in conversations between teachers and students, or in debates between rival wisdom teachers. For that reason, I have included the names of the most important characters and a brief overview of their ideas in the following synopses.

The reader should also be aware that another significant feature of the Upaniṣads is the authors' fondness for drawing mystical

The Classical Upaniṣads. Signe Cohen, Oxford University Press. © Oxford University Press 2024.
DOI: 10.1093/oso/9780197654156.003.0004

connections. The Upaniṣadic authors see the human body reflected in the cosmos, and the cosmos in the human body, and they see analogies to parts of rituals in the body, the universe, and even in language itself. While these mystical identifications of seemingly disparate parts of reality may seem disorienting to a modern reader, they are an integral part of the Upaniṣadic thinkers' attempts to understand the true nature of the world. The idea that there exists a deeper unity behind all the shifting forms of the external world is central in the Upaniṣads, and this unity also expresses itself in the sometimes surprising connections made between humans, gods, the natural world, abstract principles, rituals, and language itself.

Bṛhadāraṇyaka Upaniṣad

The name *Bṛhadāraṇyaka* means "the great wilderness" or "the great forest," but the name also suggests an affinity with late Vedic ritual texts called Āraṇyakas ("forest books"). These texts deal with powerful and dangerous rituals, performed in the forest, rather than in the village. The *Bṛhadāraṇyaka Upaniṣad*, the oldest and longest of the preserved Upaniṣadic texts, is divided into six chapters (*adhyāyas*). The Upaniṣad itself forms the concluding section of the late Vedic ritual text *Śatapatha Brāhmaṇa*. Like the *Śatapatha Brāhmaṇa*, the *Bṛhadāraṇyaka Upaniṣad* is preserved in two recensions, the *Kāṇva* and the *Mādhyaṃdina*. The eighth-century commentator Śaṅkara refers to the first two chapters of the *Bṛhadāraṇyaka Upaniṣad* as the "Honey Section," the middle two as the "Yājñavalkya Section," and the last two as the "Supplement Section" (*khila-kāṇḍa*). The designation of the last two chapters as a "supplement" may indicate that Śaṅkara believed chapters 5 and 6 to be a later addition to the text.

The first chapter of the text fuses old Vedic ritual imagery with speculations about the creation of the world, *ātman* ("the self"), the cosmic force *brahman*, and the life breath (*prāṇa*). The opening passage of the *Bṛhadāraṇyaka Upaniṣad* compares the world itself to the sacrificial horse from the old Vedic *aśvamedha* ritual. The eye of the horse is identified with the sun, its breath with the wind, and various parts of its body with time and space. The chapter also contains several half-abstract, half-mythological creation narratives, tracing the origin of the world back to Death (1.2), *ātman* (1.4.1–8 and 1.4.17), or *brahman* (1.4.11).

Bṛhadāraṇyaka Upaniṣad 1.5.17–20 contains an interesting description of what happens when a man dies. A dying man should tell his son: "You are *brahman.* You are the sacrifice. You are the world," and the man's life breath (*prāṇa*) will then enter his son. The son will deliver his father from all his misdeeds, which underscores the importance of having sons.

The second chapter of the text begins with a dialogue between the would-be wisdom teacher Dṛpta Bālāki and Ajātaśatru, the king of Kāśī. Bālāki attempts to explain *brahman* to the king, but it turns out that the king is wiser than the Brahman, and Ajātaśatru becomes Bālāki's teacher instead. Bālāki identifies *brahman* with the person in the sun, the person in the moon, the person in the lightning, the person in space, the person in the wind, the person in fire, the person in the waters, the person in the mirror, the person in the sound of a man's footsteps, the person in the directions of the sky, the person in the shadow, and the person in the body. But Ajātaśatru identifies *brahman* with *ātman* and explains that all things emanate from the *ātman* just like threads sent forth from a spider (2.1.20). The teachings of Ajātaśatru foreshadow those of the text's main character, Yājñavalkya. The second chapter also introduces Yājñavalkya himself, a wisdom teacher whose teachings about *ātman*, the eternal self, are central to the text. *Bṛhadāraṇyaka Upaniṣad* 2.4 presents Yājñavalkya and his two wives, Maitreyī and Kātyāyanī. When Yājñavalkya decides to leave home for good and devote himself to his philosophy, he offers to share his property between his two wives. Maitreyī has no interest in his material possessions but instead asks Yājñavalkya to explain to her everything that he knows. Yājñavalkya, pleased, sits down with her and explains the nature of the *ātman*. Yājñavalkya's philosophy in this text is a radical one: the *ātman* is all things, and when the *ātman* is fully understood, all subject-object distinctions disappear. The interconnectedness of all things is also highlighted in section 2.5, which uses the metaphor of honey to express the essence of something: "The *ātman* is the honey of all beings, and all beings are the honey of the *ātman*. . . . It is the immortal, it is *brahman*, it is the whole" (2.5.14).

In the third chapter of the text, King Janaka of Videha hosts a contest at his court where rival wisdom teachers attempt to explain *brahman*. The king promises a grand prize of a thousand cows, with gold pieces tied to their horns, to the philosopher who emerges victorious from the debate. To the outrage of the other contestants, Yājñavalkya is so confident in his own knowledge that he orders his students to bring the royal cows home for him before the contest has even begun. But it soon becomes apparent that Yājñavalkya is indeed the greatest wisdom teacher among them. Through a series of dialogues, he defeats the other contestants one by one by displaying superior knowledge of the cosmos, death, *brahman*, and *ātman*.

The first person to challenge Yājñavalkya is the priest Aśvala, whose questions are grounded in ritual (How can the patron of the sacrifice free himself from the grip of death, from the grip of day and night, and from the grip of the light and dark fortnights?). In his responses to Aśvala, Yājñavalkya displays his knowledge of ritual but also shows his interlocutor that there is a deeper, more symbolic meaning to the sacrificial ritual by identifying the sacrificial priests with parts of the human body and with the cosmos itself.

Something extraordinary happens during the interchange with Jāratkārava Ārtabhāga, Yājñavalkya's second interlocutor. Ārtabhāga asks what happens when a person dies, and instead of answering in front of the assembled Brahmans, Yājñavalkya pulls him aside and gives him the answer in private. Their ensuing conversation is not given in full, but the text notes that "what they talked about was *karma*, and what they praised was *karma*" (3.12.13). It seems, then, that Yājñavalkya's doctrine of *karma* is a secret that can only be shared in a private setting. Yājñavalkya addresses Ārtabhāga as "my dear," which is a common way for teachers or fathers to address their students or sons, perhaps hinting that Ārtabhāga is Yājñavalkya's own student.

Yājñavalkya's third challenger is Bhujyu Lāhyāyani, who tells of an encounter with a man whose daughter was possessed by a supernatural spirit, a *gandharva*. Bhujyu Lāhyāyani and his companions asked the *gandharva* about the whereabouts of the Parīkṣitas, the ancient kings of the Kuru-Pañcāla kingdom. The question seems to imply that the *gandharva* may know the fate of the righteous kings after death and their precise location in the afterlife. We are never told how the *gandharva* responded, but Bhujyu Lāhyāyani now directs the same question to Yājñavalkya, perhaps to test how his knowledge compares to that of a *gandharva*. Yājñavalkya gives an answer that shows his detailed knowledge of cosmology (including the location of a gap as wide as a razor's edge by the cosmic ocean) but then takes a larger view and suggests that in the grand scheme of things, "both individual things and the totality of things are just the wind," introducing his own philosophy of the oneness of all things.

The next challenger, Uṣasta Cākrāyaṇa, asks Yājñavalkya to explain *ātman* and *brahman*, which the wisdom teacher does. The fifth challenger, Kahola Kauṣītakeya, repeats the question, and Yājñavalkya explains the absolute identity between *ātman* and *brahman* in even more detail.

Among the many wisdom teachers who challenge Yājñavalkya at Janaka's court, there is also one woman, Gārgī Vācaknavī. Gārgī asks Yājñavalkya about that which lies beyond the visible world, using the metaphor of weaving: "Tell me, since this whole world is woven back and forth on water, on what is water woven back and forth?" When Yājñavalkya tells her that the answer is "air," Gārgī asks on what the air is woven. With each answer from Yājñavalkya, Gārgī pushes further, until she gets to the final element of them all, which is *brahman* itself. But Gārgī does not stop there; she asks, "On what are the worlds of *brahman* woven back and forth?" At that point, Yājñavalkya answers: "Do not ask beyond, Gārgī, or your head will split apart" (3.6). At that, Gārgī falls silent. Yājñavalkya's threat of her head shattering is not an idle one. Several late Vedic texts describe heads shattering when someone tries to enter an area of knowledge that lies beyond their comprehension, and the very last contestant Yājñavalkya faces at King Janaka's court does in fact end up dying from a shattered head after he persists in asking unreasonable questions. In Gārgī's case, it seems that the problem with her question is that it goes beyond the limits of the knowable; *brahman* itself is the ultimate reality in the *Bṛhadāraṇyaka Upaniṣad*, and there can be nothing beyond it. While Yājñavalkya's other interlocutors are given one chance each to challenge the sage, Gārgī alone gets to question him a second time.

Yājñavalkya is also questioned by his own teacher, the learned Uddālaka Āruṇi, who asks him about "the inner controller" (*antaryāmin*). Yājñavalkya responds that the inner controller is none other than the *ātman* itself.

The last of Yājñavalkya's challengers is Vidagdha Śākalya. Vidagdha Śākalya asks Yājñavalkya about the number of deities in the world, which suggests that he is still caught up in a theistic world view and does not understand the oneness of *ātman*. At the end of his dialogue with Yājñavalkya, Vidagdha Śākalya comes to a tragic end as his head shatters apart. In the text, his shattered head is presented as a direct result of his ignorance.

In the fourth chapter of the *Bṛhadāraṇyaka Upaniṣad*, Yājñavalkya has a long dialogue with king Janaka in private and explains to him the absolute identity of *ātman* and *brahman*. He teaches the king that the self can only be described in negative terms (*neti neti*, "not this . . . not that," 4.2.4). The dialogue between Yājñavalkya and his wife Maitreyī is repeated in this chapter.

The fifth chapter of the *Bṛhadāraṇyaka Upaniṣad* contains a story about the creator god Prajāpati and his children, who are the gods, humans, and demons. He teaches them all, and at the end of their study, he shares with each group of children a single syllable: *da*. The gods interpret *da* as *dāmyata* ("show restraint), while the humans interpret it as *datta* ("give"), and the demons as *dayadhvam* ("be compassionate"). This section of the *Bṛhadāraṇyaka Upaniṣad* inspired the concluding section ("What the Thunder Said") of T. S. Eliot's well-known poem *The Waste Land* (1922), which ends with two Sanskrit lines:

> *Datta. Dayadhvam. Damyata.*
> *Shantih. Shantih. Shantih*
> ("Give, show restraint, be compassionate. Peace, peace, peace")

The sixth chapter of the *Bṛhadāraṇyaka Upaniṣad* tells the story of Śvetaketu, the son of Āruṇi, who has been taught by his father. But when Śvetaketu is questioned by Jaivali Pravāhaṇa, he realizes that he does not know about the path of the soul after death. He confronts his father, and both of them become students of Jaivali and learn about the two paths after death: those who have the correct knowledge will go to the world of *brahman*, while those who do not and just offer sacrifices and practice austerities will go the world of the fathers, the moon, and eventually return to earth as rain and be reborn. The sixth chapter of the Upaniṣad also contains descriptions of rites relating to sex, pregnancy, and birth, including a ritual to harm a wife's lover. The text ends with a lineage of teachers and students.

Chāndogya Upaniṣad

The *Chāndogya Upaniṣad*, a prose text in eight chapters, is affiliated with the *Sāmaveda* and forms the concluding part of the *Chāndogya*

Brāhmaṇa. The name of the text is derived from *chandoga*, "one who sings in verse," a person who chants from the *Sāmaveda*.

The *Chāndogya Upaniṣad* is preoccupied with sacred sounds, and the first chapter of the text is devoted to the Vedic High Chant (*udgītha*), which is here identified with breath, the syllable *oṃ*, and space. Intriguingly, the text frequently compares ritual chanting to the sounds that animals make. Section 1.12 describes dogs gathering and singing a sacred chant together in order to obtain food. While this passage has often been interpreted as satirical, poking fun of the chanting of Brahman priests, it is worth noting that animals are frequently associated with wisdom and religious insight in the *Chāndogya Upaniṣad*.

The second chapter of the text is devoted to the *Sāman* ritual chant and its cosmic meaning. The various parts of the chant are identified with the earth, the fire, the intermediate region, the sun, and the sky, and mastery of the chant is therefore equated to mastery over the cosmos (2.2). The parts of the chant are further identified with wind, gathering of clouds, falling rain, lightning and thunder, and the cessation of rain, which suggests that mastering the *Sāman* chant also allows a person to control the weather (2.3). The chant is also identified with different forms of water, which will provide the chanter with an ample supply of water, with the seasons, which will allow the chanter to live through many seasons, with animals, which will allow the chanter to be rich in animals, and with the vital functions, which will allow the chanter to "win the most extensive worlds" (2.4–7).

The third chapter of the text identifies the sun as the honey (essence) of the gods and goes on to describe how this honey of the sun can be extracted from the sacred texts of the *Ṛgveda*, *Yajurveda*, *Sāmaveda*, and *Atharvaveda*. The Upaniṣad describes how different groups of Vedic gods, the Vasus (the gods accompanying the thunder god Indra), the Rudras (storm gods), the Ādityas (the offspring of Aditi, the goddess of Infinity), the Maruts (gods of lightning), and the Sādhyas (a class of demigods), subsist on this divine honey.

Chāndogya Upaniṣad 3.12 focuses on the Gāyatrī chant, which is identified with all of creation. Section 3.13 describes the five breaths: the out-breath (*prāṇa*), inter-breath (*vyāna*), in-breath (*apāna*), link-breath (*samāna*), and up-breath (*udāna*). These breaths are described as openings in the heart through which deities can enter. The out-breath is identified with the sun, the sight, and the eastern direction, the inter-breath with the moon, hearing, and the southern direction, the in-breath with fire, speech, and the western direction, the link-breath with rain, the mind, and the northern direction, and the up-breath with space, the wind, and the upward direction. These breaths are said to be the five servants of *brahman* itself and the doorkeepers of the heavenly world.

Section 3.16 compares a human being to a Vedic sacrifice. The first twenty-four years of a man's life are identified with the morning pressing of the sacred drink Soma, the next forty-four years of his life with the midday pressing of Soma, and his last forty-eight years with the third pressing of Soma. The text assures us that a person who knows all this information will live to the age of 116 (3.16.7). The numbers are no doubt symbolic here; the years relate to the number of syllables in commonly used Vedic meters.

The last section of chapter 3, 3.19, contains an intriguing abstract creation story. In the beginning, the world was non-existence (*asat*) and also existence (*sat*). This existence-non-existence then develops into an egg, which after a year splits in two. The bottom half becomes the earth, and the top part becomes the sky, while the egg's outer membrane becomes mountains, the inner membranes become clouds and mist, the egg's veins become rivers, and the amniotic fluid becomes the ocean. The "chicken" that is born from this cosmic egg is the sun itself.

The fourth chapter introduces some colorful Upaniṣadic characters: the wealthy wisdom-seeker teacher Jānaśruti, the eccentric Raikva the Gatherer, and Satyakāma Jābāla. When Jānaśruti overhears a flock of wild geese speak of the knowledge of Raikva the Gatherer, he wants to become Raikva's student. Raikva turns out to be a homeless man living under a cart, but when Jānaśruti offers him cows, gold, and a carriage in return for his teaching, Raikva calls him a *Śūdra* (person of low rank) and tells him to go away. It is only when Jānaśruti offers Raikva his daughter in marriage that Raikva agrees to share his wisdom, and he explains the importance of air among the elements and the life breath in the body. Another wisdom seeker in this chapter is Satyakāma, the son of the single mother Jābālā. Satyakāma wants to become a Vedic student, and he asks his mother about his lineage. She tells him that she doesn't know who his father is, so he can just call himself Jābāla, "the son of Jābālā." When Satyakāma tells his prospective teacher Hāridrumata the truth about his uncertain parentage, Hāridrumata takes his honesty as proof of his Brahman lineage and accepts him as a student. But when his human teacher goes traveling, Satyakāma is taught about *brahman* by a series of unusual teachers: a bull, the fire, a goose, and a water bird. It is noteworthy that three of his teachers are animals, who apparently know the full truth about *brahman* and are capable of teaching the boy (4.4.5–4.5.2).

Chāndogya Upaniṣad 5 begins by declaring that the breath is the highest of all the vital functions. Then follows a narrative about the young boy Śvetaketu and his father, Uddālaka. Śvetaketu arrives at the assembly of learned men at the court and is questioned by King Pravāhaṇa Jaivali. When he can't answer any of the king's questions, Śvetaketu goes home and gets his father, and they both become the king's students. Pravāhaṇa Jaivali tells them about the two different paths of the self after death, one that leads to *brahman,* and one that leads to rebirth (5.10.1–6).

One of the best-known narrative episodes of the *Chāndogya Upaniṣad,* from chapter 6, also features Śvetaketu and his father Uddālaka Āruṇi (6.13). Śvetaketu returns home after completing his study of the Vedas, proud of his newly acquired knowledge. But when his father asks him about that through which the unheard becomes heard and the unknown becomes known, Śvetaketu cannot answer. His father therefore teaches the boy about the nature of the *ātman* by dissolving salt in water and explains that just as the salt is present everywhere in the water, even if it cannot be seen, so the invisible self is present in all things.

Chapter 7 features Nārada, a man who has studied all the Vedas, but is ignorant of the *ātman* and therefore seeks instruction from the wisdom teacher Sanatkumāra. Sanatkumāra explains that everything in the world ultimately stems from the *ātman*.

Chapter 8 contains more reflections on the nature of *ātman* and *brahman*. The Vedic creator god Prajāpati is here an enlightened wisdom teacher, and both the god Indra and the demon Virocana seek to learn about the *ātman* from him. While Virocana accepts an initial superficial identification of *ātman* with the body, Indra keeps coming back until he learns that *ātman* is identical with *brahman*.

Aitareya Upaniṣad

The *Aitareya Upaniṣad* is a short prose text in three chapters that forms part of the older *Aitareya Āraṇyaka*. The text is affiliated with the *Ṛgveda*. The three chapters of the Upaniṣad explore the concept of *ātman* from different angles. In the first chapter, *ātman* appears as a primordial creator who brings the worlds and humans into being: "In the beginning, this world was just *ātman* alone, and no one else blinked. He thought: 'Let me create the worlds'" (1.1.1). The creation of the world in the *Aitareya Upaniṣad* is closely associated with sacrifice and echoes the idea found in the *Ṛgveda* that the world is created from the body of a primordial man. But this primordial sacrifice is reinterpreted and rendered more abstract in the *Aitareya Upaniṣad*. The *ātman* is said to have three "states of sleep" in 1.3.12, which foreshadows the later idea of the four states of the self in the *Māṇḍūkya Upaniṣad*.

The second chapter of the *Aitareya Upaniṣad* describes the three births of the self. These three "births" are conception, birth, and rebirth after death. The first "birth" is the man's ejaculation of semen during conception, the second is the man nourishing the woman who carries his child, and the third is rebirth (2.4).

The third chapter of the *Aitareya Upaniṣad* identifies the *ātman* with *brahman*, the gods, all living beings, and with cognition (*prajñāna*). We can trace a progression in the text's depiction of *ātman* as a mythological figure akin to a deity in the first chapter, via corporeal essence in the second chapter, to an abstract concept in the third.

Kauṣītaki Upaniṣad

The *Kauṣītaki Upaniṣad* forms books 3–6 of the late Vedic text *Kauṣītaki Āraṇyaka*. The text is formally affiliated with the *Śāṅkhāyana* school of the *Ṛgveda*. The *Kauṣītaki Upaniṣad* consists of four prose chapters with a few interspersed verses.

The first chapter features the young Śvetaketu, who is sent by his father Āruṇi to be the officiating priest for Citra Gāṅgyāyani. But when Citra Gāṅgyāyani asks him questions he cannot answer, Śvetaketu asks to become his pupil instead. Citra tells Śvetaketu about the two possible paths after death. When the dead arrive at the moon, those who can answer the moon's question—"Who are you?"—pass into the heavenly realm, while those who can't are born again as animals or humans in accordance with their actions or their knowledge (1.2). The correct answer to the moon's question, Citra reveals, is "I am you." A person who knows this answer will pass through various worlds and arrive at the world of *brahman* itself. *Brahman* will again ask: "Who are you?," and the person will answer: "I am who you are."

The second chapter of the text contains reflections on *brahman* as the life breath but also descriptions of a series of rituals through which a person can obtain a desired object, win someone's love, get rid of sin, ensure long life for one's children, and so forth. The description of a "father-son ceremony" in 2.15 is particularly noteworthy; here, a dying father bequeaths his vital functions, as well as his *karma*, to his son.

In chapter 3, the wisdom seeker Pratardana approaches the god Indra, who is here an enlightened teacher. Indra identifies himself with *prāṇa* and *ātman*.

In chapter 4, the would-be wisdom teacher Bālāki visits king Ajātaśatru of Kāśī and offers to teach him about *brahman* (cf. the similar episode in *Bṛhadāraṇyaka Upaniṣad* 2). Bālāki identifies *brahman* as a person in the sun, the moon, and so forth. The king is not impressed, however, and says that he would rather know about the one who created all these persons. At this point, Bālāki realizes that the king is wiser than he is and asks Ajātaśatru to be *his* teacher instead. Ajātaśatru notes that it would be a reversal of normal practice for a Brahman to be the student of a Kṣatriya, but still he assents to become Bālāki's teacher. The text culminates with Ajātaśatru's teachings about *brahman* as *ātman*.

Taittirīya Upaniṣad

The *Taittirīya Upaniṣad* is affiliated with the *Taittirīya* school of the *Yajurveda* and comprises chapters 7, 8, and 9 of the *Taittirīya Āraṇyaka*. It is a prose text in three chapters. It is likely that that the first chapter of the Upaniṣad was originally a separate text. The fourteenth-century commentator Sāyaṇa treats the first chapter as separate from the other two and calls the first chapter *Saṃhitopaniṣad* ("The Upaniṣad of Combination") and the last two chapters *Vāruṇyopaniṣad* ("The Upaniṣad of the Son of Varuṇa"). Others refer to the first chapter of the text as *Śikṣopaniṣad* ("The Upaniṣad of Learning") or *Śikṣāvallī* ("The Vine of Learning").

The first chapter of the Upaniṣad emphasizes the compatibility between traditional Vedic learning and the study of secret teachings (*upaniṣad*). The chapter begins and ends with an invocation of various Vedic gods, and the Vedic wind god Vāyu is identified with *brahman* itself. *Brahman* is also identified as the fourth and highest Veda (1.5.3), identical to the sacred sound *oṃ* (1.8). Section 1.5 introduces four *mantras* that become well known in later Hinduism: *bhūr*, *bhuvas*, *suvar*, and *mahas*. These *mantras* are identified with different parts of the universe, the elements, the Vedas, and the human breaths.

The second and third chapters of the text identify food as the primordial substance out of which the world is created (2.2.1), and food is even identified with *brahman* itself (2.2, 3.2). Food is further identified with the elements, and with the life breath (2.2, 3.2, 3.8–9). The *Taittirīya Upaniṣad* claims that the *ātman* consists of breath (2.2.1).

In a significant passage, the *Taittirīya Upaniṣad* presents the idea of a fivefold self (*pañcakośa*, "the five sheaths") in 2.2–5: food, breath, mind, perception, and joy. A dying person will reach each one of these selves in turn, culminating in the encounter with the *ātman* consisting of joy.

The third chapter of the text introduces the wisdom seeker Bhṛgu, the son of the Vedic god Varuṇa. Bhṛgu asks his father to explain *brahman* to him, and Varuṇa repeatedly sends him away to practice austerities. Through these ascetic practices, Bhṛgu understands *brahman* as food, life breath, mind, perception, and finally bliss.

Īśā Upaniṣad

The *Īśā Upaniṣad* consists of only eighteen stanzas. The text forms the concluding section to the *Vājasaneyi Saṃhitā* of the *Śukla (White) Yajurveda* and is also called the *Saṃhitā Upaniṣad*. Like the *Bṛhadāraṇyaka Upaniṣad*, it is transmitted in two different versions, a *Mādhyaṃdina* and a *Kāṇva* recension.

The text is named after the first word, *īśā* ("by the Lord") and signals the text's theistic orientation. In this Upaniṣad, *brahman* is a personal god, who dwells in all things in the created world: "The whole world is to be permeated by the Lord" (1).

This god is described through a series of paradoxes. He does not move but is swifter than the mind (4), he moves and does not move, is both far away and near, and he is both inside and outside the world (5). This divine being is identified with the *ātman* of all living beings and can therefore be found within oneself (6). This *ātman* is beyond all dualities; it is beyond ignorance and learning, beyond being and non-being, beyond becoming and destruction (9–14). Humans who seek immortality must likewise learn to move beyond a dualistic understanding of the world: "Into blind darkness go those who worship ignorance, but those who rejoice in wisdom enter darkness deeper still" (9).

The second stanza of the *Īśā Upaniṣad* outlines a view of action (*karma*) that becomes very influential in later Hinduism: "Merely performing actions (*karma*) in this world/you should want to live a hundred years. Thus, and not otherwise, does *karma* does not cling to you" (2). The doctrine of *karma,* or the idea that all actions will eventually come back to the person who performed them, becomes an essential part of later Hindu theology. In classical Hinduism, *karma* is that which ties living beings to an endless cycle of death and rebirth, and humans therefore need to find a way to rid themselves of all *karma*, positive and negative. The *Īśā Upaniṣad* suggests that a person can be free from *karma* by acting with detachment ("merely performing actions"), an idea that foreshadows the theology of the *Bhagavadgītā*, which advocates acting with detachment and surrendering all the fruits of one's actions to a deity (Kṛṣṇa).

The third stanza of the text states that those who kill the *ātman* go to worlds that are wrapped in blind darkness. It is not entirely clear whether this is a prohibition against suicide (killing oneself) or against the killing of any living being (killing the self). Read in conjunction with the cryptic line from stanza 1, "eat what has been abandoned" (by the Lord), which could be a reference to only eating that which does not contain a divine life force, that is, adopting vegetarianism, it is likely that stanza 3 is intended to prohibit the killing of any living being, not just oneself.

The last four stanzas of the text, 15–18, form an appendix to the main text of the Upaniṣad. These stanzas, which contain prayers to the Vedic gods Pūṣan (a minor sun god), and Agni (the fire) are also found in *Bṛhadāraṇyaka Upaniṣad* 5.15.1–4.

Kena Upaniṣad

The *Kena Upaniṣad* is a prose text affiliated with the *Sāmaveda.* The text is divided into four chapters, two in verse and two in prose. It is named after the first word of the text, *kena* ("by whom"): "Directed by whom, compelled by whom, does the mind soar?" (1.1).

Since the Upaniṣad is appended to the *Talavakāra Brāhmaṇa* (a text also known as the *Jaiminīya Upaniṣad Brāhmaṇa*), it is also called the *Talavakāra Upaniṣad.*

The two first chapters of the text claim that the highest principle, *brahman*, is impersonal and without attributes. This *brahman* is "different from that which is known and beyond that which is unknown" (1.4). While *brahman* is the origin of all language, it is itself something that cannot be expressed: "That which cannot be expressed by speech, through which speech is expressed—know that that alone is *brahman*" (1.5). The Upaniṣad's name, *kena*, resonates throughout the text, where *brahman* is repeatedly said to be that *through which* things occur, the ultimate agent of all actions.

In contrast to the depiction of *brahman* as a wholly abstract agent principle in the first two chapters of the text, chapters 3 and 4 present a very different, anthropomorphic *brahman.* But the text's overall point, that *brahman* is the one that makes all action possible, is also central in the last half of the text. Here, we are told that *brahman* won a victory on behalf of the gods. The gods, not understanding that *brahman* was the one that made the victory happen, took credit for the victory themselves, and *brahman* must show them the truth. *Brahman* therefore challenges Agni, the god of fire, to burn a single blade of grass, but Agni finds himself unable to do so. Vāyu, the Vedic god of wind, is likewise unable to blow the blade of grass away. The gods are puzzled, but the thunder god Indra, with the help of the enlightened goddess Umā, discovers that the one that challenged the gods was *brahman* itself, who is the force underlying everything in the world, including the fire and the wind. Therefore, even the gods cannot perform a single action without *brahman*.

In later Hindu mythology, Umā (also called Pārvatī) is the consort of the god Śiva, and her brief appearance in the *Kena Upaniṣad* foreshadows her significance in later Hinduism. But it is worth noting that Umā is a wholly independent goddess in the *Kena Upaniṣad*; there is no mention of Śiva. Umā is further depicted as an enlightened wisdom teacher in this text; she alone understands the true nature of *brahman* and can explain it to Indra, the wisest of the male gods, in this Upaniṣad.

Kaṭha Upaniṣad

The *Kaṭha Upaniṣad* is a verse text in six chapters affiliated with the *Kāṭhaka* school of the *Black Yajurveda*. The frame narrative of the Upaniṣad, about the boy Naciketas who visits Yama, the Lord of the Dead, is based on an older Vedic narrative, originally from the *Kāṭhaka Brāhmaṇa*, but now attested in the *Taittirīya Brāhmaṇa* 3.11.8.

The first chapter of the *Kaṭha Upaniṣad* tells the story of Naciketas, his father, and his journey to the realm of the dead. Naciketas' father gives away all his possessions, and the boy innocently asks his father: "To whom will you give me?" Naciketas asks again until his father becomes angry and responds: "I give you to death." Naciketas proceeds to go to the realm of the dead, although the text does not tell us how. When he arrives there, Yama, the Lord of the Dead, is not home, and the boy must wait for three days without any food or drink. To make up for his inadvertent lack of hospitality toward the Brahman boy, Yama offers Naciketas three wishes, one for each day he had to wait. Naciketas' first wish is to be able to return to his father and have his father greet him with joy. His second wish is to learn about a fire-ritual that leads to heaven. Death readily assents to both his wishes and even offers to name the ritual after Naciketas. But the boy's third wish makes Yama hesitate. Naciketas asks Yama to resolve the question about what happens to a person who is dead: does that person exist or not? At this point, Yama offers him other gifts instead: sons and grandsons, livestock, elephants, wealth, power, a long life, dancing girls, and chariots. But Naciketas is not to be distracted by these lesser gifts and insists on knowing the mystery of death. It is worth noting that in the older version of the story, preserved in the *Taittirīya Brāhmaṇa*, Naciketas' third wish is different; here, he merely wants to know how to ward off recurring death.

In the next five chapters of the Upaniṣad, Yama explains to Naciketas the truth about life and death and the eternal *ātman*. After his initial hesitation to reveal the secret knowledge, Yama praises Naciketas for insisting on yearning for knowledge and not being satisfied with ignorance. He explains that the *ātman* is eternal and does not die when the body dies. In the third chapter, Yama compares the *ātman* to a rider in a chariot. The self is the rider, the body the chariot, the intellect the charioteer who steers the vehicle, the mind the reins, and the senses the wild horses that must be controlled, an image that is also found in Plato's *Phaedrus* (246–253) as well as the Pāli Theravāda Buddhist text *Visuddhimagga*. Yama also identifies this *ātman* with *brahman* itself, and he describes the *ātman* as "a person the size of a thumb . . . always dwelling within the hearts of men" (6.17). The text concludes with the statement that Naciketas attained *brahman* after receiving this knowledge from Yama, and that he therefore became free from both old age and death. And so, says the last stanza, will anyone else who knows this teaching about the *ātman* (6.18).

Muṇḍaka Upaniṣad

The *Muṇḍaka Upaniṣad* is a verse text in three chapters affiliated with the *Atharvaveda.* The title, *Muṇḍaka*, "ones who cuts or shaves," likely refers both to the text's central metaphor of "cutting" or "shaving" away the knot of ignorance and to the practice of shaving one's head as part of an ascetic lifestyle. The *Muṇḍaka Upaniṣad* refers to a ceremony called *śirovrata* ("the vow of the head"), which suggests that the text originated within an ascetic movement where shaving one's head was a common practice. The text explicitly connects the practice of austerity and asceticism with reaching liberation (1.2.11).

The first chapter of the text differentiates between two forms of knowledge. The lower form of knowledge is familiarity with the four Vedas, rituals, phonetics, grammar, etymology, metrics, and astrology. The higher form of knowledge, however, is understanding *brahman* (1.5), which is the ultimate goal according to the *Muṇḍaka Upaniṣad. Brahman* is something that is completely beyond ordinary sensory perception; it is "that which cannot be seen or grasped, colorless, without sight or hearing, without hands or feet, eternal and omnipresent" (1.6).

The second chapter describes *puruṣa*, the primeval person from which all things originate, including gods, humans, and animals, and the text equates this person with the inner self (*antarātman*). The rest of the chapter is devoted to *brahman*, which is attained through the knowledge of *ātman* (2.2.4). In a striking image, *Muṇḍaka Upaniṣad* 2.2.4 likens the sacred syllable *oṃ* to a bow and suggests that when *ātman* is placed upon it as an arrow, it will strike the target, which is *brahman* itself.

The third chapter describes different ways in which someone can know *brahman* and through this knowledge become *brahman* itself and attain immortality (3.2.9). In this chapter, *puruṣa* is even said to be the ultimate cause of *brahman* itself (3.1.3). This *puruṣa* cannot be grasped by the senses but is accessible through meditation (3.1.8).

A line from *Muṇḍaka Upaniṣad* 3.1.6, *satyam eva jayate* ("truth alone conquers"), is part of the State Emblem of India and appears on currency, official government letterhead, and Indian passports.

Śvetāśvatara Upaniṣad

The *Śvetāśvatara Upaniṣad* is a verse text in six chapters, formally affiliated with the *Black Yajurveda*. The text is named after a sage, Śvetāśvatara, who is mentioned in 6.21: "By the power of his penance, and by the grace of God, the wise Śvetāśvatara first realized *brahman*."

The *Śvetāśvatara Upaniṣad* introduces several ideas that are not known from other Upaniṣadic texts, such as the identification of the highest principle with a personal god (Rudra/Śiva), the idea that *brahman* itself may be created by a deity, the concept of a threefold *brahman*, and the notion of *pradhāna*, the primordial material from which the world is made.

The first chapter of the text reintroduces Gārgī's rejected question from *Bṛhadāraṇyaka Upaniṣad* 3: What is the cause of *brahman*? The answer the text offers is a complicated one. Everything is created by a personal god, but this god is simultaneously part of *brahman*. *Brahman* contains within itself a triad, which consists of the lower *ātman*, the higher *ātman*, and *pradhāna* (matter). Knowledge of this tripartite *brahman* leads to liberation from rebirth (1.7–8). The idea of a threefold *brahman* is unique to the *Śvetāśvatara Upaniṣad*.

The higher *ātman*, which is identified with the god Rudra/Śiva, is the divine creator of all, including *brahman*, but at the same time *brahman* is the universe in its totality, encompassing both the lower, unenlightened *ātman* and the higher enlightened *ātman*. In the *Ṛgveda*, Rudra is a wild and unpredictable god who can both bring diseases and heal the sick. He is called *śiva* ("kind" or "benevolent") in hymns that implore him to be gentle to his worshippers and not strike them with illness and misfortune. Over time, the adjective *śiva* became an alternative name for the deity, which later replaces the original name. In the *Śvetāśvatara Upaniṣad*, Rudra/Śiva is for the first time in ancient Indian literature praised as the highest god and the creator of all. The text is therefore seminal in the development of Śaivism (the worship of Śiva) in India. The lower self is "not lord" and bound to the world, while the higher self is identified with Śiva himself. This model of the two *ātmans* underscores that while the individual self is ultimately to be identified with the divine, it is ignorant of its own divine nature and in need of enlightenment to reach its higher state. *Pradhāna* ("matter") in the *Śvetāśvatara Upaniṣad* is an important precursor to the concept of *prakṛti* ("nature"), which is central in Sāṃkhya and Yoga philosophy. In these later systems of thought, *prakṛti* is encompasses all the physical and mental components of the world that are different from pure consciousness (*puruṣa*).

The second chapter of the text describes an early form of Yoga that involves correct posture, breathing techniques, and control of one's mind as a means to understanding the true nature of *ātman*/*brahman*. This chapter opens with an evocation of the Vedic sun god Savitṛ, whose control over mind and thoughts becomes a paradigm for human practice. Several of the stanzas in this chapter contain forms of the verbal root *yuj* ("to yoke, to control"), from which the noun *yoga* is also derived.

The third, fourth, and fifth chapters identify the *ātman* with Rudra and claim that people who know him as the Lord become immortal (3.7). Rudra is specifically said to be the source and origin of the gods (3.4), and he is identified with *puruṣa* and *brahman*. The third chapter describes the *ātman* itself as without gender: "It is neither a woman, nor a man, nor a hermaphrodite. It is ruled over the whatever body it obtains" (5.10).

The final chapter of the text returns to the question that was asked in the opening stanza of the Upaniṣad: What is the cause of *brahman*? The answer, claims the *Śvetāśvatara Upaniṣad*, is "the greatness of God in the world" (6.1). This God is all-knowing and without attributes, the creator, and the architect of time (6.2). The sixth chapter of the Upaniṣad identifies God (Rudra) as the prime mover and the cause of all things, but those who are wise can also perceive him in their own self. The One God is equated with the "inner self" (*antarātman*) of all beings (6.11), but at the same time, he is someone in whom a person can seek refuge: "He who created *brahman* in the beginning and gave him the Vedas, he who manifests himself by his own intelligence, in that God do I, seeking liberation, seek refuge" (6.18).

Māṇḍūkya Upaniṣad

The *Māṇḍūkya Upaniṣad* is a prose text in twelve sections and the shortest of all the Upaniṣads. The name of the text comes from that of a Vedic sage, Maṇḍuka (literally "the frog"). The text is formally affiliated with the *Atharvaveda*, but this association seems to be a mere formality, since the text has no clear connection to the *Atharvaveda*. The sixth-century CE commentary on the *Māṇḍūkya Upaniṣad*, the *Kārikā* of Gauḍapāda (also known as the *Āgama Śāstra*), is a foundational text in Advaita Vedānta philosophy and the earliest systematic presentation of Advaita teachings. According to Indian tradition, Gauḍapāda was the teacher of Govindapādācārya, who was Śaṅkara's teacher. Gauḍapāda's

Kārikā is the only pre-Śaṅkara commentary on the Upaniṣads that has survived.

The main themes in this Upaniṣad are the sacred syllable *oṃ* and the four states of consciousness. The Upaniṣad identifies *oṃ* with the entire world and breaks the syllable down into three phonemes: *a*, *u*, and *m*. These three parts of *oṃ* are identified with three states of consciousness: wakefulness, dream, and dreamless sleep, while the syllable in its totality is identified with a mystical fourth state of consciousness, *turīya* ("the fourth"), understood as complete unity with the *ātman*. Wakefulness is defined as being fully aware of the external world, dream as perceiving only the internal world, and dreamless sleep as having no desires and seeing no dreams and therefore being "a single mass of perception." The fourth state is said to be ungraspable, unthinkable, and indescribable, and identical with the *ātman* itself.

Although the *Māṇḍūkya Upaniṣad* is a very brief text, it has been immensely influential. The later *Muktikā Upaniṣad* states that to achieve spiritual liberation (*mokṣa*), studying the *Māṇḍūkya Upaniṣad* is enough (1.1.26). Significantly, the *Māṇḍūkya Upaniṣad* is often read with its *Kārikā* (explanatory commentary), which articulates a strong Advaita Vedānta stance (see chapter 8). According to Gauḍapāda's commentary, all *ātmans* are the same, and any perceived difference between them a mere illusion. *Ātman-brahman* is the only true reality, and everything else is created by the mind.

Praśna Upaniṣad

The *Praśna Upaniṣad* ("The Upaniṣad of Questions") is a prose text in six chapters, with a few verses interspersed. The text is affiliated with the *Atharvaveda*.

In each of the six chapters of the text, a wisdom seeker asks a question of the legendary teacher Pippalāda and receives an answer. While the earlier questions are grounded in a mythological worldview, the later questions become increasingly philosophical and abstract. The six men who ask the questions are all presented as learned sages, "searching for the highest *brahman*" (1.1).

In the first chapter of the text, Kabandhī Kātyāyana asks Pippalāda where living beings come from. In Pippalāda's version of creation, the primordial creator god, Prajāpati ("The Lord of Creatures"), longs for living beings and creates an ancestral couple: *prāṇa* (the life breath) and *rayi* (substance). The life breath is associated with the sun, but also with austerity and a quest for understanding *ātman*. Substance, on the other hand, is associated with ritual offerings, children, and family. In a way, this primordial duality, *prāṇa* and *rayi*, represents a tension at the heart of the Brahmanical tradition, between renunciation and a life devoted to the quest for knowledge on the one hand, and the life of a pious householder on the other. But the text also offers a more material, less abstract explanation of where living beings come from: Prajāpati is himself food, and from food comes semen, and from semen comes all living beings.

The second sage, Bhārgava Vaidarbhi, asks which deity is supreme among those that support a living being. In response, Pippalāda identifies *prāṇa* as the highest deity.

In the third chapter, Kausalya Āśvalāyana asks where this *prāṇa* comes from and how it enters the body. In response, Pippalāda explains the relationship between the *prāṇa* and the *ātman* and outlines a doctrine of the five breaths.

In the fourth chapter, the discussion turns to the question of agency. Sauryāyaṇī Gārgya wants Pippalāda to identify the true agent of a person's actions and the true subject of that person's experiences. Pippalāda identifies the breaths as that which keeps a person awake, the mind as the part that experiences dreams, but *ātman* or *puruṣa* as the true agent of all actions.

The fifth chapter focuses on the sacred syllable *oṃ*. Pippalāda explains to Śaibya Satyakāma that the syllable *oṃ* is made up of three sounds, *a*, *u*, and *m*. Pippalāda identifies the first sound, *a*, with the *Ṛgveda*, the first and second sounds together, *au*, with the *Yajurveda*, and the three sounds together, *auṃ* (=*oṃ*), with the *Sāmaveda*. But it is only by knowing the syllable as a totality, *oṃ*, over and above its constituent sounds, that a person can reach the world of *brahman*. Pippalāda implies that the complete truth about reality is only partially revealed in the first three Vedas. There is a strong implied suggestion that the full truth is only revealed in the fourth Veda, the *Atharvaveda*, a text with which this Upaniṣad is affiliated.

The last chapter of the text deals with the idea of a person consisting of sixteen parts. Pippalāda reveals to Sukeśa Bhāradvāja that the sixteenfold person is "the highest *brahman*," who is present "right here, within the body." This revelation of the nature of *brahman* is the culmination of Pippalāda's teachings. The number 16 is a significant one in India and symbolizes wholeness and completion. Many Vedic rituals require sixteen priests, a human being is as tall as sixteen bricks, and the moon has sixteen phases (*kalās*) in Hindu astronomy. The person consisting of sixteen parts therefore stands for the full and complete person.

Prāṇa, or life breath, is a central concept in the *Praśna Upaniṣad*. This breath is identified with the Vedic gods Prajāpati, Indra, and Rudra, but is also said to arise from *ātman* itself. The progression of the questions asked of Pippalāda in the text suggests that understanding *prāna* is an important step toward understanding *ātman* itself.

The Maitrī Upaniṣad

This Upaniṣad, a prose text in six chapters, is also known as the *Maitri*, *Maitreya*, *Maitrāyaṇa*, *Maitrāyaṇī*, or *Maitrāyaṇīya*

Upaniṣad. It is formally affiliated with the *Maitrāyaṇīya* school of the *Black Yajurveda*, although the later *Muktikā Upaniṣad* lists the *Maitrī* as one of the Upaniṣads of the *Sāmaveda*. Śaṇkara did not compose a commentary on the *Maitrī Upaniṣad*, but there are commentaries on the text by Vidyāraṇya (fourteenth century) and Rāmatīrtha (seventeenth century).

The central theme in the *Maitrī Upaniṣad* is the discovery of *ātman*. The first chapter introduces the frame narrative of the text, which features king Bṛhadratha who wants to discover the true nature of *ātman*. He asks the sage Śākāyanya to explain *ātman* to him, and the sage, after some initial reluctance, does so.

In the second chapter, Śākāyanya explains that the Vedic creator god Prajāpati entered all living creatures as the fivefold breath. Śākāyanya also uses the parable of the chariot, known from the *Kaṭha Upaniṣad*, and compares the body to a chariot, the mind to the charioteer, the *ātman* to the driver of the chariot, and the senses to wild horses that must be reined in.

The third chapter differentiates between two forms of *ātman*, a higher enlightened form, and a lower unenlightened form. It is the lower self, here called *bhūtātman* ("the being-self"), that is reborn and experiences the fruit of *karma* (3.2). The *bhūtātman* is influenced by the three *guṇas* (qualities) of nature: light, passion, and darkness (*sattva*, *rajas*, and *tamas*), while the higher, immortal self remains unaffected.

The fourth chapter of the text reflects on the worship of various deities. The different gods are just different forms of the one divine *brahman* (4.5–6), but a person must eventually move beyond the worship of deities to attain union with the highest *ātman*.

The fifth chapter equates everything, including the gods, with the *ātman* and reflects further on the three *guṇas* (qualities of nature). The sixth chapter describes the inner and the outer *ātman* and states that humans should meditate on both these selves, using the syllable *oṃ*.

Śaṅkara and the Creation of an Upaniṣadic Canon

The eighth-century philosopher Śaṅkara composed commentaries to eleven of the older Upaniṣads: *Bṛhadāraṇyaka*, *Chāndogya*, *Taittirīya*, *Aitareya*, *Śvetāśvatara*, *Īśā*, *Kena*, *Kaṭha*, *Praśna*, *Muṇḍaka*, and *Māṇḍūkya*. Śaṅkara's commentaries been profoundly influential for the interpretation of these Upaniṣads in later Hindu thought.

Intriguingly, Śaṅkara composed two commentaries on the *Kena Upaniṣad*, the *Padabhāṣya* ("Word Commentary") and the *Vākyabhāṣya* ("Sentence Commentary"). We do not know why he chose to compose two separate commentaries on this text, but not on any of the other Upaniṣads. It has been speculated that only the *Padabhāṣya* is the original work of Śaṅkara, but as Mayeda (1967) has demonstrated, the two commentaries are complementary rather than redundant, and they are both characterized by the style, idiosyncratic vocabulary, and philosophical ideas known from the other commentaries ascribed to Śaṅkara. It seems reasonable, therefore, to attribute the authorship of both these commentaries to Śaṅkara himself.

Śaṅkara's commentary on the *Bṛhadāraṇyaka Upaniṣad* is based on the *Kāṇva*, rather than the *Mādhyaṃdina* recension of the text, which may in turn have contributed to the popularity of the *Kāṇva* recension relative to the *Mādhyaṃdina* one in later Indian philosophy. Most translations of the text into other languages are based on the *Kāṇva* recension.

While linguistic evidence suggests that the *Kauṣītaki Upaniṣad* is as old as some of the other older Upaniṣadic texts, it is not included among the Upaniṣads that Śaṅkara commented on. It seems that Śaṅkara was familiar with the *Kauṣītaki Upaniṣad*, however, since he cites the text several times in his commentary on the *Brahmasūtra*. It is likely that Śaṅkara's reason for not composing a commentary on this text, even if he was familiar with it, was theological. In his commentaries, Śaṅkara argues that *brahman* is an impersonal divine force rather than a personal god, and it is likely that the *Kauṣītaki Upaniṣad*'s theistic nature made it difficult to compose a commentary on the text that was in alignment with Śaṅkara's Advaita Vedānta philosophy. Additionally, the inclusion of magical rites for winning a woman's love, becoming rich, or getting children in the *Kauṣītaki Upaniṣad* are also likely to have been less than appealing to the philosopher.

Śaṅkara did, however, compose a commentary on the *Īśā Upaniṣad*, a text with undeniably theistic tendencies. But for Śaṅkara, the "lord" (*Īśā*) of the text is not a personal god, but rather *ātman* itself.

Śaṅkara's *Upaniṣadbhāṣyā*, the collection of his commentaries of the Upaniṣads, is one of the finest examples of Indian commentarial literature. Śaṅkara also composed commentaries on two other texts, the *Brahmasūtra* and the *Bhagavadgītā*, and together with his Upaniṣad commentaries, these are among the foundational texts of Advaita Vedānta philosophy, a school of thought that is based on the idea of an absolute identity of *ātman* and *brahman*.

In Śaṅkara's reading, the Upaniṣads all present *ātman* and *brahman* as completely one, without a difference, and *brahman* as an impersonal divine force rather than a personal divine being. In Śaṅkara's view, *ātman-brahman* constitutes all of reality. Not only does Śaṅkara interpret the Upaniṣads in light of his own non-dualist philosophy; his philosophy grows out of his reading of the older Upaniṣads.

Śaṅkara's commentary on the Upaniṣads has been enormously influential in India, not just because his reading of these texts formed the basis for Advaita Vedānta philosophy, but also because his commentaries were instrumental in creating the *idea* of a general "philosophy of the Upaniṣads," the notion that there is a set of doctrines that all the classical Upaniṣads have in common, regardless of their *śākhā*-affiliation. While *ātman* and *brahman* are central concepts in all the classical Upaniṣads, the absolute identification of the two concepts owes more to Śaṅkara's reading than to the text of the Upaniṣads themselves. But the very idea that the Upaniṣads should be studied together, and that they articulate a single doctrine, regardless of each text's school affiliation, is itself groundbreaking. While a similar notion of the Upaniṣads as a unified body of texts seems to inform the older *Brahmasūtra* as well (see chapter 8), the first full articulation of this idea is found in the works of Śaṅkara.

Śaṅkara's commentaries, which embedded the Upaniṣadic texts themselves, were also instrumental in preserving the texts of the Upaniṣads. It is likely that one of the reasons why so many variant readings are found in the text of the *Kauṣītaki Upaniṣad* compared to other Upaniṣadic texts is precisely that an authoritative version of the text had not been established through Śaṅkara's commentaries.

The later Vedānta philosophers Rāmānuja (1017–1137) and Madhva (1238–1317) also wrote extensively on the Upaniṣads. While Rāmānuja did not write separate commentaries on the Upaniṣads, he quoted extensively from the eleven Upaniṣads in Śaṅkara's "canon" in his work and contributed to their popularity. Madhva composed commentaries on ten Upaniṣads: *Bṛhadāraṇyaka*, *Chāndogya*, *Taittirīya*, *Aitareya*, *Īśā*, *Kena*, *Kaṭha*, *Praśna*, *Muṇḍaka*, and *Māṇḍūkya*. These are the same Upaniṣads that Śaṅkara commented on, except for the *Śvetāśvatara Upaniṣad*, whose identification of Śiva with *ātman*/*brahman* may not have appealed to the passionate Viṣṇu-devotee Madhva.

Śaṅkara's "canon" of eleven Upaniṣads is not the only one known to us, however. As mentioned in the first chapter, the Mughal emperor Dara Shikoh's 1657 translation of the Upaniṣads into Persian, contains fifty texts, although two of them are not Upaniṣads at all (*Ṛgveda* 10.90, the Hymn to Cosmic Man [*Puruṣa*] and the *Śatarudriya*, the list of a hundred names of the god Rudra from the *Vājasaneyī Saṃhitā* 16, 1–66 of the *Yajurveda*). The remaining texts included in *Sirr-i-akbar* include the eleven Upaniṣads commented on by Śaṅkara, the *Kauṣītaki* and *Maitrī Upaniṣads*, as well as later

Upaniṣads. Like Śaṅkara, Dara Shikoh draws on the *Kāṇva* recension of the *Bṛhadāraṇyaka Upaniṣad*.

The medieval *Muktikā Upaniṣad* lists 108 Upaniṣads. The *Muktikā Upaniṣad* itself lists thirteen of these texts as *mukhya* ("principal") Upaniṣads: the *Īśā*, *Kena*, *Kaṭha*, *Praśna*, *Muṇḍaka*, *Māṇḍūkya*, *Taittirīya*, *Aitareya*, *Chāndogya*, *Bṛhadāraṇyaka*, *Śvetāśvatara*, *Maitrāyaṇīya* (*Maitrī*), and *Kauṣītaki Upaniṣads*. In other words, the *Muktikā Upaniṣad* recognizes the eleven Upaniṣadic texts commented on by Śaṅkara as well as *Kauṣītaki* and *Maitrī* as the main Upaniṣads.

The other Upaniṣads listed by the *Muktikā Upaniṣad* include Vaiṣṇava Upaniṣads (e.g., *Mahānārāyaṇa*, *Nṛsiṃhatapanīya*, *Rāmatāpanīya*, *Avyakta*, *Kṛṣṇa*) that identify *ātman*/*brahman* with the god Viṣṇu, Śaiva Upaniṣads that identify *ātman*/*brahman* with the god Śiva (*Kaivalya*, *Akṣamālikā*, *Atharvaśiras*, *Kālāgnirudra*, *Atharvaśikhā*), and Śākta/Devī Upaniṣads (*Sītā*, *Devī*, *Tripurā*, *Bhāvanā*) that identify *ātman*/*brahman* with various goddesses. The *Muktikā Upaniṣad* also classifies some of these later Upaniṣads as Yoga Upaniṣads, a category that includes *Haṃsa Upaniṣad*, *Yogatattva Upaniṣad*, *Yogakuṇḍalinī Upaniṣad*, and *Dhyānabindu Upaniṣad*. Other Upaniṣads in this collection relate to renunciation (*Nirvāṇa*, *Jābāla*, *Paramahaṃsa*). Paul Deussen (1897) referred to these as Saṃnyāsa (renunciation) Upaniṣads, and other Western scholars have since adopted the term. It should be noted, however, that this is not an Indian category that is used in the Sanskrit tradition itself. The *Muktikā Upaniṣad* is familiar with several collections of Upaniṣads; it states that in order to obtain liberation, reading the *Māṇḍūkya Upaniṣad* alone should be sufficient, but if it is not, a person should then study "the ten Upaniṣads" (*Īśā*, *Kena*, *Kaṭha*, *Praśna*, *Muṇḍaka*, *Māṇḍūkya*, *Taittirīya*, *Aitareya*, *Chāndogya*, and *Bṛhadāraṇyaka*), and if that is also not enough, "the thirty-two Upaniṣads," and finally, if a person is still not enlightened, all the 108 Upaniṣads in the *Muktikā Upaniṣad*'s list. It is not clear exactly which texts were included in the "thirty-two Upaniṣads", although one may speculate that this refers to the thirty-two texts in the *Muktikā Upaniṣad*'s list affiliated with the *Kṛṣṇa Yajurveda*.

Despite the existence of more expanded Upaniṣadic canons, the "classical" eleven texts known to Śaṅkara, the *Kauṣītaki Upaniṣad*, and the *Maitrī Upaniṣad* have been particularly influential in Indian philosophy and religion.

5
Social and Political Context

The Geographical Context

Where were the classical Upaniṣads composed? Based on place names mentioned in the texts, we know that they were likely composed in an area of north India between the Himalaya mountains in the north and the Vindhya mountains in the south, the Indus River in the northwest, and the Bay of Bengal in the east.

The older Vedic texts that preceded the Upaniṣads were generally composed further to the west, and the western areas like Kuru-Pañcāla are still regarded as centers of Vedic orthodoxy in the Upanishads. But new and interesting ideas are beginning to arise among thinkers in the eastern areas like Kosala and Videha. This growth of new cultural centers in the east is reflected, for example in the *Bṛhadāraṇyaka Upaniṣad*'s narrative about the contest at the court of King Janaka of Videha, where the local priest Yājñavalkya outshines the Brahmans from the Kuru-Pañcāla region.

The oldest of the classical Upaniṣads, the *Bṛhadāraṇyaka*, frequently mentions the Videha religion in eastern India, which corresponds roughly to the modern state of Bihar. Chapters 3 and 4 of the *Bṛhadāraṇyaka Upaniṣad* take place at the court of King Janaka of Videha, and Brahmans from the Kuru (modern Haryana) and Pañcāla (modern Uttar Pradesh) regions further west visit his court. There is some geographical rivalry implied in this text, and Yājñavalkya demonstrates that he is consistently more knowledgeable that the Brahmans of Kuru and Pañcāla (see, e.g., *Bṛhadāraṇyaka Upaniṣad* 3.9.19). But there are knowledgeable Brahmans in the Kuru and Pañcāla regions as well; chapter 2 of

The Classical Upaniṣads. Signe Cohen, Oxford University Press. © Oxford University Press 2024.
DOI: 10.1093/oso/9780197654156.003.0005

the *Bṛhadāraṇyaka Upaniṣad* describes a wisdom teacher from Pañcāla, Jaivali Pravāhaṇa, who becomes the teacher of Śvetaketu and his father Āruṇi. The same characters are mentioned in *Chāndogya Upaniṣad* 5.3.1, and yet again their geographical location is identified as Pañcāla. The *Chāndogya Upaniṣad* also tells the story of a couple from Kuru, Uṣasti Cākrāyaṇa and his wife Āṭikī, who are starving due to locusts destroying the crops in the land. Uṣasti approaches the king, who is ready to perform a sacrifice, and demonstrates that he has deeper knowledge of the sacred chants than the officiating priests (1.10). Kuru is mentioned again in a cryptic verse from *Chāndogya Upaniṣad* 4.17.9, where a Brahman protects the men of Kuru "like a mare." From these small geographical clues, it seems that the *Bṛhadāraṇyaka Upaniṣad* may have originated in the Videha region, while the *Chāndogya Upaniṣad* shows stronger ties to the Kuru-Pañcāla regions further west.

The city of Kāśī (modern-day Varanasi in Uttar Pradesh) is mentioned in both the *Bṛhadāraṇyaka* and the *Kauṣītaḳi Upaniṣad.* The *Bṛhadāraṇyaka Upaniṣad* (2.1) presents the king of Kāśī, Ajātaśatru, as a wise man who knows far more than the learned Brahman who comes to teach him. The mention of fierce warriors of Kāśī and Videha in *Bṛhadāraṇyaka Upaniṣad* 3.8.2 underscores the power of the eastern regions in the text.

The *Kaṭha* school of Vedic recitation, which produced the *Kaṭha Upaniṣad*, likely flourished in the eastern Panjab, while the *Taittirīya* school was active further east in Pañcāla. Since the *Śvetāśvatara Upaniṣad* is not part of a known larger Vedic textual corpus, it is very difficult to determine the text's geographical origin.

The *Kauṣītaki Upaniṣad* describes the would-be wisdom teacher Bālakī as a "learned and well-traveled man" (4.1), and the places he has visited before coming to the city of Kāśī include Uśīnara, Satvan, Matsya, Kuru and Pañcāla, and Videha. Uśīnara was located Gandhāra (present-day Afghanistan and northwest Pakistan) in the northwest, and Matsya in today's Rajasthan in the west. It is not clear where Satvan was, but from the context, it is possible that it was located somewhere between Gandhāra and Rajasthan, that is, somewhere in current-day eastern Pakistan. It seems, then, that a "well-traveled man" at the time of the Upaniṣads would have traveled across a broad swath of northern India/Pakistan.

Buddhist texts refer to sixteen Great Realms (*mahājanapada*) that existed in Northern India prior to the time of the Buddha. These sixteen are Aṅga, Assaka (Aśmaka), Avanti, Cedī, Gandhāra, Kāśī, Kamboja, Kosala, Kuru, Magadha, Malla, Matsya, Pañcāla, Śūrasena, Vajji (Vṛji), and Vatsa. Among these, the Upaniṣads are familiar with Kāśī, Kosala, Kuru, Matsya, Pañcāla, and Gandhāra but make no mention of the realms farther away from the Kuru-Pañcāla center, such as Kamboja in the north, Cedī, Avanti, or Aśmaka in the south, or Magadha, Aṅga, and Vṛji in the east.

Daily Life in the Upaniṣads

The older Upaniṣads were composed during a period of growing urbanization and trade in northern India, but agriculture was still the main livelihood. Rice was the main crop, but barley, millet, lentils, wheat, and sesame are also mentioned. *Bṛhadāraṇyaka Upaniṣad* (6.4.15–18) mentions cooked rice mixed with yoghurt and butter, cooked rice mixed with sesame seeds and butter, and cooked rice mixed with meat and butter. It is unlikely that meat was a mainstay of the diet, but it does seem to have been consumed in India in this time period. Honey is also mentioned in several passages. The well-known "Honey Section" of the *Bṛhadāraṇyaka Upaniṣad* (2.5) uses "honey" in the sense of "lifegiving" essence, which suggests that this food was highly valued: "The earth is the honey of all beings, and all beings are the honey of the earth." The text goes on to identify not only the earth, but also the waters, fire, wind, the sun, the directions of the sky, the moon, lightning, thunder, space, *dharma* (law), truth, humanity, and eventually *ātman* itself, as the "honey" or essence of all beings.

Some of the older Upaniṣads have a particular obsession with food. In the worldview of the Upaniṣads, food is not just something that people consume to stay alive, but a cosmic and spiritual substance as well. Food even takes its place in the evolution of the world in *Taittirīya Upaniṣad* 2.1:

> From the self, space arose, from space air, from air fire, from fire waters, from waters earth, from earth plants, from plants food, and from food man. Man is made from the essence of food.

Not only are humans dependent on food to live; they are born from food and will again return to food: "All beings on earth are born from food. They live by food alone once they are born, and in the end, they will return to food" (*Taittirīya Upaniṣad* 2.2). It is easy to interpret this passage as a reference to the fact that food sustains all living beings, and that those living beings will after death become food for animals and insects. But food means more than just physical nourishment: "They who worship *brahman* as food, they will get all food for themselves" (*Taittirīya Upaniṣad* 2.2). The idea that food can be equated with the cosmic power *brahman* itself is striking. The third chapter of this Upaniṣad even equates *brahman* with food. This passage tells the story of Bhr̥gu, the son of the Vedic god Varuṇa, who asks his father to teach him about *brahman.* Varuṇa defines *brahman* as "food, life breath, sight, hearing, mind, and speech" (3.5.3). Bhr̥gu meditates on what his father tells him and comes to understand all these five concepts as forms of the divine *brahman*. The text continues (3.7):

> The rule is that one should not make light of food. The life breath is food, and the body is the eater of food. The body is based on the life breath, and the life breath on the body. Therefore, food is based on food. When someone knows this food based on food, he will be well established. He will be someone who had food

> and eats food. He will become a great man through his offspring, his cattle, and the radiance of his knowledge. He will become a great man through his fame. The rule is that one should not reject food. Water is food, and fire is the eater of food. Fire is based on water, and water on fire. Therefore, food is based on food. When someone knows this food based on food, he will be well established. He will be someone who had food and eats food. He will become a great man through his offspring, his cattle, and the radiance of his knowledge. He will become a great man through his fame. The rule is that one should make a lot of food. The earth is food, and space is the eater of food. Space is based on earth, and earth on space. Therefore, food is based on food. When someone knows this food based on food, he will be well established. He will be someone who had food and eats food. He will become a great man through his offspring, his cattle, and the radiance of his knowledge. He will become a great man through his fame.

This intriguing passage introduces some common-sense advice about food: don't make light of it, don't reject it, and prepare enough of it. But these "rules" about food are placed in a larger cosmic context as food is equated with the life breath itself as well as with the elements of fire, water, earth, and space. The emphasis on becoming someone who has food suggests some anxieties surrounding food security—anxieties that, our Upaniṣad assures us, can be allayed through having the correct knowledge about the food's mystical identity with the elements and with *brahman* itself.

The very self of a person consists of five layers: the self made of food, the self made of life breath, the self made of mind, the self made of perception, and the self made of bliss. A man who knows this, the *Taittirīya Upaniṣad* states, will "depart from this world" and travel through these five selves, "eating whatever he wants and taking on whatever form he wants", while singing an ecstatic chant (3.10):

I am food! I am food! I am food!
I eat food! I eat food! I eat food!
I set the rhythm! I set the rhythm! I set the rhythm!
I am the firstborn of truth
Born before the gods,
In the navel of the immortal.
The one who gives me
Will eat me.
I am food!
I eat the one who eats the Good!
I have conquered the whole world!
I am like a light in the firmament.

Here, both cosmic matter and immortality itself are articulated in terms of food. The *Bṛhadāraṇyaka Upaniṣad* also seems to be familiar with the idea of *brahman* itself being identified with food, although this text puts a slightly different spin on the idea (5.12). The authors of the *Bṛhadāraṇyaka Upaniṣad* note that "some people" say that *brahman* is food, but that this is not correct. Instead, they argue that *brahman* must be understood as *both* food and life breath together. Elsewhere, this text calls both food and life breath "deities" (3.9.8), which suggests that food is perceived as a life-sustaining force. The *Bṛhadāraṇyaka Upaniṣad* also defines *ātman* as "the eater of food and the giver of wealth" (4.4.24). The *Chāndogya Upaniṣad* 1.11.9 also calls food "a deity." The identification of *brahman* with food is also mentioned in *Chāndogya Upaniṣad* 7.9.2.

Several Upaniṣadic passages suggest that certain kinds of knowledge will lead to an abundance of food ("When a man knows this, his food will never decrease," *Bṛhadāraṇyaka Upaniṣad* 2.2.2, "When a man know this, he becomes the eater of the whole world, and the whole world becomes his food," *Bṛhadāraṇyaka Upaniṣad* 2.2.4, "When a man knows this hidden connection of the sāman chants, speech will give him the milk that is the milk of speech, and he will possess and eat food," *Chāndogya Upaniṣad* 1.13.4; cf.

Chāndogya Upaniṣad 2.8.3 and 2.12.2, 2.14.4). Here, food seems to represent abundance and joy and fulfillment.

The *Aitareya Upaniṣad* describes how *ātman* creates the worlds. At one point, he also creates food to sustain what he has created, but then the food that emerges from the waters tries to escape. The self tries to capture the food by means of speech, but he can't; as the text states, if he had captured food by speech, one could become full by just speaking of food (*Aitareya Upaniṣad* 1.3.3). The *ātman* then desperately tries to capture the run-away food by means of out-breath, sight, hearing, skin, mind, and finally his penis, before he finally succeeds in catching it with his in-breath. The idea of food as an essential component of the cosmos itself can be traced back to the Vedic sacrifice where humans offer food and drink to the gods and are blessed with abundant food in return.

In short, food is perceived both as bodily nourishment and divine principle in the Upaniṣads. The importance of food is also underscored in passages that describe the relationship between guests and hosts. Feeding one's guests is essential, and even Death himself is worried when a young Brahman boy shows up at his house unannounced and is therefore left to wait without food and water until his host returns home (*Kaṭha Upaniṣad* 1). Guests, the *Taittirīya Upaniṣad* admonishes, should be treated like gods (1.11.2). A later passage in the same text declares: "The rule is that one should never turn anyone away from one's home. Therefore, one should get a lot of food in every way possible" (3.10.1). Hospitality to guests, even unexpected and uninvited ones, is paramount.

Animal husbandry was important in Upaniṣadic times, and a person's wealth was often measured in how many cows they owned. *Taittirīya Upaniṣad* (1.4.1–2) contains a prayer for wisdom, clothes, cows, food, and drink, with a request that Prosperity will come to the speaker, "rich in sheep and cows." The epitome of generosity was to give away numerous cows, as the generous king Janaka does in the *Bṛhadāraṇyaka Upaniṣad*. There are references to domesticated horses, goats, and sheep, and elephants and horse-drawn chariots are also mentioned. The texts distinguish clearly between wild animals (*Bṛhadāraṇyaka Upaniṣad* 1.4.16; *Chāndogya Upaniṣad* 2.9.7) and domestic ones (*Chāndogya Upaniṣad* 7.2.1, 7.7.1, 7.8.1, 7.10.1). Tiger, lions, wolves, rhinoceroses, and boars are mentioned (*Chāndogya Upaniṣad* 6.10.2; *Kauṣītaki Upaniṣad* 1.2). But wild animals do not appear to have been a major threat; the wild animals flee from humans (*Chāndogya Upaniṣad* 2.9.7). The old Vedic horse sacrifice (*aśvamedha*) is still referenced (*Bṛhadāraṇyaka Upaniṣad* 1.2.7) but appears to be more of a metaphor than a description of a contemporary practice. There are also several references to dogs in the Upaniṣads. There is a passing reference to a theoretical situation of dogs and birds consuming a person's heart (*Bṛhadāraṇyaka Upaniṣad* 3.9.25), but an intriguing passage in the *Chāndogya Upaniṣad* also compares dogs to Vedic priests (1.12):

> Next, there is the High Chant of the dogs. One day Baka Dālbhya—or maybe Glāva Maitreya—went to perform his recitation, and a white dog appeared before him. Other dogs gathered around the white dog and said: "Please, sir, find food for us by singing. We are very hungry." And he said to them: "Come back and meet me here in the morning." Then Baka Dālbhya—or maybe Glāva Maitreya—watched that place. Then the dogs came in, slinking in quietly just like priests slink in quietly in a row, holding each other's backs and sang the chant called Bahiṣpavamāna. They sat down and chanted huṃ. They chanted: "*Oṃ*, let us eat. *Oṃ*, let us drink. *Oṃ*, may the gods Varuṇa, Prajāpati and Savitṛ bring us food here. Lord of food, bring us food! Bring it here, bring it, bring it, *oṃ*."

In mildly satirical passage, it appears that dogs squeaking and begging for food strike the authors as being like priests chanting to obtain food and plenitude. There is certainly a humorous element present in this comparison, but the text suggests that the vocalization of hungry dogs and the chants of priests have something else in common other than making sounds: they can bring about the desired result. The idea that dogs, like priests, can "sing" for their food, suggests that the authors were familiar with dogs begging for food.

Birds are also frequently mentioned in the Upaniṣads. Geese seem to be a particular favorite of the Upaniṣadic authors; the highest principle *ātman/brahman* is even compared to a goose (*haṃsa*) that dwells in the middle of the world (*Śvetāśvatara Upaniṣad* 6.15). The idea that the goose is a symbol for the soul/self is often found in later Hindu thought as well. There has been a great deal of scholarly debate over the precise translation of the Sanskrit *haṃsa*. Western scholars used to translate this term "swan," but the translation "goose" has now become far more common. The Sanskrit word is distantly related to both the German *Ganse* and the English *goose*. Although mute swans do migrate to India in the winter, swans are quite rare on the subcontinent, and it is likely that the *haṃsa* in Sanskrit text was intended to designate a more common goose instead. The *Śvetāśvatara Upaniṣad* compares the individual *ātman* to a goose that flutters around within the vast cosmic wheel of *brahman* (1.6).

Playing dice, singing, and instrumental music are mentioned as pleasant pastimes in the Upaniṣads. According to *Chāndogya Upaniṣad* 4.1.4, the one who gets the highest throw in dice wins everything, which suggests that the dice game played in this time period was similar to that described in the Vedic hymn sometimes referred to as the Gambler's Lament (*Ṛgveda* 10.34). Although the rules of the game are not entirely clear from the extant texts, it appears to have been played with 150 dice, made from the nuts of the *vibhītaka/vibhīdaka* or myrobalan tree, *Terminalia bellerica*, which often have flattened sides, like dice from elsewhere in the world. The players reach into the gaming hollow or the game board and grab a random number of dice. The winner ends up with a number of dice that is evenly divisible by four. The losing "throw" involves having one die left over when the dice are divided by four.

The poor gambler in *Ṛgveda* 10.34 ends up losing both his property and his wife, although everything he has lost appears to be restored to him by the end of the hymn.

The *Bṛhadāraṇyaka Upaniṣad* mentions drums, conches, and lutes (4.5.8–10), while the *Chāndogya Upaniṣad* mentions "the world of singing and music" as one of the possible worlds a person could desire to obtain, along with "the world of perfumes and garlands" and "the world of food and drink" (8.2.6–8). The *Chāndogya Upaniṣad* also mentions singing and playing the lute as a means of obtaining wealth (1.8.6), which suggests that some people may have made their living as professional singers and musicians. Among the gifts Death offers to the boy Naciketas (instead of the knowledge Naciketas wants from him) are young women, chariots, and lutes (*Kaṭha Upaniṣad* 1.25).

The Upaniṣads are mostly preoccupied with the lives of teachers and students, but we catch little glimpses of family life and larger social structures as well. Social relations in the Upaniṣads are summed up in *Taittirīya Upaniṣad* 1.11.2: "Treat you mother like a god. Treat your father like a god. Treat your teacher like a god. Treat your guests like gods."

The social bond that is more important than any other in the Upaniṣads is that between teachers and students. The importance of the student-teacher relationship is emphasized by the genealogies in the Upaniṣads (*Bṛhadāraṇyaka Upaniṣad* 2.6, 4.6, 6.5; *Muṇḍaka Upaniṣad* 1.1–2). Significantly, these are never genealogies of parents and children, but rather lists of teachers and students.

The Upaniṣadic studentship is modeled on the older Vedic education but introduces some significant new features. A boy from the three upper classes would study the Vedas, maybe with a group of other boys, with a Brahman teacher, and the boys would live at the teacher's house for the duration of their student days. In *Chāndogya Upaniṣad* 6.1, we hear about a boy returning home at age twenty-four after completing twelve years of education. According to

Taittirīya Upaniṣad 1.11.1–2, a teacher should say the following when a student has completed his education:

> Speak the truth, observe *dharma*, do not neglect your private Veda recitation. Give a gift to the teacher, and do not cut off your family line. Do not neglect the truth, do not neglect *dharma*, do not neglect your health or wealth, do not neglect your private or public Veda recitation. Do not neglect rites to gods or ancestors.

But while the older Upaniṣads are familiar with the world of Vedic education, they also operate with a different, informal model of studentship, where students must find a worthy teacher on their own and beg him to accept them. Many of the Upaniṣadic students are not young boys, but adult men, who have realized that whatever knowledge they have acquired through traditional means is not sufficient. In *Chāndogya Upaniṣad* 7.1, the student Nārada approaches the wisdom teacher Sanatkumāra for instruction. Nārada summarizes his own previous education as follows:

> "Sir, I have studied the *Ṛgveda*, the *Yajurveda*, the *Sāmaveda*, and the *Ātharvaṇa* [*Atharvaveda*] as the fourth, histories and old legends as the fifth among the Vedas, ancestor rituals, mathematics, augury, treasure-finding, dialogues, monologues, the science of the gods, the science of rituals, the science of spirits, the science of government, the science of astrology, and the science of serpents. I have studied all these things." But he added: "Here I am, someone who knows all the Vedic formulas, but do not know the self."

Nārada is well-versed in the various branches of knowledge of his time, and yet he knows that something is missing from his impressive education.

Often, a teacher is depicted as reluctant to teach, and the student must prove himself worthy by not giving up in the face of refusal or obstacles. In *Chāndogya Upaniṣad* 4.1–3, for example, the wealthy Jānaśruti Pautrāyaṇa wants to be the student of the eccentric homeless wisdom teacher Raikva, and he offers Raikva money, a chariot, cows, and finally his own daughter in order to convince the teacher to accept him as a student. Even gods and demons must seek wisdom from enlightened teachers. In *Chāndogya Upaniṣad* 8.7–12, we hear about Indra and Virocana, a god and a demon, approaching the old Vedic creator god Prajāpati to become his students. Prajāpati initially reveals only a superficial part of his knowledge, however. The demon Virocana is satisfied with the initial answer, while Indra shows his superiority as a student by insisting on coming back for deeper answers until he learns the truth about *ātman* and *brahman*. In the *Kaṭha Upaniṣad*, Yama likewise tries to offer the boy Naciketas worldly gifts instead of the ultimate truth about death. By insisting on the knowledge, rather than the riches, Naciketas shows himself as a worthy student.

But the knowledge divulged by the wisdom teachers of the Upaniṣads is not for everyone. Several passages emphasize the esoteric and secret nature of these teachings. Both the *Bṛhadāraṇyaka Upaniṣad* (6.3.12) and the *Chāndogya Upaniṣad* (3.11.4) warn that the teachings must not be disclosed to someone who is not a son or a worthy student.

The relationship between fathers and sons also plays a significant role in the Upaniṣads, although it is less significant overall than that of teachers and students. The most prominent father-son relationships in these texts are the ones where the father also acts as a teacher for his son—or fails to do so. The great Upaniṣadic philosopher Yājñavalkya cites his father as a source of authority several times (*Bṛhadāraṇyaka Upaniṣad* 4.1.2–7), and we learn that Uddālaka Āruṇi was taught by his own father (*Bṛhadāraṇyaka Upaniṣad* 3.11.4); the text states: "Therefore, a father should impart this truth only to his oldest son or a worthy student." The six sages who approach the great Pippalāda to learn about the ultimate reality in the *Praṣna Upaniṣad* ultimately recognize him as their "father" in a spiritual sense: "They praised him and said: 'You are our father, for you have brought us to the farthest shore beyond ignorance'" (6.8).

While some Upaniṣadic fathers teach their sons well at home, there are also examples of sons who must go elsewhere to get the insights that their fathers are not able to provide.

Uddālaka Āruṇi and his son Śvetaketu provide an excellent example of a good father-son relationship in the Upaniṣads (*Bṛhadāraṇyaka Upaniṣad* 6.2; *Chāndogya Upaniṣad* 5.3; *Kauṣītaki Upaniṣad* 1). As mentioned in previous chapters, when Śvetaketu discovers that what his father has taught him at home is not sufficient, he runs back to his father and tells him that king Jaivali Pravāhaṇa (called Citra Gāṅgyāyani in the *Kauṣītaki Upaniṣad*) asked him questions he couldn't answer. Uddālaka Āruṇi does what a good father should do under the circumstances; when his ignorance is exposed, he joins his son in becoming the king's student. But elsewhere in the *Chāndogya Upaniṣad* (6.1–16), Uddālaka Āruṇi is himself presented as an enlightened wisdom teacher who instructs his son Śvetaketu about the nature of reality.

The boy Naciketas, on the other hand, has a somewhat complicated relationship with his father in the *Kaṭha Upaniṣad*. While Uddālaka Āruṇi teaches his son Śvetaketu to the best of his ability, Naciketas' father Uśan Vājaśravas does not seem particularly concerned with his son's education. Instead of answering his son's questions as a good teacher should do, Uśan Vājaśravas forces his son to find a better teacher, which in this case turns out to be Death himself. It is rather touching that Naciketas asks Death to return him to his father, and for his father's anger to be appeased, which suggests that the boy is still very fond of his temperamental father.

The young Satyakāma Jābālā (*Chāndogya Upaniṣad* 4.4) doesn't know who his father is, but he is able to find himself suitable teachers, even if some of those teachers are somewhat unusual (a bull, the fire, a wild goose, a waterbird, and a human teacher). Although fathers are far more prominent than mothers in the Upaniṣad, mothers are also mentioned on serval occasions; *Bṛhadāraṇyaka Upaniṣad* 1.5.7 identifies the father with the mind, the mother with speech, and the child with breath—all essential components of the person.

We hear less about husbands and wives in the Upaniṣads than about fathers and sons, but a few significant examples should be mentioned. *Chāndogya Upaniṣad* (1.10) tells of a poor man, Uṣasti Cākrāyaṇa and his wife Āṭiki. The two of them are hungry due to the crops' being destroyed by hailstorms, and Uṣasti Cākrāyaṇa begs an elephant owner for food. The elephant owner is in the process of eating beans, and he offers Uṣasti Cākrāyaṇa the leftovers from his plate. Although eating someone else's leftovers is considered impure, Uṣasti Cākrāyaṇa is desperate, and he accepts the beans. But he only eats some of them and brings the rest home to his wife; even she "had already eaten well" (1.10.5). The text implies that Uṣasti Cākrāyaṇa had given her the food he had and gone hungry himself. Even so, he brings a portion of the beans home to his wife, which suggests that he is putting her needs above his own. His wife Āṭiki is equally unselfish, however; she puts them aside and feed them to him the next morning. The couple's actions in this narrative suggest a strong mutual affection and willingness to make sacrifices for the sake of one's partner.

As we have seen, the wisdom teacher Yājñavalkya wishes to leave both his wives, Maitreyī and Kātyayanī, presumably to devote himself to a religious life, and he offers to divide his property between them (*Bṛhadāraṇyaka Upaniṣad* 2.4 and 4.5). Maitreyī, however, does not care for material possessions but instead insists that Yājñavalkya shares his knowledge of *ātman* with her. Yājñavalkya teaches her, and for all practical purposes, she becomes his student. As with the father-son relationship, it seems that the ideal husband-wife relationship is also ultimately that of a teacher and student.

Children are important in the Upaniṣads. *Bṛhadāraṇyaka Upaniṣad* 6.4 contains several rituals and spells associated with conception and childbearing and even provides instructions for what to feed the pregnant woman to get "a son with fair complexion," a "son with ruddy complexion," "a son with dark complexion," a learned and long-lived daughter, or a learned and famous son.

Human sexuality is strongly associated with procreation in the Upaniṣads. The description of sexual intercourse in *Bṛhadāraṇyaka Upaniṣad* 6.4 is accompanied by *mantras* for the man to utter to make sure that his partner becomes pregnant. But the idea of celibacy is also found in the Upaniṣads. The *Chāndogya Upaniṣad* distinguishes between three kinds of person who live in accordance with *dharma*: those who practice sacrifice, Vedic recitation, and gift-giving; those who are devoted to austerity (*tapas*); and celibate students living at their teachers' house (2.23). A later passage in the same Upaniṣad declares that only those who lead the life of a celibate student (*brahmacarya*) will obtain the world of *brahman* (8.4.3).

But the life of a celibate student seems to have posed challenges of its own. The *Chāndogya Upaniṣad* cites an older verse that lists stealing gold, drinking alcohol, killing a Brahman, having sexual relations with one's teacher's wife, or associating with a person who does any of these things as evil (5.10.9). Having sexual relations with one's teacher's wife (rather than with a married woman in general) seems oddly specific, but we should bear in mind that adolescent male students, who were expected to be celibate, often lived at their teachers' house until the completion of their education. One can imagine that this rule prohibiting relations with one's teacher's wife, which is often cited in Sanskrit texts, was put in place to ensure that no temptations arose from pubescent boys living under the same roof as a woman they were not related to.

Ultimately, however, all social bonds are irrelevant compared to the highest reality. For a person who knows the *ātman*, "a father is not a father, a mother is not a mother, worlds are not worlds, gods are not gods, and the Vedas are not the Vedas" (*Bṛhadāraṇyaka Upaniṣad* 4.3.22).

Class and Social Structure in the Upaniṣads

As Lindquist (2018a) points out, it is difficult to draw any firm conclusions about social realities in the time of the Upaniṣads based on the texts, which are literary compositions with a religious purpose. We can study what the Upaniṣads have to say about class and social structures, but we have no way of knowing to what extent that corresponds to the lived reality in the time period.

As mentioned in chapter 2, society is divided into four main social classes called *varṇas* in post-Vedic Brahmanical religion: Brahmans (priests), Kṣatriyas (kings and warriors), Vaiśyas (farmers and merchants), and Śūdras *Śūdras* (servants). Although these four groups of people are mentioned already in the *Ṛgveda*, it is not likely that a "caste system" as such was highly developed in the Vedic or Upaniṣadic period. It is quite possible that the four *varṇas* were ritual categories in the oldest time period that later became occupational designations.

The famous *Puruṣasūkta* ("Hymn to Man," *Ṛgveda* 10.90) describes a primordial human sacrifice that results in the creation of the world. In this hymn, a cosmic giant simply called *Puruṣa* ("man") is sacrificed to the gods in the beginning, and the universe is then created from various parts of his body (12):

> The *Brahman* was his mouth. The ruler was made into his two arms. As to his thighs—that is what the freeman was. From his two feet the servant was born.

The priests are here associated with the mouth of the primordial man because it is their duty to recite the sacred texts, the rulers and warriors are associated with strength and therefore the arms of *puruṣa*, the freemen or farmers are connected with fertility and therefore the area around the genitalia of the cosmic man, and the servants are associated with the feet and therefore the lowest part of *puruṣa*. But does this mean that a rigid social ṣtratification existed already in the Vedic period? Likely not. While these *varṇas* and the further subdivisions into *jātis* (birth groups associated with professions) later become rigid categories in India, it is not at all clear that these categories were as rigid and hierarchical in the Vedas or Upaniṣads as they would later become.

One Upaniṣadic passage attempts to untangle the relationship between Brahmans and kings (Kṣatriyas):

> In the beginning, this world was only one, *brahman* alone. Because it was only one, *brahman* was not yet fully developed. It created the ruling power (*kṣatra*). . . . Therefore, there is nothing higher than the ruling power. At a royal consecration, a Brahman bows down before a Kṣatriya. . . . But the priestly power [*brahman*] is the source of the ruling power, and therefore, even if a king becomes exceedingly powerful, he will return in the end to the priestly power as his own source. (*Bṛhadāraṇyaka Upaniṣad* 1.4.11)

Here, there is some obvious tension between the socialpower of the king and the religious power of the priest. But the Upaniṣad notes that *brahman* was still not fully developed with the creation of the priestly power and the ruling power. It therefore created the Vaiśyas, who are associated with the "gods who are listed in groups" (1.4.12), that is, the Vasus ("the bright ones," a group of eight gods), the Rudras (a group of eleven storm gods), Ādityas (a group of seven gods, the sons of Aditi, the goddess of infinity), the All-gods (the collective Vedic pantheon), and the Maruts (storm gods). It is likely that the Vaiśyas are associated with these nature gods due to their association with agriculture and fertility. But the *Bṛhadāraṇyaka Upaniṣad* goes on to state that *brahman* was still not fully developed and therefore created the Śūdras. The Śūdras are associated with the Vedic sun deity Pūṣan ("the nourisher"). It is noteworthy that while all four groups are mentioned, there is no sense in this passage that Vaiśyas or Śūdras are in any way inferior to Brahmans or

Kṣatriyas; rather, they all need to exist for the divine *brahman* to be fully manifested in the world.

The Upaniṣads are particularly concerned with Brahmans and Kṣatriyas. Brahmans are traditionally associated with rituals and Vedic recitation, knowledge, and studying, but the primary role of a Brahman in the Upaniṣads is not that of a priest, but rather that of a teacher. In fact, the Upaniṣads repeatedly assert that it is one's knowledge and one's place in a teacher-student lineage that makes a person a true Brahman, rather than one's birth. In the *Chāndogya Upaniṣad*, the Brahman Āruṇi tells his son Śvetaketu to go off and become a student, since there is no one in their family who has not studied "and in a Brahman only by birth" (6.1.1). In Āruṇi's view, being a Brahman is as much about the proper education as it is about one's family lineage.

Although there are many wise Brahmans in the Upaniṣads, not all who are wise are Brahmans, and not all Brahmans are wise. There are several examples in the Upaniṣads of Kṣatriyas who are wiser and more knowledgeable than Brahmans. In the *Chāndogya Upaniṣad*, for example, king Pravāhaṇa Jaivali teaches a doctrine of five fires and claims that these powerful ideas are unknown to Brahmans, which is why Kṣatriyas are the ones who rule the world (5.3.7). In *Bṛhadāraṇyaka Upaniṣad* 2.1, King Ajātaśatru becomes the teacher of the Brahman Dṛpta Bālāki, and in *Chāndogya Upaniṣad* 5.11, Uddālaka Āruṇi refers a question he can't answer about *ātman* and *brahman* to the king Aśvapati Kaikeya.

Brahmans often face each other in debates (*brahmodyas*) in the Upaniṣads. These verbal sparring matches, like the one at King Janaka's court in *Bṛhadāraṇyaka Upaniṣad* 3, are far more aggressive than the dialogues between teachers and students and have as their goal to determine the relative authority of the Brahmans involved. Black (2007) differentiates between two types of *brahmodyas* in the Upaniṣads, private ones where the loser becomes the student of the winner, and public ones where the winner may obtain wealth or prestige.

The Upaniṣads redefine the traditional role of Brahmans; the "true" Brahmans are not merely ritual specialists, as in Vedic times, but *teachers*, who can impart salvific knowledge to their students and patrons. But because ritual training is less significant than knowledge of the self, this also means that Brahmans are no longer unique in the new role that they fill in the Upaniṣads. Many of the Upaniṣadic teachers are Brahmans, but others are Kṣatriyas or even non-humans.

The *Chāndogya Upaniṣad* (5.10.7) associates a person's social class with reincarnation and *karma*:

> People whose conduct is pleasant here will enter a pleasant womb, such as that of a Brahman, Kṣatriya, or Vaiśya woman. But people with bad conduct will enter a bad womb, such as that of a dog, a pig, or a Caṇḍāla woman.

This passage suggests that it is good to be reborn as a person of the Brahman, Kṣatriya, or Vaiśya class, while the Śūdra class is not mentioned. Perhaps by implication, it is considered less than ideal to be reborn as a Śūdra. A Caṇḍāla, however (i.e., a person regarded as untouchable) is put at the same level as an animal. Caṇḍālas are mentioned alongside thieves and abortionists in *Chāndogya Upaniṣad* 4.3.22. This implies that a person's birth was a factor in their social status at the time of the Upaniṣads, even though this passage describes the state of a person who is fully embraced by the self, for whom none of these social categories have any meaning. But although the *varṇas* are ultimately meaningless in the Upaniṣads when seen from the perspective of the salvific knowledge of *ātman*'s unity with *brahman*, they do appear to have been a not insignificant part of people's lived reality.

The post-classical *Vajrasūcī Upaniṣad* (9) goes even further than the classical Upaniṣads in defining a Brahman by the person's knowledge of the self, rather than by birth:

> Then who is a Brahman? It is he who perceives the self, just like a fruit held in the palm of one's hand, as without a second, without the distinctions of birth, quality, or action . . . in the form of truth, knowledge, bliss, and eternity, by itself, without conceptual cognition, but the basis of endless conceptual cognition, the one who is the inner self of all beings, who pervades the inside and the outside of all things like ether, who has the nature of bliss, immeasurable, to be realized only through experience, manifesting itself directly and through the fulfillment of nature, he who gets rid of the faults of desire, attachment, and so forth, and possessed the qualities ties of calm and so forth, he who is rid of the states of being, spitefulness, greed, expectation, confusion, and so forth, he whose mind is unafflicted by pride, who and so forth. He alone who has these qualities is a Brahman. This is the view of the *śruti* and *smṛti* texts, and legends and history. Achieving the state of a Brahman is otherwise impossible. Meditate on *brahman*, the self who is being, consciousness and bliss, one without a second.

Several Upaniṣads depict kings (who are Kṣatriyas) as the teachers of Brahmans. In the *Chāndogya Upaniṣad* 5.11.1–5.24.4, Aśvapati Kaikeya is one of two kings who teaches the Brahman Uddālaka Āruṇi. Even though he is the one teaching, Aśvapati is generous to the Brahmans, both those who teach and those who perform sacrifices. Likewise, Uddālaka Āruṇi and his son Śvetaketu become the students of the king alternatively called Jaivali Pravāhaṇa (*Bṛhadāraṇyaka Upaniṣad* 6.2.1–8), Pravāhaṇa Jaivali (*Chāndogya Upaniṣad* 1.8.1–2.8), and Citra Gāṅgyāyani (*Kauṣītaki Upaniṣad* 1.1–2). King Ajātaśatru is approached by the Brahman Gārgya who wants to be his teacher, but after it emerges that the king is wiser than the Brahman, Gārgya becomes Ajātaśatru's student instead (*Bṛhadāraṇyaka Upaniṣad* 2.1.1–20 and *Kauṣītaki Upaniṣad* 4.1–20).

This reversal of older norms is quite remarkable and has led several scholars to suggest that the Upaniṣads may have been composed by Kṣatriyas rather than by Brahmans. Since the older Upaniṣads were composed and transmitted within the traditional Vedic schools of recitation, there is little evidence to support this claim, however. Rather, it is likely that the trope of Kṣatriyas teaching Brahmans in the Upaniṣads must be understood as an illustration of the general idea that knowledge is far more important than birth. King Pravāhaṇa Jaivali claims that the knowledge he has imparted to Uddālaka Āruṇi was not previously known by Brahmans (*Chāndogya Upaniṣad* 5.3.7). This claim should not be taken at face value since the teachings of Pravāhaṇa Jaivali are, in fact, based on older Vedic texts transmitted by Brahmans.

Monarchy was the prevailing form of government at the time when the Upaniṣads were composed, and kings are often mentioned in the texts. King Janaka of Videha is mentioned in the *Bṛhadāraṇyaka Upaniṣad* (as well as in the older *Śatapatha Brāhmaṇa*), King Jaivali Pravāhaṇa of Pañcāla in the *Bṛhadāraṇyaka Upaniṣad* and the *Chāndogya Upaniṣad*, King Ajātaśatru of Kāśī in the *Bṛhadāraṇyaka Upaniṣad* and the *Kauṣītaki Upaniṣad*, and King Bṛhadratha in the *Maitrī Upaniṣad*. These kings are associated with smaller geographical regions rather than large empires and are depicted as local rulers who are taking an interest in the ideas of wisdom teachers in their kingdoms. Although a king Ajātaśatru ruled over Magadha in the fifth century BCE, there is no evidence to connect him with the king of Kāśī depicted in the Upaniṣads. A legendary king Bṛhadratha was said to be the first ruler over Magadha and there was also a king Bṛhadratha who ruled over the Maurya Empire from around 187–180 BCE. It is unlikely that the Bṛhadratha of the *Maitrī Upaniṣad* is to be identified with either of these kings, however; like the other Upaniṣadic kings, we must understand him as a literary character whose function is to embody the search for wisdom. The Upaniṣads are primarily interested in kings as men who can lend support to wisdom teachers and demonstrate that a thirst for wisdom is more important than political power. One of their main functions is to serve as dialogue partners for the wisdom teachers of the Upaniṣads. A king's court may also serve as a venue for philosophical debate, as seen in the well-known contest scene at King Janaka's court in *Bṛhadāraṇyaka Upaniṣad* 3.

But a king's patronage is also important for the wisdom teachers, as demonstrated by the same the contest scene, which ends with Yājñavalkya walking away with a thousand cows and a substantial amount of gold after demonstrating his superior wisdom.

Gender in the Upaniṣads

Ancient Indian society was male-dominated, and the world we glimpse in the Upaniṣads is no exception. Most of the characters, human and divine, in the Upaniṣads are men, and male perspectives on life are privileged. There are, however, a few significant female characters in the Upaniṣads. But these are literary characters in texts likely composed by men, and it is difficult to draw any conclusions about women's lives in the time of the Upaniṣads based on these texts.

The two best-known female characters in the Upaniṣads are Gārgī and Maitreyī, who both appear in the *Bṛhadāraṇyaka Upaniṣad* in conversation with the prominent male wisdom teacher Yājñavalkya (see chapter 4). Yājñavalkya is pleased with his wife Maitreyī's yearning for knowledge and proceeds to teach her about the nature of the self. Their ensuing conversation is not a dialogue between equals, however, but rather a teacher's lecture to an eager student. Before he begins his exposition of *ātman*, Yājñavalkya tells Maitreyī how dear she is to him, but adds, "While I'm explaining, try to concentrate" (2.4), which implies that he sees her as an unfocused student, rather than an actual conversation partner. Yājñavalkya's other wife, Kātyāyanī, does not get a speaking part in the narrative; apparently, she has no questions to ask and is content with receiving part of her husband's material property instead. We also note that although Yājñavalkya shares his teachings with

Maitreyī, the question of her joining him on his journey is not raised; presumably, Yājñavalkya will become a homeless wanderer devoted to the pursuit of knowledge, while Maitreyī stays home, a little wiser than before.

Another woman, Gārgī Vācaknavī, is one of the many challengers to Yājñavalkya during the contest scene at King Janaka's court in *Bṛhadāraṇyaka Upaniṣad* 3 (see chapter 4). It has often been noted that Gārgī is the only woman who speaks during this scene, and that she is the only one who gets to challenge Yājñavalkya twice. While Yājñavalkya emerges as the obvious winner of the wisdom contest at Janaka's court, Gārgī is a close runner-up; she alone among all the other participants can grasp the ultimate point of Yājñavalkya's teachings, that *brahman* is the ultimate foundation and source of all things.

Yājñavalkya's initial silencing of Gārgī has often been read as gendered; he is a man silencing a woman who is bold enough to speak up in an assembly of men. But in the larger context of the *Bṛhadāraṇyaka Upaniṣad*, the issue does not seem to be Gārgī's gender but rather the nature of her question. She has asked about something that is simply impossible; Yājñavalkya can't answer the question about the cause of *brahman* because *brahman* is itself the ultimate cause.

As I have argued elsewhere (Cohen 2008, 83), it may be significant that the female figures in the *Bṛhadāraṇyaka Upaniṣad* carry names associated with the Vedic tradition. Yājñavalkya's two wives, Maitreyī and Kātyāyanī, are named after schools of Vedic recitation. Kātyāyanī's name is related to that of Kātyāyana, the author of a *Śrautasūtra* of the *White Yajurveda*, while Maitreyī's name recalls the *Maitrāyaṇīya* school of the *Black Yajurveda*. I have proposed that Yājñavalkya functions as a representative of the authority of the *White Yajurveda* school in the *Bṛhadāraṇyaka Upaniṣad*, as seen in the contest scene in Janaka's court where he defeats opponents associated with other branches of Vedic transmission. It is therefore possible to read both Maitreyī and Kātyāyanī as literary representations of two branches of textual transmission. Perhaps the silent Kātyāyanī has no questions to ask Yājñavalkya because she represents the same branch of the textual tradition that he does, that of the *White Yajurveda*, while Maitreyī, as a representative of the related *Black Yajurveda*, needs to be lovingly instructed in the correct teachings. It is possible to read Gārgī as a representation of a textual tradition as well. Her patronym Gārgī associates her with the Ṛgvedic sage Garga and the Ṛgvedic textual tradition.

But while both Maitreyī and Gārgī are exemplary students in the *Bṛhadāraṇyaka Upaniṣad*, in that they accept instruction from Yājñavalkya, the *Kena Upaniṣad* offers a brief glimpse of a female wisdom teacher, the goddess Umā. Here, she is the one who explains to the god Indra the nature of *brahman* itself (4.4). In later Hindu mythology, Umā or Pārvatī is best known as the wife of the powerful god Śiva. But in the *Kena Upaniṣad*, Umā is not a consort but a wisdom teacher with an understanding of *brahman*. This brief glimpse of the female divine teacher in the *Kena Upaniṣad* foreshadows the identification of the goddess with the highest *brahman* in later sectarian Upaniṣads.

But there are also female figures in the Upaniṣads who do not get to speak for themselves at all. As mentioned previously, the beautiful daughter of King Jānaśruti Pautrāyaṇa is nothing more than a form of currency, along with gold and cows, for her father as he is attempting to become the student of the homeless teacher Raikva (*Chāndogya Upaniṣad* 4.1–3). Raikva accepts the offer of the king's daughter in exchange for sharing his teachings, but nobody asks how the daughter herself feels about being given to a homeless man living under a cart. The Upaniṣadic narrative is not very interested in the daughter; the text's concern is with the teacher–student relationship between the king and the sage.

We learn something about gender in the social world of the Upaniṣads in passages that describe male and female bodies and their role in conception and birth. *Aitareya Upaniṣad* 2, for example, has a curiously male-oriented view of conception and pregnancy: an embryo first comes into being as semen in a man, and then comes into the woman's body. When she is pregnant, the woman is nourishing a man's self (*ātman*) that has entered her. As he cares for his pregnant partner, the man is nourishing his own self that is in her. Here, the man is both the creator of and the model for the unborn child, while the woman is reduced to the role of receptacle and caretaker for his child.

Creation is often associated with male deities or principles in the Upaniṣads. In *Bṛhadāraṇyaka Upaniṣad* 6.4.2–3, the Vedic creator god Prajāpati creates woman "as a firm basis" for a man's semen. Prajāpati creates woman and has intercourse with her, and this act becomes the paradigm for man's intercourse with woman. In this narrative, woman is a secondary creation, made for the purpose of sexual intercourse with man. But this intercourse itself has a profound religious meaning. In *Bṛhadāraṇyaka Upaniṣad* 6.4.3, sexual intercourse is equated with the Vedic Soma sacrifice, in which juice made from a sacred plant was offered to the gods:

> Her vulva is the sacrificial ground, her pubic hair the sacrificial grass, her labia majora the Soma-press, and her labia minora the fire in the center. A man who knows this and has intercourse attains a world equal to that of one who performs a Soma sacrifice. He takes unto himself the good deeds of the women he sleeps with. But the women take unto themselves the good deeds of a man who has intercourse without knowing this.

Here, the woman's genitals are equated with the sacrificial ground itself, and for the man, sexual intercourse can therefore be the ritual equivalent of a Vedic Soma sacrifice. This is only the case, however, if the man truly understands the religious nature of the encounter. Strikingly, the text says nothing about what the woman's perception of their encounter is, or if any knowledge is required on her part. It is interesting to note that the man's spiritual gain from this knowledge is a woman's loss; if he knows the true ritual meaning of the sexual encounter, he will acquire his partner's good deeds as his own, while a lack of knowledge on his part means that he will transfer his good deeds to her. The woman, it appears, has no control over what happens to her own good deeds.

Another passage from the same chapter of the *Bṛhadāraṇyaka Upaniṣad* (6.6–8) states:

> When a woman has changed her clothes once her period is over, she is the most auspicious among women. When she has changed her clothes once her period is over, one should therefore approach that radiant woman and ask her to have intercourse. If she refuses, he should bribe her. But if she still refuses, he should beat her with a stick or his hands and force her and say: "I take away the radiance from you with my own virility and radiance." Then she will lose her radiance. But if she does as he wants, he should say: "I give radiance to you with my own virility and radiance." Then they will both become radiant.

This passage makes it all too clear that a woman's consent, while desirable, is not necessary to have sex. The endorsement of sexual violence in this passage suggests that men and women were far from equal partners at the time when the Upaniṣads were composed. The passage above is followed by a love spell for a man to recite during intercourse if he wants a woman to love him, which also implies dubious consent.

The Upaniṣad further suggests that it is the man who will decide whether a sexual act should result in a child:

> If he does not want her to become pregnant, he should put his penis inside her, put his mouth against hers, breathe into her mouth and breathe in, saying: "I take back my seed from you with

> my virility and seed." And then she will be without seed. But if he wants her to become pregnant, he should put his penis inside her, put his mouth against hers, breathe in first, and then breathe out, saying: "I put the seed in you with my virility and my seed." And then she will become pregnant.

The woman does not appear to have a say in this process. It is also the man who controls what kind of offspring they will get, even though they both participate in the rites: if a man wants a son with fair complexion who knows one of the Vedas, he should make the woman thresh rice and cook it with milk, and they should both eat it with butter. If he wants a son with a reddish complexion who knows two of the Vedas, he should make her cook the rice with yoghurt, and they should both eat it with butter. If he wants a son with a dark complexion who knows three of the Vedas, he should make her cook the rice with water, and they should both eat it with butter. If he wants a learned daughter, he should make her cook the rice with sesame seeds, and they should both eat it with butter. But if he wants a son who knows all four of the Vedas, he should make the woman cook the rice with meat, and they should both eat it with butter (6.4.14–18). Even though the woman participates fully in these magical rites, they are presented in the text as something that happens on the man's initiative and to fulfill his desires. It is intriguing to note that only sons can master the Vedas; one can certainly get a learned daughter as well, but the nature of her learning is not specified here. This passage does suggest, however, that while the Vedas were seen as the domain of men, this was not true of all learning.

But not all marriages were happy; *Bṛhadāraṇyaka Upaniṣad* also contains a ritual spell for a man whose wife has a lover (4.4.12). After kindling fire in an "unbaked pot" on top of a bed of reeds, arranged in an order that is "the opposite of normal," the jilted husband should dab butter on the tips of the reeds and offer them in the fire with the spell:

> You made an offering in my fire. I rob you of your out-breath and your in-breath.
> You made an offering in my fire. I rob you of your sons and your cattle.
> You made an offering in my fire. I rob you of your sacrifices and good deeds.
> You made an offering in my fire. I rob you of your hopes and dreams.

The woman is here again equated with the ritual fire, and the husband claims ownership over both her body and all her lover's possessions. The text goes on to warn that if a man is cursed by a Brahman who knows this ritual, he will leave this world without both his manhood and his good deeds. Therefore, concludes the Upaniṣad, one should keep away from the wives of learned Brahmans.

But in the final instance, gender is seen as irrelevant in the Upaniṣads; the highest *ātman* itself is "neither a woman nor a man nor non-binary but is ruled by whatever body it has" (*Śvetāśvatara Upaniṣad* 5.10). Similarly, the life breath (*prāṇa*) is called both "father" and "mother" in the *Praśna Upaniṣad* (2.11, 2.13).

6
Central Ideas in the Upaniṣads

Ātman

One of the most significant concepts in the Upaniṣads is *ātman*, which can be translated as "self." *Ātman* signifies the self or essence of a living being, but it can also be used as a reflexive pronoun: "myself," "yourself," "herself." Etymologically, the term *ātman* is related to "breath," and it seems to have originated in the idea of the life breath as the essence of a person. *Ātman* is the inner essence of a person, located in the heart (*Chāndogya Upaniṣad* 3.14.2–4, 6.8.7).

Knowledge of *ātman* and its ultimate identity with *brahman*, the cosmic divine force, leads to freedom from death (see, e.g., *Bṛhadāraṇyaka Upaniṣad* 2.5.20). *Ātman* is the "inner controller" of all human beings, and ultimately the agent of all human action:

> It sees but cannot be seen; it hears but cannot be heard, it thinks but cannot be thought of, it perceives but cannot be perceived. Other than that, there is no one who sees, no one who hears, no one who thinks, and no one who perceives. It is your *ātman*, which is the inner controller, the immortal. Everything other than that is suffering. (*Bṛhadāraṇyaka Upaniṣad* 3.7.23)

A person who knows the *ātman* will gain knowledge of the entire world (*Bṛhadāraṇyaka Upaniṣad* 2.4.5). This is because in an enlightened state, free of duality, all reality has become one with the *ātman*:

The Classical Upaniṣads. Signe Cohen, Oxford University Press. © Oxford University Press 2024.
DOI: 10.1093/oso/9780197654156.003.0006

> When this whole world has become the *ātman*, then whom and how will one smell? Whom and how will one see? Whom and how will one hear? Whom and how will one address? Of whom and how will one think? Whom and how will one perceive? (*Bṛhadāraṇyaka Upaniṣad* 2.4.14)

According to the *Īśā Upaniṣad*, all *ātmans* are ultimately one and the same:

> When one sees all beings
> Within the *ātman*
> And the *ātman* within all beings,
> It will not conceal itself.
> When one knows,
> One's *ātman* becomes all beings.
> What confusion or sorrow can there be
> For one who has seen this oneness? (6–7)

This *ātman* is smaller than the smallest thing and larger than the largest, and it is located in the heart of all living beings (*Kaṭha Upaniṣad* 2.20 and 4.2).

The *Śvetāśvatara Upaniṣad* differentiates between two forms of *ātman*, a lower unenlightened form, and a higher, fully enlightened self. The lower self is "not lord" (*anīśa*) and bound to this world but can be liberated when it realizes its own nature (1.8).

According to most textual passages from the Upaniṣads, *ātman* is the inner, immortal essence of a person or animal, that which is reincarnated, and that which is finally liberated. But certain Upaniṣadic passages also suggest that *ātman* can be other things as well: *ātman* can be the body, a personal god, an object of worship, and the creator of the universe.

In some of the oldest Upaniṣads, *ātman* occasionally means "body" (see, e.g., *Bṛhadāraṇyaka Upaniṣad* 1.1.1, 1.2.1, 1.2.3, 1.2.4, 1.2.5, 1.2.7, 1.4.4; *Chāndogya Upaniṣad* 1.2.14, 1.6.3, 1.7.1, 3.18.1;

Aitareya Upaniṣad 2.2; *Kauṣītaki Upaniṣad* 2.12, 4.2, 4.10), but this usage disappears from the later classical Upaniṣads. Instead, *ātman* comes to signify an eternal immaterial part of the person, something that will survive after the physical death of the body. This *ātman* of all living beings is identified with the cosmic divine principle *brahman*.

But in some of the older Upaniṣads, especially those formally affiliated with the *ātman* can also be understood as a god. The theistic conceptions of *ātman* in the classical Upaniṣads can be divided into two distinct types: *ātman* as a divine, primordial creator, and *ātman* as a personal deity involved in salvation. The first type of theism is common to several of the older Upaniṣads, but particularly prominent in the Upaniṣads affiliated with the *Ṛgveda*, whereas the second type develops gradually in the Upaniṣads formally affiliated with the *Black Yajurveda*.

Some passages in the Upaniṣads depict *ātman* as a primordial creator. For example, in *Bṛhadāraṇyaka Upaniṣad* 1.4.1–3, the creation of the world is described as follows:

> In the beginning there was only *ātman*, in the form of a person. Looking around, he saw nothing other than himself. In the beginning, he uttered: "I am." . . . He has no joy. Therefore, one who is alone has no joy. He desired a second. He became as large as a man and a woman embracing. He made that self fall into two parts. From that husband and wife arose. For, like Yājñavalkya said, this body is half of itself, like one of the two halves of a fragment. So this space is filled by a wife. He united with her. From that human beings were born.

Likewise, the *Aitareya Upaniṣad* 1.1 describes the creation of the universe as a conscious act by a primordial *ātman*:

> The *ātman* was all this, the one, in the beginning. No one else winked. He thought: "Let me create the worlds!"

In other passages, however, the creation of the universe is described, not as a conscious creative act by *ātman*, but rather as a spontaneous evolution from *ātman*:

> As a spider sends out its thread, and as sparks spring from the fire, so do all the breaths, all worlds, all gods, and all beings spring from the *ātman*. (*Bṛhadāraṇyaka Upaniṣad* 2.1.20)

> From the *ātman* comes the life breath, from the *ātman* comes hope, from the *ātman* comes memory, from the *ātman* comes space, from the *ātman* comes heat, from the *ātman* comes water, from the *ātman* come appearing and disappearing, from the *ātman* comes food, from the *ātman* comes strength, from the *ātman* comes perception, from the *ātman* comes reflection, from the *ātman* comes thought, from the *ātman* comes resolve, from the *ātman* comes mind, from the *ātman* comes speech, from the *ātman* comes name, from the *ātman* come *mantras*, from the *ātman* come actions—this whole world comes from the *ātman*. (*Chāndogya Upaniṣad* 7.26.1)

> From this *ātman*, indeed, space arose, from space air, from air fire, from fire, water, from water earth, from earth plants, from plants food, and from food the person. (*Taittirīya Upaniṣad* 2.1.1)

Although it is possible to regard the descriptions of *ātman* as the creator of the universe as psychological suggestions that human beings create their own mental universes, this is likely not what the authors of these passages had in mind. Rather, these descriptions of *ātman* as the creator are better seen against the backdrop of the Upaniṣadic quest for a principle that is both the origin and the goal of human existence. The question of origins is central in the Upaniṣads: Uddālaka Āruṇi discusses whether the world arose from being or non-being, Gārgī asks for the origin of *brahman* in the *Bṛhadāraṇyaka Upaniṣad*, and the *Śvetāśvatara Upaniṣad* suggests that there exists a god (*deva*) who is the ultimate origin of the universe, to mention a few well-known examples. Both *ātman* and *brahman* are invoked as the first principle in several Upaniṣads. By extension, both *ātman* and *brahman* may also described as creators of the universe.

But does this mean that the *ātman* or *brahman* itself was regarded as a personal creator, or are the passages where these entities are described as creating the universe merely metaphorical, examples of the Upaniṣadic mythological diction? The Upaniṣads, like many late Vedic texts, are characterized by a pervasive reification and personification of abstract principles. Are these passages describing *ātman* as a primordial creator simply further examples of this widespread personification?

In the *Atharvaveda* (19.53–54), for example, it is time (*kāla*) itself that creates offspring in the beginning. Similarly, the Vedic creator god Prajāpati is regularly identified with *manas*, the mind. But *manas* is also in late Vedic literature said to be a deity, worthy of worship (see, e.g., *Śatapatha Brāhmaṇa* 3.1.4.13). Similarly, significant concepts and ideas are often personified and mythologized in the Upaniṣads as well, and abstract concepts like hunger, speech, or death may appear as quasi-mythological characters. The Upaniṣadic descriptions of the creation of the universe from *ātman* or *brahman* may therefore simply underscore the overall importance of these central concepts. But the idea that *ātman* or *brahman* could be seen as a god, or even worshipped, is not, however, totally absent in the Upaniṣads.

In the Upaniṣads formally affiliated with the *Ṛgveda*, such as the *Aitareya Upaniṣad* and the *Kauṣītaki Upaniṣad*, this divine *ātman* or *brahman* is often identified with a deity, such as Indra. In the *Aitareya Upaniṣad*, the question of who *ātman* is, is answered: "It is *brahman*, it is Indra, it is Prajāpati, it is all the gods" (3.3). In *Kauṣītaki Upaniṣad* 3.2, Indra says, "I am the breath, the *ātman* of intelligence."

It is perhaps not surprising to encounter theistic elements in the depiction of *ātman* in the Upaniṣads transmitted in the *śākhās* affiliated with the *Ṛgveda* in particular, since the *hotṛs*, or Ṛgvedic priests, were responsible precisely for invoking the deities during the Vedic sacrifice.

But although the idea of *ātman* as a creator is present in several of the older Upaniṣads, the notion of *ātman* as a personal god and savior with the ability to help the worshipper transcend the bonds of *saṃsāra* does not emerge until the middle Upaniṣads of the *Yajurveda*, such as the *Kaṭha* and the *Śvetāśvatara Upaniṣad.*

The inner *ātman* is identified as the highest deity in *Kaṭha Upaniṣad* 2.12:

> Realizing god, who is difficult to see,
> hidden, being in the heart, dwelling in the deep,
> the ancient one, through the contemplation of the supreme *ātman*,
> the wise man abandons joy and sorrow.

The *ātman* is not merely something to obtain, but a deity with an active role in the salvation process in *Kaṭha Upaniṣad* 2.23:

> The *ātman* cannot be obtained
> by teaching, by intellect, or by great learning.
> Only the one he chooses can grasp him
> the one whose body the *ātman* chooses for his own.

And whereas the *Kaṭha Upaniṣad* hints a theistic conception of *ātman*, its sister text, the *Śvetāśvatara Upaniṣad*, is a theistic text throughout. Here, *ātman* is both the creator of the world and the inner self:

> That god, the maker of everything, the great *ātman*,
> always seated in the heart of the creatures. (4.17)

In the *Śvetāśvatara Upaniṣad*, theism is omnipresent. The text suggests that the universe was created by a god, and that it will eventually be destroyed by a god as well (5.3):

> This god spreads out in manifold ways
> every creature in this field and destroys them again.
> When he has created again, he who is the Lord and master
> exercises his lordship, the great *ātman*.

The *Śvetāśvatara Upaniṣad* uses the word *deva* ("god") more frequently than any other Upaniṣad. The *deva* of the *Śvetāśvatara Upaniṣad* is identified with Rudra/Śiva, although sections of the text suggest that the one god who is both the creator of the universe and the path to salvation, is the *ātman* itself (6.11):

> One god, hidden in all creatures,
> all-pervading, the inner *ātman* of all beings . . .

Gradually, this text was then transformed into a Śaiva text by identification of the divine *ātman* with the god Rudra/Śiva. The emerging theism in the Upaniṣads of the *Black Yajurveda* can be seen as the forerunner of the theism of the *Bhagavadgītā*, a text that is closely linked to both the *Kaṭha* and the *Śvetāśvatara Upaniṣad*, both thematically and through shared stanzas. The devotional theism we encounter in the *Bhagavadgītā* did not emerge in a literary vacuum; it has its roots in the emerging theism of the classical Upaniṣads.

Puruṣa, the Person

There is a complex interrelationship in the classical Upaniṣads between the concepts of *ātman* ("the self") and *puruṣa* ("the person"). In some passages, the two terms appear to be identical, whereas other Upaniṣadic texts differentiate between the two. Overall, *puruṣa* becomes a more important term in the later classical Upaniṣads than in the earlier ones.

But what exactly is *puruṣa*? The most basic meaning of *puruṣa* is simply "man" or "human being." As we have seen, in one hymn of the *Ṛgveda*, 10.90, *puruṣa* is a cosmic giant whose body is dismembered by the gods to create the universe. In this hymn, *puruṣa* is the origin of the physical world, and this hymn may very well have served as the starting point for the later idea that *puruṣa* is the highest principle.

The idea that *puruṣa* is the ultimate reality is suggested, but ultimately rejected, in some of the earliest Upaniṣads. In *Bṛhadāraṇyaka Upaniṣad* (2.1) and *Kauṣītaki Upaniṣad* (4.19), the would-be wisdom teacher Dṛpta Bālāki identifies many different *puruṣas* as *brahman*, but he is corrected by the wise king Ajātaśatru, who identifies *brahman* with *ātman* instead. Even the supreme wisdom teacher of the *Bṛhadāraṇyaka Upaniṣad*, Yājñavalkya, at one point calls *ātman* a "*puruṣa* within the body" (2.5), but overall, the *Bṛhadāraṇyaka Upaniṣad* privileges *ātman* over *puruṣa*.

The *Chāndogya Upaniṣad* identifies a golden person (*puruṣa*) in the sun with the Vedic High Chant (*udgītha*) (1.6.6–8). When the creator god Prajāpati is approached by the god Indra and the demon Virocana (*Chāndogya Upaniṣad* 8.7), he initially teaches them that the *puruṣa* in the eye is the *ātman*. Virocana accepts this answer, but Indra pushes further and keeps coming back until Prajāpati reveals to him the ultimate truth: that *ātman* is *brahman*. Here, the notion of *puruṣa* is clearly presented as an inferior teaching compared to the doctrine of *ātman*'s identity to *brahman*.

But the concept of *puruṣa* is picked up again in some of the Upaniṣads affiliated with the *Black Yajurveda*. The *Kaṭha Upaniṣad* identifies *puruṣa* as the highest principle (3.10–11), which foreshadows the idea of *puruṣa* as the ultimate principle of consciousness in the later Hindu philosophical schools of Sāṃkhya and Yoga. According to the *Śvetāśvatara Upaniṣad*, *puruṣa* is "higher than *brahman*" (3.7) and the text declares: "I know that great *puruṣa*, of the color of the sun, beyond the darkness. Only a man who knows him will pass beyond death" (3.8). The *Muṇḍaka Upaniṣad* identifies *puruṣa* as the highest principle and first cause of the universe:

> The *puruṣa* is divine.
> He has no visible form.
> He is inside and outside, unborn, without breath or mind.
> He is brilliant, and further than the furthest imperishable.
> From him come breath and mind
> And all the senses,
> Wind, fire, and ether,
> And the earth that carries all things. (2.1.2–3)

This rise of *puruṣa* to the highest principle, ultimately identical to or even superior to *ātman* and *brahman* in the Upaniṣads of the *Black Yajurveda*, may be associated with the emergence of an early form of Sāṃkhya-Yoga philosophy in the environment that produced these Upaniṣadic texts.

The Upaniṣads of the *Black Yajurveda* contain many technical terms and ideas that later come to be associated with Sāṃkhya and Yoga philosophy, as formulated in the *Sāṃkhyakārikā* of Īśvarakṛṣṇa and the *Yogasūtras* of Patañjali. While these proto-Sāṃkhya and proto-Yoga terms and ideas foreshadow the later systematic philosophies of the twin schools of Sāṃkhya and Yoga, the terms are often used more loosely in the Upaniṣads. In classical Sāṃkhya and Yoga, *puruṣa* acquires a very specific technical meaning and is defined as pure consciousness, an eternal cosmic principle contrasted with *prakṛti* or "nature." Salvation, in the full-fledged Sāṃkhya-Yoga system, is achieved when *puruṣa* is recognized to be completely separate from *prakṛti*.

But *puruṣa* is not only the highest principle in the *Black Yajurveda* Upaniṣads; it is also identified with the individual self of a person in a way that is reminiscent of classical Sāṃkhya and Yoga. Several passages in the *Kaṭha Upaniṣad* identify *puruṣa* with the individual *ātman* of a human being (*Kaṭha Upaniṣad* 3.11, 4.12, 6.8). The term *puruṣa* is also used in a similar sense in *Śvetāśvatara Upaniṣad* 3.13, where the cosmic *puruṣa* is identified with a thumb-size person inside the heart, an echo of the *Taittirīya Upaniṣad*:

> A person the size of a thumb inside the body,
> always dwells in the heart of people.
> He has been contemplated with heart, with insight,
>   and with thought.
> Those who know this become immortal.

Brahman

The term *bráhman* is used in older Vedic texts, in a slightly different meaning from the one it acquires in the Upaniṣads. In the Vedas, *bráhman* is a prayer or ritual speech act, but also the power behind that speech act. *Brahman* is also associated with speech in the Upaniṣads, so there seems to be a continuation of the older idea of *brahman* as speech here.

But in the Upaniṣads, *brahman* is above all a divine power that permeates the world. *Brahman* is the highest principle in many of the classical Upaniṣads, and ultimately identical to the self (*ātman*) within the person. In his debate with Gārgī in *Bṛhadāraṇyaka Upaniṣad* 3, Yājñavalkya, the text's supreme authority figure, rejects the idea that *brahman* has a cause; *brahman* itself *is* the cause of all things, the first principle.

But the theistic *Śvetāśvatara Upaniṣad* picks up on Gārgī's rejected question from the *Bṛhadāraṇyaka Upaniṣad* 3 and answers it; in this Upaniṣad, *brahman* itself is created by a personal god, here identified with Rudra/Śiva. The question of whether *brahman* is personal of impersonal is a central one in the Upaniṣads. Some of the classical Upaniṣads, such as the *Aitareya*, *Kauṣītaki*, *Kena*, and

Īśā, regard *brahman* as a personal being who can be worshipped. But this idea is firmly rejected by other Upaniṣadic passages, especially those portions of the *Bṛhadāraṇyaka Upaniṣad* that deal with the teachings of Yājñavalkya.

Brahman is often understood as the source of the universe in the Upaniṣads, both in a causal sense and in the sense of the material stuff from which the world is made. But *brahman* is also that which contains everything, including the universe itself. As the *Chāndogya Upaniṣad* (1.3.14) states: "All this is indeed *brahman*." *Brahman* is described both as the universe in its totality and as a sacred principle beyond the visible world that humans must seek to obtain. Although most Upaniṣads see *brahman* as an impersonal principle rather than a personal god, the *Kauṣītaki Upaniṣad* describes *brahman* as a person sitting on a throne and holding a conversation with the dead in the afterlife (1.6). This anthropomorphized depiction of *brahman* as something more akin to a god than a divine force may be the reason why the great commentator and philosopher Śaṅkara, who composed commentaries on the other oldest Upaniṣad, did not write a commentary on the *Kauṣītaki Upaniṣad*. Śaṅkara was insistent that *brahman* had to be understood as an impersonal force without qualities rather than a personal deity, and it is quite difficult, even for an expert exegete like Śaṅkara, to glean that message from the *Kauṣītaki Upaniṣad*.

In the *Kena Upaniṣad*, we find two different views of the nature of *brahman*. The first two chapters of the text describe a completely abstract *brahman* that cannot be captured in words: "It is different from that which is known and beyond that which is unknown" (1.4). This *brahman* is "that which cannot be expressed by speech" (1.5). But in the last two chapters of the text, *brahman* is a mysterious, half-personified being. *Brahman* wins a victory for the gods, but the gods fail to recognize that they had only been victorious through the power of *brahman* and took credit for their own victory. To help them understand, *brahman* "made itself visible to them" (3.2). The gods have no idea who—or what—*brahman* is. When Agni, the Vedic god who is fire personified, tries to show *brahman* his own power, his ability to burn, he finds himself incapable of burning even a single blade of grass. Vāyu, the god of wind, is likewise unable to lift a blade of grass in front of *brahman*. Indra, the Vedic thunder god, approaches *brahman*, but loses sight of it. Finally, the goddess Umā explains to the three puzzled gods that what they had encountered was *brahman*, and that *brahman* is the one who gives the gods themselves their power. Here, *brahman* is depicted as some sort of holy energy that powers even the actions of the gods.

In the *Praśna Upaniṣad*, six sages approach the wisdom teacher Paippalāda to learn about the nature of *brahman*. While several Upaniṣads present *ātman* as the unknown principle that wisdom seekers must discover, the *Praśna* and the *Muṇḍaka Upaniṣads* both present *ātman* as the known and *brahman* as the unknown whose nature must be discovered. The *Praśna Upaniṣad* suggests that *brahman* has two forms, a higher and a lower (5.2), an idea that is also found in the *Muṇḍaka Upaniṣad* (2.2.8) as well as the later *Maitrī Upaniṣad*.

The most complex model of *brahman* in the Upaniṣads is that of the tripartite *brahman* in the *Śvetāśvatara Upaniṣad*. This text introduces the idea that *brahman* is made up of three components:

> There are two male unborns, one who knows and one who is ignorant, one who is lord and one who is not lord. There is one unborn female, joined to the enjoyer and the objects of enjoyment. The *ātman* is limitless, of every form, but without activity. When someone finds these three, he will find *brahman*. (1.9)

These three principles that make up *brahman* are usually interpreted as the lower, unenlightened *ātman*, the higher enlightened *ātman*, and a female principle (akin to the *prakṛti* of Sāṃkhya and Yoga philosophy) that represents primordial nature.

Time in the Upaniṣads

The new genre of the Upaniṣads that emerged out of late Vedic literature demanded a shift in the literary conceptions of time as well. We can see within the Upaniṣads a gradual transition from the older Vedic "ritual time," where both time and space are intimately connected with the performance of sacrificial rituals, to what we may call "ontological time," where time becomes a cosmic and ontological entity that takes its place alongside such philosophical concepts as being, *ātman*, and *brahman* as part of a larger soteriological framework.

The *Bṛhadāraṇyaka Upaniṣad* fuses time and space into an integrated whole in the striking image that opens the text:

> The dawn is the head of the sacrificial horse. The sun is its eye, the wind is its breath, and its open mouth is the fire common to all men. The year is the body (*ātman*) of the sacrificial horse, the sky is its back, the intermediate region is its belly, the earth is its underbelly, the quarters of the sky are its flanks, the intermediate quarters are its ribs, the seasons are its limbs, the months and half-months are its joints, the days and nights are its feet, the stars are its bones, the clouds are its flesh, the sand is the food in its stomach, the rivers are its intestines, the hills are its liver and lungs, the plants and trees are its hairs, the rising sun is its front part, and the setting sun is its back part. (1.1)

This passage identifies various parts of the visible world—sun, wind, sky, stars, clouds, plants—with the body of a horse about to be ritually sacrificed, but it also views the year, the changing seasons, months and fortnights, days and nights, as parts of the same cosmic horse. The various measurements of time are here identified with the parts of the horse associated with movement, such as limbs, joints, and feet, but ultimately not separate from other parts of the cosmos. Time and space merge into one living being in this

Upaniṣadic passage, inseparable parts of a whole. Significantly, time is here closely associated with both ritual and with calendrical divisions such as months, half-months, and years; time has not yet become an abstraction, separate from the rhythms of daily life.

The various calendrical divisions of time, such as day, night, fortnights, and months, are part of the cosmic architecture of the worlds through which a person travels after death in *Bṛhadāraṇyaka Upaniṣad* 6.2.15–16. Here, a person of knowledge travels after death from the (funeral) fire to the day, to the fortnight of the waxing moon, to the six months when the sun travels north, and then to the world of the gods, the sun, and the region of lightning. The afterlife journey of a person who has no such knowledge but instead offers pious sacrifices, on the other hand, goes through smoke, night, the fortnight of the waning moon, the six months when the sun travels south, the world of the fathers, and the moon, and then back to the earth as rain. Significantly, divisions of time such as days, nights, and fortnights are here parts of the fabric of the cosmos itself, as much a part of the empirical world as the sun or the moon.

We can observe through the older Upaniṣads that time gradually becomes an abstraction, something apart from seasons, processes, and activities. In the *Bṛhadāraṇyaka Upaniṣad*, however, divisions of time such as past and future are still closely tied to ritual: "Saying 'to what has been, *svāhā*!' he makes an offering in the fire and pours the rest into the mixture. Saying 'to what will be, *svāhā*!' he makes an offering in the fire and pours the rest into the mixture" (6.3.3).

The (ritual) year often functions as a stand-in for time in general in the *Bṛhadāraṇyaka Upaniṣad*, as in the creation myth narrated in 1.2.4:

> He [Death] had a desire: "May a second body (*ātman*) be born for me!" With his mind, he had intercourse with speech, and Death had intercourse with hunger. That which was the semen became the year. Before that, the year did not exist.

How are we to interpret this curious image of time, here represented by the year, as the offspring of death, language, and hunger? Perhaps the underlying idea here is that our concept of time originates in a recognition of transience and decay (death), in conjunction with desire (hunger) and the ability of language to create abstractions. By assigning a mythological beginning to the year, and by implication to time itself, this Upaniṣad hints that time is not an eternally existing thing, but a construct.

But the *Bṛhadāraṇyaka Upaniṣad* also speculates that time itself may be the origin of all things. In *Bṛhadāraṇyaka Upaniṣad* 1.5.14–15, the creator god Prajāpati is himself likened to the year and its components:

> Prajāpati is the year, consisting of sixteen parts. His nights consist of fifteen parts, but his sixteenth part is constant. With his nights, he waxes and wanes. On the night of the new moon he enters into all that has life, and is born again in the morning.

The creator god Prajāpati is here identified with time itself in the form of the year and its lunar months, which brings to mind the well-known hymn to time in the *Atharvaveda* 19.53, which identifies Time (*kāla*) as the father of the creator god Prajāpati and claims time as the ultimate origin of all things. The idea that the creator god Prajāpati consists of sixteen parts can be traced back to the *Vājasaneyī Saṃhitā* of the *Yajurveda* (8.36); cf. *Śatapatha Brāhmaṇa* 7.2.2.17. Since the number 16 is frequently associated with totality in Vedic literature, it makes sense that the originator of all things is also made up of sixteen parts. But in this passage from the *Bṛhadāraṇyaka Upaniṣad*, it is interesting to note that of the sixteen parts that make up the totality of the year, fifteen parts wax and wane, while one part remains constant (*dhruva*). This notion that time can be divided into a transient part and a constant, unchanging one, foreshadows the later Upaniṣadic idea that fleeting, transitory time can be contrasted with something eternal and timeless.

The *Bṛhadāraṇyaka Upaniṣad* also delves deeper into the idea of time as something closely intertwined with suffering. The lesser philosopher Aśvala observes in his debate with Yājñavalkya, the protagonist of the text, in *Bṛhadāraṇyaka Upaniṣad* 3.1.4 that "this whole world is gripped by days and nights" and asks how a patron of a sacrifice can free himself from this cruel grip of time. The movement of time is here explicitly tied to ritual, as so often in the older Vedic texts, but in this passage, time is also viewed as a form of suffering, something a person might wish to free himself from. In his response to Aśvala, the sage Yājñavalkya points to principles beyond the mutations of time, such as fixed ritual roles and the sun, wind, and moon, timeless elements that offer comfort and stability to the person caught in the grip of time. But later in the same text, Yājñavalkya introduces Gārgī (apparently the only woman among the philosophers gathered at King Janaka's court to discuss the nature of the self) to the idea that the passage of time itself is under the command of a higher "imperishable" principle: "At the command of this imperishable, Gārgī, moments and hours, days and nights, half-months and months, seasons and years stand apart" (3.8.9). While Aśvala articulates the predicament of a person controlled by time, Yājñavalkya points to a higher reality that controls time itself. Yājñavalkya argues in his dialogue with Gārgī that it is the self (*ātman*), 'before which the year revolves, along with its days" (4.4.16), establishing the eternal, unchangeable nature of the *ātman* as something that is set apart from and higher than the passing of time.

In their dialogue about the ultimate origin of all things in *Bṛhadāraṇyaka Upaniṣad* 3.8, Gārgī pushes Yājñavalkya to explain the origins of both the material world and of time itself: "That which is above the sky, that which is below the earth, and that which is between heaven and earth, and that which they call past, present, and future—on what, Yājñavalkya, are these woven back and forth?"(3.8.6). Gārgī here uses the metaphor of weaving to indicate a cosmic construction of reality. Yājñavalkya's answer is that all of these things she lists, including the divisions of time such as past, present, and future, are "woven back and forth" on space, hinting, perhaps, that he views space as the origin of time. But the ultimate origin of all things, including both space and time, is, according to Yājñavalkya, the highest *brahman* itself. While some parts of the *Bṛhadāraṇyaka Upaniṣad* still resonate with older notions of time as liturgical and ritual, we can also trace a gradual development of a notion of time as an ontological principle in this text, especially in the statements ascribed to Yājñavalkya.

The *Chāndogya Upaniṣad* similarly posits that a higher reality exists beyond the mutations of time; this text claims that when someone "knows *upaniṣad* of *brahman* in this way—for him the sun does not rise or set; for him it is always day" (3.11.3). Here, timelessness is not just associated with *brahman* itself, but also with a person who possesses the correct knowledge of *brahman*. The idea that knowledge can help a human being access an eternal reality is of course central to all the Upaniṣads.

The *Chāndogya Upaniṣad* further suggests that time and *brahman* belong to two entirely different modes of reality, separated by the *ātman*:

> This self is a dam, a divider, to keep these worlds apart. Days and nights do not pass across this dam, and neither do old age, or death, sorrow, or good and bad deeds. All evil turns back from it, for this world of *brahman* is free from evil. (8.4.1)

The idea that the divisions of time and old age and death have no access to the world of *brahman* indicates that *brahman* is located outside of time altogether. But how are we to understand the image of *ātman*, the self, that is the dividing line between these two realities? Perhaps what is implied here is the idea that the self of a human being belongs simultaneously to two different realities, the realms of time, death, and suffering, and the realm of the eternal.

While we still see some remnants of the idea of time as closely tied to days and nights and the rhythms of the physical world in the *Chāndogya Upaniṣad*, later classical Upaniṣads such as the *Śvetāśvatara* present time as something entirely distinct from the physical world. Here, time is no longer the ritual year or the passing of days and nights, but an abstract idea. This Upaniṣad speculates about the possible origin of *brahman* itself, the invisible cosmic force that permeates all things: "What is the cause of *brahman*? . . . Should we think of it as time, self-nature, necessity, coincidence, the elements, birth, or the person (*puruṣa*)?" (1.1–2). The theory of time as the ultimate origin of all things is likely drawn from *Atharvaveda* 19.53–54, as discussed previously. This passage in the *Śvetāśvatara Upaniṣad* implies that a form of *kālavāda*, a doctrine of time as the highest principle and origin of all things, existed by the time this *Upaniṣad* was composed.

But while time is listed first among all the potential sources of *brahman* and of the world itself in the *Śvetāśvatara Upaniṣad*, this text ultimately rejects this idea of time as origin in favor of a personal god as the ultimate cause of the universe: "Some wise men say it is self-nature, but others, who are deluded, say it is time. But it is the greatness of god in the world by means of which this wheel of *brahman* is turned around" (6.1). This god, Rudra/Śiva, is called the "architect of time" (*kālakāra*, 6.2 and 6.16), which suggests that time is here seen as part of creation itself rather than a cosmic cause. Rudra's creative work is here likened to that of a magician or an illusionist (*māyin*), and the list of things from which he creates the world includes the past and the future, as well as such ritual components as meters, sacrifices, rites, and religious observances (4.9), which hints that time itself is in this Upaniṣad simply a part of the material stuff of the universe. The creator/illusionist himself is, however, beyond time altogether; he is "beyond the three times" (i.e., past, present, and future, 6.5). Intriguingly, the very word for "illusion," *māyā*, is connected with measurement; the noun is derived from the verbal root *mā*, "to measure." While the term *māyā* usually means something like "creative power" or "the power to measure out space and time" in older Vedic language, *māyā* is used in the sense of "illusion" in these stanzas of the *Śvetāśvatara Upaniṣad*, as in later Advaita Vedānta philosophy (see chapter 8). In stanza 4.10, *māyā* (illusion) is identified with primordial matter, while the illusionist that creates the world is identified with Rudra/Śiva. The use of the significant term *māyā* here hints that the measuring out of finite space and time is somehow the work of a divine illusionist and suggests that time is something associated with a fleeting existence in *this* world, rather than with the highest reality.

Moreover, while the god Rudra/Śiva is the creator of time in this Upaniṣad, he is also its destroyer: "For one is Rudra. . . . He stands opposite all beings. After drawing in all beings, he stands as the protector at the end of time" (3.2). The notion that time has an end, and that Rudra/Śiva is instrumental in bringing it about, is a radical innovation in this text, which foreshadows the later Hindu idea of Śiva as the destroyer at the end of a *yuga*, annihilating the universe before it is created anew.

While other classical Upaniṣads are less theistic than the *Śvetāśvatara* in their outlook, they also embrace the idea of a divine reality beyond time. The *Māṇḍūkya Upaniṣad* proposes that the past, the present, and the future are all part of the sacred all-encompassing syllable *oṃ*. But this Upaniṣad also adds, intriguingly, that "whatever else that is beyond the three times, that is also just *oṃ* (1). This idea that there is something located beyond the three times hints at a budding concept of the timeless, which will be further developed in later texts like the *Maitrī Upaniṣad*. The *Māṇḍūkya Upaniṣad* suggests that the past, present, future, and the timeless are all parts of the *ātman*, and that these four parts of the self also correspond to four states of consciousness: the waking state, sleep, dreamless sleep, and the mystical fourth, or *turīya* state.

By implication, then, both time and timelessness are here regarded as aspects of both the self and of consciousness, and the timeless associated with the deepest form of consciousness.

The *Maitrī Upaniṣad* revisits the older concept of time as closely tied to the physical world: "Food is the origin of all the world. Time is the origin of food. The sun is the origin of time" (6.14). The idea that time is the origin of food is perhaps based on the observation that it takes time for crops to grow and ripen, but this Upaniṣad also takes a more abstract view of time when it suggests that the sun itself is the origin of time, since "[w]ithout measure there is no knowledge of the thing to be measured" (6.14). This passage implies that we only have a concept of time because the shifting of days and nights gives us the ability to measure it. This doesn't necessarily mean that time is nothing but a human construct, but rather that we would be unable to know time if we could not measure it. The *Maitrī Upaniṣad* further states that time is that which "cooks" (ripens) all living creatures (i.e., brings them to the end of their natural life cycle, 6.15), but also proposes that there is another reality that lies beyond time altogether: "*Brahman* has two forms: time and non-time" (6.15). This concept of a non-time (*akāla*), something opposed to and distinct from time (*kāla*), implies that while the cosmic force *brahman* may be experienced in this world, there is also a part of *brahman* that lies beyond the empirical realm associated with the measurement of time.

The *Maitrī Upaniṣad* plays with the terms *kāla* ("time") and *kala* ("part, division") and uses the pun to make a larger theological point: "That which is before the sun is non-time, without parts. Of the partite (*brahman*) the form is the year" (6.15). The underlying idea here is that time is that which can be measured by the movement of the sun and the division into days and nights, while there also exists a timeless, unmeasurable aspect of the same cosmic reality of *brahman*.

Although eternity—as an abstract noun—is not a term that is often used in Indian philosophy, the *idea* of the eternal is nevertheless easy to identify in the classical Upaniṣads. *Brahman* is, for example, specifically called eternal, *sanātana*, in *Kaṭha Upaniṣad* 5.6 and *Muṇḍaka Upaniṣad* 1.1.6. The frequent references to *brahman* as imperishable (*akṣara*) in the Upaniṣads similarly suggest that *brahman* is beyond all mutations of time. *Brahman* is "the lord of what was and what will be; he is both today and tomorrow" (*Kaṭha Upaniṣad* 4.13). The *ātman* is also described as "without beginning or end, beyond the great, and eternal" (*Kaṭha Upaniṣad* 3.15), while the sacred syllable *oṃ* is likewise referred to as "different from what has been and what will be" (*Kaṭha Upaniṣad* 2.14). The classical Upaniṣads cited here often play with the term *akṣara*, which can mean both "syllable" and "imperishable." The syllable *oṃ* is *akṣara* in both senses of the word; it is a sacred syllable associated with an unchanging reality beyond time.

We can trace through the Upaniṣads a gradual process of untangling the idea of time from the rhythms of the natural world, the changing seasons, and the ritual year, a process that already began in the Hymns to Time in the *Atharvaveda*. This abstraction of time parallels other abstractions in the Upaniṣads. The idea of *ātman*, the self of a living being, begins with a notion of self that is indistinguishable from the physical body in some passages in the older Upaniṣads and gradually becomes a transcendent and wholly immaterial entity as distinct from the body. Similarly, the notion of time comes to transcend the physical realities of seasons and days and nights and becomes an abstract philosophical concept in the Upaniṣads. This shift in Upaniṣadic notions of time is intricately connected to the gradual separation of the Upaniṣads from the corpus of the Vedic ritual texts and their eventual emergence as a new genre of texts, a genre that demands new notions of space and time. In the oldest Upaniṣads, we still see an older notion of liturgical and ritual time, echoing the rhythms of the natural year, while time becomes more abstract as the Upaniṣads refine their narratives of transcendence and grow increasingly occupied with a higher reality behind the visible forms of the natural world.

While the earliest Upaniṣads are often concerned with ritual time, as are the Brāhmaṇas that precede them, later Upaniṣadic texts are increasingly preoccupied with the invisible, transcendent reality behind and beyond the visible forms of this world. Over time, time itself is perceived as one such form of transcendent reality, and ultimately, as a gateway to an even higher reality beyond. The abstraction of time, just like the abstraction of *karma* or *ātman*, is part of a larger turning of the literary gaze away from the empirical world and toward the underlying reality, the timeless *brahman* itself.

Karma and Reincarnation in the Upaniṣads

The term *kárman* is used in Vedic Sanskrit to designate a ritual action. We should note that the term *kárman* is most frequently used in the Vedic texts affiliated with the *Yajurveda*, such as the *Taittirīya Saṃhitā*, the *Taittirīya Brāhmaṇa*, the *Taittirīya Āraṇyaka*, the *Kaṭha Saṃhitā*, and the *Śatapatha Brāhmaṇa*. This is perhaps only to be expected, since ritual actions are the domain of the *adhvaryu*, the priest of the *Yajurveda*.

Even though the word itself is used, the *karma* doctrine of later Hinduism is not attested in the Vedas. The term *karma* is first used in the sense of religiously efficacious action with the power to influence a person's future life in the Upaniṣads. In classical Hinduism, *karma* is a law that governs all action; a person who does good will reap positive benefits in the future, while a person who does evil will reap negative consequences. The karmic results of a particular action may occur within the same lifetime as the original action, or they may lead to a better or worse rebirth.

Reincarnation is first mentioned in *Bṛhadāraṇyaka Upaniṣad* 6.2.16, where we learn that those who win the heavenly world through their sacrifices and gifts will travel into the smoke, the night, the fortnight of the waning moon, the dark half of the year, the world of the fathers, the moon, and eventually into the rain, and into food, and when that food is eaten, they pass into man and woman and become a human embryo before being born again. A person who has the correct knowledge, however, will pass into the fire, and then into the day, the fortnight of the waxing moon, the light half of the year, the world of the gods, the sun, the lightning, and eventually the world of *brahman*. Those who reach the world of *brahman* will not be reborn at all, but rather stay in that world (6.2.15). The mention of sacrifices and gifts suggests that rebirth is a sort of karmic reward for these actions, although the path that leads to rebirth is inferior to that which leads to the world of *brahman*. This passage foreshadows the idea found in later Hinduism that the ultimate goal of human existence is freedom from death and rebirth altogether.

The text says nothing about the fate of those who do not get to be reborn through sacrifices and gifts if they do not have the knowledge to obtain the world of *brahman*. A parallel passage in *Chāndogya Upaniṣad* 5.10.1–6 does, however, address the question of those who do not enter either of the two paths—that of gift offerings leading to rebirth in human form, or that of knowledge that leads to entry into the world of *brahman*: "There are also those who don't go on either of these two paths. They become tiny creatures going around here forever. Be born, die—that is the third state" (*Chāndogya Upaniṣad* 5.10.8). This inferior third state appears to involve an endless series of rebirths, with no hope of escape, while those who are reincarnated in human form presumably will have the opportunity to follow the path of knowledge and seek liberation from the cycle in the future. But while the passages in the two Upaniṣads are otherwise quite similar, *Chāndogya Upaniṣad* ties the notions of *karma* and reincarnation to social class: "People who beave pleasantly here will enter a pleasant womb, like that of a Brahman, Kṣatriya, or Vaiśya woman. But those who behave disgustingly will enter a disgusting womb, like that of a dog, pig, or Caṇḍāla woman" (5.10.7). It is possible that the fusion of reincarnation and *karma* that we find in the *Chāndogya Upaniṣad* represents a more recent development that is absent in the older *Bṛhadāraṇyaka Upaniṣad.* Elsewhere, *Bṛhadāraṇyaka Upaniṣad* (4.4.3) compares the self to a caterpillar, who crawls across a leaf, and simply continues on to the next leaf, just as the self continues on to the next life.

Where did the idea of reincarnation in the Upaniṣads come from in the first place? There is no explicit notion of reincarnation in the Vedas, but the idea of rebirth seems to grow out of the older Vedic idea of re-death (*punarmṛtyu*), a repeated death in the afterlife after the initial bodily death (*Kauṣītaki Brāhmaṇa* 25.1; *Śatapatha Brāhmaṇa* 2.3.3.9 and 10.1.4.14; *Taittirīya Brāhmaṇa* 3.11.8.6). Immortality is often mentioned as a goal in Vedic literature. This immortality is conceptualized as an eternal world, filled with eternal and abundant food, and without the threat of re-death. Achieving this goal is associated with a person's *sukṛta*, the sum of their correctly performed ritual actions. When *sukṛta* runs out, a person may experience a new death (see Lopez 1997). The idea of a person's *karma* influencing reincarnation is therefore not entirely alien to Vedic literature, even if it is not made explicit.

But when a person's fate in the afterlife is tied to one's previous actions in the *Brāhmaṇas*, these are exclusively ritual actions. In the Upaniṣads, however, this idea is extended to encompass *all* actions, and the idea of *karma* as we find it in later Hinduism (and Buddhism and Jainism) is born.

The *Kauṣītaki Upaniṣad* also talks about a "circle of life" that involves rebirth in a different form:

> All those depart go from this world go to the moon. Because of their breaths, the moon grows larger when it is waxing, and when it's waning, it leads them to birth. The moon is the door to the heavenly world. It allows those who can answer its question to pass on. Those who cannot answer its question become rain, and they rain down to earth. They are born again as a worm or a moth or a bird or a tiger or a lion of a fish or a rhinoceros or a human,

> or some other being, in accordance with their actions and their knowledge. (1.2)

Here, both knowledge and actions help determine a person's next birth, but the most crucial knowledge is that which helps a person answer the moon's question, "Who are you?" The correct answer to that is an enigmatic verse involving semen, mothers, and the seasons of the year, but the final line of the verse is very clear: "Who am I? I am you!" (1.2). It is this knowledge of identity between oneself and the moon, and perhaps by implication between oneself and *brahman*, that leads to freedom from the cycle of rebirth.

In the *Kaṭha Upaniṣad*, Death himself finally reveals the secret of death and rebirth to the boy Naciketas:

> Come, I will tell you this secret
> and everlasting truth
> about what happens to the *ātman*
> when it reaches death.
> Some enter a womb in which
> The embodied self becomes corporeal.
> Others pass into a stationary object
> According to their actions and knowledge. (5.6–7)

A similar distinction between those who are reborn and those who escape the cycle can be found in *Muṇḍaka Upaniṣad* 1.2.10–11:

> Those who think of sacrifices and gifts as best,
> Not knowing any better in their delusion,
> Enjoy their good deeds in the back of the sky,
> But return again to this world.
> But those who practice asceticism and faith in the forest,
> Calm and wise, living on alms,
> They go spotless through the gate of the sun
> Where the immortal *puruṣa* is, the *ātman*.

Knowledge and Liberation in the Upaniṣads

The idea that a person can become immortal through a particular form of knowledge is prominent in the Upaniṣads. This salvific knowledge (*jñāna*) leads to freedom from death and reincarnation and is particularly associated with the insight that *ātman* and *brahman* are one. While the older Brāhmaṇa texts that preceded the Upaniṣads emphasized the correct knowledge as a way to make religious rituals effective, the Upaniṣads regard knowledge as the path to spiritual liberation. While older Vedic texts were concerned with knowledge as well, the Vedic knowledge is often an applied one, to be used in a ritual context. The knowledge valued in the Upaniṣads is a far more abstract one, less concerned with actions than with understanding. It seems likely that the emphasis on knowledge in the Upaniṣads initially grew out of the desire to seek a deeper understanding about certain parts of the Vedic rituals, as the desire that is often articulated in the Brāhmaṇa texts. But in the Upaniṣads, knowledge is defined as an understanding of the outer and inner world in general, rather than ritual expertise.

The *Muṇḍaka Upaniṣad* distinguishes between two forms of knowledge:

> There are two forms of knowledge to be known, say those who know *brahman*: the higher and the lower. The lower is the *Ṛgveda*, the *Yajurveda*, the *Sāmaveda*, the *Atharvaveda*, phonetics, ritual, grammar, etymology, meter, and astrology, while the higher is that by which the syllable *oṃ* is understood. (1.4–5)

The Sanskrit term for knowledge, frequently used throughout the Upaniṣads, is *jñāna*, a term that is etymologically related to the Greek *gnosis*. Knowledge in the Upaniṣads is a path to salvation and immortality, not merely knowledge for its own sake. This Upaniṣadic knowledge is a form of absolute absorption, an altered state of being:

> As a man embraced by a beloved woman ceases to know anything outside or within, in the same way a man embraced by the knowing self ceases to know anything outside or within. (*Bṛhadāraṇyaka Upaniṣad* 4.3.21)

The Upaniṣads speculate about the connection between things in the natural world, such as wind and water, aspects of the human body, such as breath, psychological concepts such as consciousness, and abstract principles such as being (*sat*), non-being (*asat*), *brahman*, and *ātman*. The Upaniṣads are concerned with knowledge of an absolute, unchanging reality behind all the shifting forms of the world of the senses, and they speculate about the origin of the world. But above all, the Upaniṣads are concerned with knowledge of the highest, absolute reality, that which underlies all changing appearances.

But this knowledge is radically different from all other forms of knowledge, which involve a knowing subject and a known object. While several Upaniṣads do discuss both *ātman* and *brahman* as something to be known, other Upaniṣadic texts suggest that knowledge of *ātman* implies a breaking down of the very distinction of subject and object:

> For when there seems to be a duality, there one sees the other, smells, hears, speaks to, understands, and knows the other. But when everything has become one's own self, how could one smell, see, hear, address, understand, or know anyone? How could one know that, through which all is known; how could one know the knower?" (*Bṛhadāraṇyaka Upaniṣad* 2.4.14)

As the philosopher Yājñavalkya points out, the ultimate reality cannot be an object of knowledge because it is ultimately the subject of all knowledge:

> Truly, Gārgī, the imperishable sees, but is not seen, hears but is not heard, understands but is not understood, and knows but is

> not known. Other than that, there is no seer, other than that there is no hearer, other than that there is no one who understands, and other than that there is no one who knows. (*Bṛhadāraṇyaka Upaniṣad* 3.8.11)

The same idea is expressed in the *Chāndogya Upaniṣad*:

> If someone sees no other, hears no other, knows no other, that is fullness (*bhūman*). If he sees, hears, and knows another, that is scarcity (*alpam*). The fullness is immortal, and the scarcity is mortal. (7.24.1)

What does it even mean to speak of the knowledge of *ātman* or *brahman*, if they cannot be understood as objects of knowledge? The Upaniṣadic texts imply that knowing the ultimate reality is radically different from all other sorts of knowledge; it is not knowing an object, but rather being transformed into the all-knowing subject that *is* that reality.

Knowledge of the absolute reality, and of one's own unity with the ultimate subject of the self, is transformative and ultimately leads a person to immortality. As the final stanza of the *Kaṭha Upaniṣad* (6.18) assures us:

> After Naciketas has received this knowledge
> and the entire method of Yoga taught by Death,
> he reached *brahman* and became free from old age and death,
> and so will others who know this teaching of the self.

Mantras, Sound, and Sacred Language

The Upaniṣads are permeated by speculations about the mystical efficacy of language and ritual speech. Numerous *mantras*, or sacred utterances, are found sprinkled throughout the Upaniṣadic texts, both the well-known *oṃ* and more obscure ones such as *hiṃ* or *huṃ*. Language is in the Upaniṣads not just a tool to describe the world, but an integral part of the cosmos itself. When the *Taittirīya Upaniṣad* claims that "this whole world is *oṃ*" (1.8), this tells us something significant about the Upaniṣadic worldview: a powerful sound can capture the essence of the entire cosmos.

Like the Vedas, Brāhmaṇas, and Āraṇyakas before them, the Upaniṣads were passed on orally from teachers to students. Writing was never highly valued in ancient India, perhaps because the spoken language itself was considered sacred from Vedic times onward, personified as the goddess Vāc ("Speech").

Although the oldest among the classical Upaniṣads still identify language with the cosmos itself, speculations simultaneously begin to arise about the possibility that something may exist that is beyond the reach of language:

> That which one cannot express by speech,
> by which speech itself is expressed—
> Know that only that is *brahman*,
> And not that which they worship here. (*Kena Upaniṣad* 1.5)

In the *Kena Upaniṣad*, the cosmic divine force *brahman* is the origin of language, but ultimately itself beyond language. The idea that both *ātman* (the inner self) and *brahman* (the divine force) are ineffable is expressed in the famous Upaniṣadic phrase: *Neti neti* ("Not this, not that"):

> This *ātman* is neither this nor that (*neti neti*). It is ungraspable, for it cannot be grasped. It is immortal, for it does not die. (*Bṛhadāraṇyaka Upaniṣad* 4.4.22)

The limitations imposed by language are, however, overcome by means of the non-linguistic utterances of the Upaniṣadic *mantras*. *Mantras* are sacred sounds of immense power that function as shortcuts to the highest reality of *ātman/brahman*. Some scholars have explained *mantras* as non-linguistic utterances, others as linguistic units or ritual speech acts. We should note that the term *mantra* is used in Indian literature to mean several different things. A *mantra* can be a quotation from the Vedas, used in a ritual context. In this case, a *mantra* has a clearly identifiable lexical meaning, even if that meaning may later be forgotten. A *mantra* may also be a brief exclamation used in a ritual sense, such as *svāhā* ("hail" or "blessing!") and the threefold *vyāhṛti* ("utterance") of *bhūr*, *bhuvaḥ*, *svaḥ*. These *mantras* possess a lexical meaning, but also a mystical power beyond the semantic meaning of the word. The semantic meaning of *bhūr*, *buvaḥ*, *svaḥ* is "earth, atmosphere, and heaven," yet the utterance takes on a mystical significance that far transcends the literal meaning. The *Chāndogya Upaniṣad* suggests that *bhūr*, *buvaḥ*, *svaḥ* represent the essence of the Vedas, extracted by the creator god Prajāpati himself from the holy texts (*Chāndogya Upaniṣad* 4.17.1–3). And lastly, a *mantra* can be a religiously significant utterance without any apparent lexical meaning, such as *oṃ*. *Mantras* represent a cosmic non-linguistic language that creates a connection to the reality that lies beyond language. *Brahman* is, for example, said to be indescribable, and yet identical to the sacred non-linguistic syllable *oṃ* (*Praśna Upaniṣad* 5.2).

The *Kaṭha Upaniṣad* suggests that *oṃ* is the essence of all the Vedas:

> That word that all the Vedas reveal
> The word that all austerities speak of
> That which people desire when they live ascetic lives
> I will tell you that word briefly: *Oṃ*. (*Kaṭha Upaniṣad* 2.15)

The *Kaṭha Upaniṣad* (2.16), like the *Taittirīya Upaniṣad* (1.8.1), identifies *oṃ* with *brahman* itself, while the *Māṇḍūkya Upaniṣad* divides the syllable up into four parts and uses the fourfold *oṃ* as the starting point for elaborating on the idea of the four states of the *ātman*: wakefulness, sleep, dreamless sleep, and a mystical state beyond all these. The fourth state, associated with the deepest possible insight into reality, is here identified with the syllable *oṃ* in its entirety (12). "The *ātman* itself is *oṃ*," claims the *Māṇḍūkya Upaniṣad*. "Anyone who knows this enters into the *ātman* by the *ātman*" (12). The *Muṇḍaka Upaniṣad* also claims that the syllable *oṃ* is a tool for salvation; it will help steer the *ātman* into its unity with *brahman*: "*Oṃ* is the bow, the arrow is *ātman*, and *brahman* the target" (2.2.4).

In fact, the cosmos itself appears to be linguistic in nature:

> It is like this as far as the worlds are concerned: The first word is the earth, the next word is the sky, and space is the *sandhi* between them. Wind is that which joins them together. This is how it is with the worlds. (*Taittirīya Upaniṣad* 1.3.1)

This passage refers to the phenomenon of *sandhi*, a peculiarity of the Sanskrit language, whereby a sound change happens at the boundary between two words. Following a set of elaborate rules, the final sound of the first word changes to become more similar to the beginning sound of the following word. But in the vision of the authors of the *Taittirīya Upaniṣad*, this approximation does not just happen between sounds, but also on a cosmic level: space is the *sandhi* between heaven and earth. The fact that the cosmos itself is seen as linguistic in nature highlights the power of the spoken word in the Upaniṣads.

The Upaniṣads are rich in wordplay that is difficult to convey adequately in translation.

> The *Sāman* (chant) is speech. It is both She (*sā*) and He (*ama*), and this gives name to and reveals the nature of the *Sāmaṇ*. Or alternatively, maybe it is called *Sāman* because it is the same (*sama*)

> size as a fly, a mosquito, an elephant, the three worlds, or the whole universe. (*Bṛhadāraṇyaka Upaniṣad* 1.3.22)

> The first being was called Man (*puruṣa*) because before (*pūrva*) all of this, he burnt (*uṣ*) all evil. (*Bṛhadāraṇyaka Upaniṣad* 1.4.1)

> The sun is *mahas*, for all the worlds are made happy (*mah-*) by the sun. (*Taittirīya Upaniṣad* 1.5.2)

> But all he saw was that man, *brahman*, the highest, and he said: "This (*idam*) I have seen (*adarśam*)." And therefore, he is called *Idandra*. His name is Idandra, but even though he is Idandra, people cryptically call him Indra, for the gods love the cryptic. (*Aitareya Upaniṣad* 1.13–14)

The authors of the Upaniṣads likely knew perfectly well that the word *Sāman* was not derived from the pronouns *sā* and *ama*, nor from the adjective *sama*. But their purpose was not to give a historically correct etymology of a term, but rather to connect the sacred chant *Sāman* through similarity of sound to other concepts and thereby express a deeper truth. In this case, the point the authors are making about the *Sāman* chant does not relate to its linguistic history, but rather to its all-encompassing nature that cannot be limited by gender or size. Likewise, a correct knowledge of *puruṣa* will lead to the removal of evil, and the correct knowledge of the *mantra mahas* will gladden like the sun, no matter what the etymological origins of these words are from a historical perspective. The name of the Vedic god Indra is not derived from a verb meaning "to see," but in the *Aitareya Upaniṣad*, like in other texts formally affiliated with the *Ṛgveda*, the Vedic thunder god Indra becomes a paradigmatic wisdom seeker. To associate Indra with vision and insight therefore makes theological, if not etymological sense. Language is here used playfully to point to larger truths, rather than as a form of erroneous historical linguistics.

Over time, *oṃ* emerges as the most significant *mantra* in the Upaniṣads. The older Vedic *Taittirīya Saṃhitā* (3.2.9.6) identifies *oṃ* as the sound the *hotṛ* (*Ṛgveda*) priest makes at the end of a verse, but what may have begun as a ritual humming took on a sacred significance of its own. The *Aitareya Brāhmaṇa* (5.32) identifies *oṃ* with heaven and the sun. *Oṃ* is often referred to as *akṣara* in the Upaniṣads, a word with a significant double meaning; *akṣara* means "syllable" but also "imperishable." The syllable *oṃ* therefore becomes a symbol of the highest, imperishable reality itself. *Chāndogya Upaniṣad* declares that "*oṃ* is the entire world" (2.23.3), while *Taittirīya Upaniṣad* (1.8) identifies *oṃ* with *brahman*. The *Kaṭha Upaniṣad* calls *oṃ* "the essence of all the Vedas" (2.15). The *Śvetāśvatara Upaniṣad* suggests that knowing a *Ṛgveda* verse in meaningless if one doesn't also know the syllable *oṃ*: "The syllable among the *Ṛgveda* verses, the syllable on which all the gods rest in the highest heaven—when someone does not know it, what use is a *Ṛgveda* verse?" (4.8). The *Muṇḍaka Upaniṣad* suggests that *oṃ* will lead the *ātman* to its final union with *brahman*: "*Oṃ* is the bow, *ātman* is the arrow, and *brahman* is the target" (2.2.4).

The *Māṇḍūkya Upaniṣad* identifies the *ātman* with *oṃ* and suggests that the syllable *oṃ*, like the *ātman*, can be divided into four parts. The four states of the self, wakefulness, sleep, dreamless sleep, and the mystical fourth state beyond all the others, are identified with the sounds *a*, *u*, and *m*, and with the syllable *oṃ* in its entirety. A person who knows this, declares the Upaniṣad, will enter the *ātman* by means of the *ātman* (12).

The *Chāndogya Upaniṣad* even suggests that *mantras* can exist among animals, perhaps because they make sounds that appear meaningful, yet are non-linguistic:

> Then the dogs came in, slinking in quietly just like priests slink in quietly in a row, holding each others' backs and sang the chant called *Bahiṣpavamāna*. They sat down and chanted *huṃ*. They chanted: "*Oṃ*, let us eat. *Oṃ*, let us drink. *Oṃ*, may the gods

> Varuṇa, Prajāpati and Savitṛ bring us food here. Lord of food, bring us food! Bring it here, bring it, bring it, *oṃ*." (*Chāndogya Upaniṣad* 1.12.4–5)

The idea of animals producing *mantras* fits well in the overall context of this Upaniṣad, where non-human entities such as animals can be wisdom teachers.

7

Narrative and Main Characters in the Upaniṣads

The Upaniṣads as Vedic Literature

As mentioned in chapter 3, some of the very oldest Upaniṣads are simply portions of larger late Vedic texts later identified as "Upaniṣads" because they deal with themes common to other Upaniṣadic texts, such as the identification of *brahman* and *ātman*. But over time, the Upaniṣads become a genre unto themselves, characterized by their philosophical speculations surrounding the concepts of *ātman* and *brahman* and their characteristic style that weaves together narratives, dialogues, mythology, and linguistic speculation.

The Upaniṣadic authors are experts at recycling older narratives and imbuing them with new meaning. The boy Naciketas visits the Lord of the Dead in the older *Taittirīya Brāhmaṇa* and learns about rituals, but in the *Kaṭha Upaniṣad* his conversation with Death is focused on the self, rather than rituals. The *Śatapatha Brāhmaṇa* tells the story of Yājñavalkya's victory in debate at the court of King Janaka, but when the story is retold in the *Bṛhadāraṇyaka Upaniṣad*, Yājñavalkya is no longer a mere master of ritual but the one who possesses the true knowledge about *ātman* as the fundamental reality. In the *Ṛgveda*, the thunder god Indra slays demons with his thunderbolt, but in the *Chāndogya Upaniṣad*, Indra shows his superiority to the demon Virocana by managing to wrestle the ultimate secrets about the nature of the self out of the old creator god Prajāpati.

The Classical Upaniṣads. Signe Cohen, Oxford University Press. © Oxford University Press 2024.
DOI: 10.1093/oso/9780197654156.003.0007

The oldest of the classical Upaniṣads (*Bṛhadāraṇyaka, Chāndogya, Taittirīya, Aitareya, Kauṣītaki*) are mainly composed in prose, with a few verses interspersed, while some of the later classical Upaniṣads are composed in verse or blend poetry and prose. The *Kena Upaniṣad*, for example, contains two chapters in verse followed by two in prose, while the *Kaṭha, Īśā, Śvetāśvatara*, and *Muṇḍaka Upaniṣads* are in verse. The later *Māṇḍūkya* and *Praśna Upaniṣads* shift back to prose.

Narrative and Dialogues in the Upaniṣads

The philosophy of the Upaniṣads is not merely framed by narratives; narratives are a primary mode of philosophical inquiry in these texts. When philosophy is separated from narrative, it becomes impersonal and general, but philosophy grounded in narrative and dialogue reveals truths inherent in lived human experience. Narrative is a vehicle for understanding the world in the Upaniṣads, and philosophical argument is developed through conversations between named characters in the texts. The larger idea that the truth about the ultimate reality can be found in the human realm through conversations about ideas informs the structure of the Upaniṣads. But while we get multiple voices in the Upaniṣads, some voices carry more authority than others. The Upaniṣadic authors signal clearly to their audience who emerges victorious from the debates featured in the texts. Yājñavalkya walks away with a thousand cows, the Brahman Dṛpti Bālāki begs a king who is his social inferior to become his teacher, and Śāṇḍilya's head literally splits apart due to his lack of knowledge.

The Upaniṣads are religious and philosophical texts expressing ideas about *ātman*, *brahman*, knowledge, and the path to liberation. These ideas may be presented in passages of abstract philosophical reflection, but some of the most important ideas are conveyed through narrative episodes, especially in dialogues between characters. Characters in the Upaniṣads are concerned with the ultimate reality, and they ask, instruct, and debate each other to get closer to the truth about this reality. The many memorable characters of the Upaniṣads not only serve to present philosophical ideas in a livelier, more personal way; they also demonstrate that even the most abstract knowledge is located in *people*, and that the path to knowledge is therefore to find the right teacher.

The Upaniṣads are filled with characters asking questions. While some questions are shown by those answering them to be based in faulty premises and therefore unanswerable, the overall message of the Upaniṣads is that it is essential to ask questions to attain the kind of wisdom that leads to immortality and freedom.

In addition to dialogues between wisdom seekers and teachers, the Upaniṣads contain dizzying passages of abstract philosophical speculation as well as mythological stories about the creation of the world, narratives that blend the abstract and the more tangible. Even when the Upaniṣadic texts discuss abstract concepts like death and time, concepts themselves can be anthropomorphized and begin to act like human characters.

Ideas about the nature of reality are often expressed in the earlier Brāhmaṇa texts as well, but in the Upaniṣads, these ideas are more often articulated through the texts' characters. While some Upaniṣadic passages discuss abstract ideas without tying these concepts to specific characters, many central ideas in these texts are expressed by characters in conversation with each other. Most dialogues are conversations between teachers and students, in which the teacher explains significant concepts to the student, but there are also debates between rival wisdom teachers, such as the well-known contest scene at the court of King Janaka in *Bṛhadāraṇyaka Upaniṣad* 3. Ideas are therefore presented and discussed by a multitude of voices. But these voices are not equal; the texts often make firm judgments about who is saying the right thing and who needs further instruction.

While the main characters in the earlier Vedic texts are gods and demons, the main characters in the Upaniṣads are teachers and students. Some of these teachers and students may be gods, but most of them are humans. Even those teachers who are gods are figures of authority because of *what* they teach, not because they are divine.

Since the Upaniṣads are deeply concerned with knowledge and its transmission, most of the narratives embedded in the texts are focused on teacher-student relationships. Most of the Upaniṣads' characters are ordinary humans, but when gods, demons, or talking animals occur in the text, they too must model their behavior on that of humans and assume the roles of teachers and students.

The central ideas of the Upaniṣads are presented through dialogues, associated with individual teachers and their students. Black (2003) differentiates between four kinds of dialogues in the Upaniṣads: those between Brahman teachers and their students, those between Brahmans and kings, those between Brahmans who debate each other, and those between Brahmans and women.

The dialogue form that occupies such a central place in the older Upaniṣads may ultimately be traced back to the so-called dialogue hymns of the *Ṛgveda*, poems where two characters are engaged in a lively debate. Some of the dialogues involving women in the *Ṛgveda* are even more spirited than those in the Upaniṣads and feature female characters who disagree strongly with their male debate partners and will not be silenced or talked into a different opinion.

The Characters of the Upaniṣads

Do any of the teachers and students of the Upaniṣads represent actual historical figures? Few scholars today will go as far as Water Ruben, who listed 109 Upaniṣadic philosophers, with suggested dates for their lives (Ruben 1947). Instead, modern scholars approach the characters of the Upaniṣads as literary creations

(Olivelle 1999; Black and Geen 2011; Lindquist 2011c, 2018b), rather than historical persons.

Many of the characters in the Upaniṣads are closely tied to Vedic *śākhās*. Yājñavalkya represents the *White Yajurveda*, Gārgī, Dṛpta Bālāki, and Śākalya the *Ṛgveda*, and Pippalāda the *Atharvaveda*. Some of the Upaniṣadic characters are also known from older Vedic texts. Yājñavalkya, the main wisdom teacher of the *Bṛhadāraṇyaka Upaniṣad*, is also featured in the older ritual text *Śatapatha Brāhmaṇa*, as are Uddālaka Āruṇi and his son Śvetaketu, who are featured prominently in the *Bṛhadāraṇyaka*, *Chāndogya*, and *Kauṣītaki Upaniṣads*. Naciketas, the main character of the *Kaṭha Upaniṣad*, is also featured in the *Taittirīya Brāhmaṇa* (3.1.8). Śāṇḍilya, who loses to Yājñavalkya in the wisdom contest at King Janaka's court, is mentioned in *Śatapatha Brāhmaṇa* 10.6.3.1. But while these characters are mainly concerned with ritual knowledge in the earlier texts, in the Upaniṣads, they are focused on knowledge of *ātman* and *brahman*—except for poor Śāṇḍilya, who is stuck in an antiquated theistic worldview, and whose head therefore shatters apart. While the Upaniṣads draw on older Vedic texts and reuse their characters, these characters become part of the Upaniṣads' larger discourse of *ātman* and *brahman*, rather than Vedic ritualists.

Among the characters in the oldest Upaniṣads, there are several kings. These kings serve several different functions in the texts: they show the importance of royal patronage for Brahmaṇ wisdom teachers, and they demonstrate that the knowledge promoted in the Upaniṣads is not the exclusive property of Brahmans. While kings were important patrons of expensive and complicated Vedic sacrifices that required several ritual experts, the royal patronage takes on a new form in the Upaniṣads. By showing kings as eager promoters of knowledge of *ātman-brahman*, rather than just hosts of large public rituals, the Upaniṣads encourage continued royal patronage even as they dismiss the importance of the old rituals the kings used to sponsor.

Main Characters in the Classical Upaniṣads

Yājñavalkya. Yājñavalkya is the most prominent character in the *Bṛhadāraṇyaka Upaniṣad*, but he is only mentioned in this Upaniṣad and in an earlier text of the *White Yajurveda*, the *Śatapatha Brāhmaṇa*. In the *Śatapatha Brāhmaṇa*, Yājñavalkya is frequently invoked as an authority on a variety of subjects, ranging from men and women eating separately to the classification of the *agnihotra* sacrifice, while the Yājñavalkya we encounter in the *Bṛhadāraṇyaka Upaniṣad* is far more interested in the true nature of *ātman*.

Yājñavalkya's knowledge is well rewarded by his royal patron. In *Śatapatha Brāhmaṇa* 11.3.1.2, King Janaka of Videha asks Yājñavalkya about the nature of the *agnihotra* sacrifice, and when Yājñavalkya answers well, the king gives him a hundred cows. In *Śatapatha Brāhmaṇa* 11.4.3.20, King Janaka offers Yājñavalkya a thousand cows for his knowledge of the Mitravindā sacrifice. A thousand cows is also the grand prize the philosopher gets from the king in the third chapter of the *Bṛhadāraṇyaka Upaniṣad*.

In the older *Śatapatha Brāhmaṇa*, there is a limit to even Yājñavalkya's knowledge, but no such limitation is hinted at in the *Bṛhadāraṇyaka Upaniṣad*. In *Śatapatha Brāhmaṇa* 11.6.2, King Janaka encounters three traveling Brahmans, Śvetaketu Āruneya, Somasuṣma Sātyayajñi, and Yājñavalkya, and asks them how each of them performs the *agnihotra* sacrifice. The king finds Yājñavalkya's answer the best, but still declares himself unsatisfied and drives away. It turns out that Janaka himself understands the *agnihotra* sacrifice better than any of the priests, and Yājñavalkya ends up running after him and insisting that he explain the ritual.

The contest scene at King Janaka's court that is so central to the *Bṛhadāraṇyaka Upaniṣad* is also found in the *Śatapatha Brāhmaṇa* (11.6.3). In the *Śatapatha Brāhmaṇa*, as in the Upaniṣadic text, Yājñavalkya is so certain of his victory that drives away the cows before the contest starts, but in the older Brahmana text, he only has a single interlocutor, the priest Śākalya.

In the *Śatapatha Brāhmaṇa*, Yājñavalkya is an expert on Vedic ritual, but in the *Bṛhadāraṇyaka Upaniṣad*, Yājñavalkya is the supreme authority on *ātman* and *brahman*. Yājñavalkya's teachings in the *Bṛhadāraṇyaka Upaniṣad* are based on the absolute unity of *ātman* and *brahman* and foreshadow the later Advaita Vedānta school of philosophy. Yājñavalkya understands *brahman* as an impersonal principle, rather than a personal god, and as absolute identical with *ātman*.

Yājñavalkya is presented as extremely confident in the *Bṛhadāraṇyaka Upaniṣad*; when he is about to enter a debate at the court of King Janaka where various wisdom teachers will compete for the grand prize of a thousand cows, each with ten old pieces tied to their horns, Yājñavalkya instructs his student to bring the cows home for him—before the debate has even started! (*Bṛhadāraṇyaka Upaniṣad* 3.1.1). The other priests are upset by this and mutter among themselves. Is this mere arrogance on Yājñavalkya's part? Is he trying to psych out his opponents before the debate has even started? It is possible that the text's authors are making the point that only Yājñavalkya has the absolute confidence in his knowledge to dare to claim the cows beforehand. But interestingly, when one of the other priests asks Yājñavalkya if he really thinks he is the most learned among them, Yājñavalkya answers: "We all bow down to the most learned man. But we are really here for the cows" (*Bṛhadāraṇyaka Upaniṣad* 3.1.2). What does this mean? Isn't Yājñavalkya himself there for the cows as well? It is possible that this passage is meant to imply that Yājñavalkya's dramatic action of claiming the cows before the debate has started is meant to reveal how upsetting this is to the other contestants, and therefore what their true motivation is for participating: not for the sake of wisdom or even the honor of being recognized as the wisest, but merely for the sake of wealth.

Yājñavalkya's own lack of interest in wealth is demonstrated in the narrative (repeated twice, in *Bṛhadāraṇyaka Upaniṣad* 2.4 and 4.5) where he prepares to leave his two wives and divides his property between them. But when Yājñavalkya later visits King Janaka alone (*Bṛhadāraṇyaka Upaniṣad* 4), the king has clearly not forgotten the man who walked away with a thousand cows, and he asks: "Why have you come? For cows or subtle debates?" (4.1.1). One can sense some sarcasm on the king's part here, indicating that he does believe that the wisdom teacher is very interested in wealth. Yājñavalkya simply answers "both." However, when he goes on to dazzle the king with his insightful teachings, he refuses all the generous gifts of cows, bulls, and elephants the king offers him and says, "My father believed that one should never accept a gift before giving instruction," which suggests that the character's ultimate motivation is the transmission of knowledge, rather than monetary wealth.

Śvetaketu, the son of Uddālaka Āruṇi, is mentioned in three different Upaniṣads, the *Bṛhadāraṇyaka* (6.2.1–8), *Chāndogya* (5.3 and 6.1–16), and *Kauṣītaki Upaniṣad* (1). In the *Bṛhadāraṇyaka* and *Chāndogya Upaniṣad* narratives, Śvetaketu is questioned by the wisdom teacher Jaivali Pravāhaṇa and realizes that his father, Uddālaka Āruṇi, has not taught him about what happens after death. Both Śvetaketu and Uddālaka Āruṇi become Jaivali Pravāhaṇa's eager students. A variant of the same story is found in *Kauṣītaki Upaniṣad*, but here, Uddālaka Āruṇi is merely called Āruṇi, and the person who instructs father and son is called Citra Gāṅgyāyani, rather than Jaivali Pravāhaṇa. In *Chāndogya Upaniṣad* 6, Śvetaketu is depicted as an arrogant twenty-four-year-old who returns home to his father after twelve years of studying and believes himself to be very learned. Āruṇi, however, realizes that his son is lacking in true knowledge and teaches him about the *ātman*.

Śvetaketu also appears as a character in the *Śatapatha Brāhmaṇa*. He is cited as an authority on the Soma sacrifice (3.4.4.13), fore-offerings (11.2.7.12), and whether students should eat honey

(11.5.5.18). In 11.6.2, 1–2, Śvetaketu is wandering around with two other Brahmans, Somaśuṣma and Yājñavalkya, when they encounter King Janaka who quizzes them about how to perform the *agnihotra*. Śvetaketu gives an answer that is satisfactory, but not as good as Yājñavalkya's. Śvetaketu is quizzed by his (unnamed) father when he is about to perform a sacrificial ritual, and must learn more about the details of the sacrifice and its meaning from his father (10.3.3). In general, Śvetaketu is presented as a learned Brahman in the *Śatapatha Brāhmaṇa*, but one who still has things to learn from his father. From this literary inheritance, the Upaniṣads construct a new Śvetaketu who demonstrates the new ideas of these texts.

As Olivelle has noted, the narratives in the *Bṛhadāraṇyaka* and *Chāndogya Upaniṣads* follow each other quite closely, while the Śvetaketu we encounter in the *Kauṣītaki Upaniṣad* is a little different (Olivelle 1999, 46). In B, Śvetaketu is rude and ignorant, while Uddālaka Āruṇi is humble, and Pravahana Jaivali fatherly and magnanimous (Olivelle 1999, 58). In the *Chāndogya Upaniṣads*, Śvetaketu is less rude, and his father humble enough to ask questions, but not to become a student again. Jaivali is also less kind in this version and humiliates the young Śvetaketu. The *Kauṣītaki Upaniṣad* emphasizes Uddalaka's ignorance, rather than Śvetaketu's rudeness. The *Bṛhadāraṇyaka Upaniṣad* depicts both father and son in unflattering light compared to Yājñavalkya.

Uddālaka Āruṇi, Śvetaketu's father, is also called Gautama ("the descendant of Gotama"). In *Chāndogya Upaniṣad* 6, he is depicted as a knowledgeable teacher, while other Upaniṣadic passages (*Bṛhadāraṇyaka* 6.2.1–8; *Chāndogya* 5.3; *Kauṣītaki* 1) show him as someone who himself needs to be taught. In his teachings, Uddālaka Āruṇi focuses on *ātman* as the essence of all things, but he does not mention *brahman*. He teaches his son Śvetaketu about *ātman* in *Chāndogya Upaniṣad* 6 by having him taste salt dissolved in water and claiming that the *ātman* is invisibly present in all things as the salt is in the water. He uses the phrase *tat tvam asi* ("you are that"), which the commentator Śaṅkara interprets as referring to the identity of the personal self with *brahman*. But Brereton (1986) has shown that according to late Vedic syntax, *tat tvam asi* should instead be rendered "you are like that," and that Uddālaka Āruṇi tells Śvetaketu that he is of the same nature as some of the things his father has described to him, like the banyan tree, whose finest essence can't even be seen. Uddālaka Āruṇi is a proponent of experiential learning; he helps his son discover truths about the self by observing the natural world. In the *Chāndogya Upaniṣad* (6.7.3), Uddālaka Āruṇi shows his son the connection between nourishment and the ability to focus on one's studies. In *Chāndogya Upaniṣad* 6.1.1, Uddālaka Āruṇi emphasizes the importance of being a Brahman by education, rather than just by birth.

Intriguingly, Uddālaka Āruṇi is depicted more positively in the *Chāndogya Upaniṣad* than in the *Bṛhadāraṇyaka Upaniṣad*. According to the *Bṛhadāraṇyaka Upaniṣad* (6.3.7), Uddālaka Āruṇi is Yājñavalkya's teacher, but when he appears as one of Yājñavalkya's interlocutors at Janaka's court (6.3), it soon becomes clear that Yājñavalkya knows far more than his old teacher. There is no direct confrontation between the two, but Uddālaka Āruṇi is eclipsed by his former student. He asks Yājñavalkya about the "inner controller," and Yājñavalkya responds by explaining the *ātman*.

It is possible, but not certain, that Uddālaka Āruṇi is identical to Naciketas' father in the *Kaṭha Upaniṣad*. Here, Naciketas' temperamental father is called Uśan Vājaśravasa and referred to as Gautama ("the descendant of Gotama"). But Uśan Vājaśravasa is not necessarily a personal name; Uśan means "the one who desires" and may simply be a reference to the character's lack of genuine generosity, while Vājaśravasa means "the descendant of Vājaśravas." But what is his actual name? Intriguingly, Naciketas is called Auddālaka Āruṇi ("the son/descendant of Uddālaka Āruṇi") in the text (1.11). It is possible, therefore, that the father in the story should be identified with Uddālaka Āruṇi (which would make Naciketas Śvetaketu's brother). On the other hand, Naciketas may also be a more distant descendant of Uddālaka Āruṇi. The identification of

Uddālaka Āruṇi with Uśan Vājaśravasa is confirmed in the retelling of the Naciketas story in *Mahābhārata* 13.70.

Uddālaka Āruṇi is also featured in the older text *Śatapatha Brāhmaṇa*. In *Śatapatha Brāhmaṇa* 9.4.1, Uddālaka Āruṇi is identified as a Brahman of Kuru-Pañcāla, whose knowledge of the sacrificial rites are challenged by Svaidāyana Śaunaka. In this text, Svaidāyana's knowledge is superior, and Uddālaka Āruṇi eventually approaches him with firewood in his hands, a symbolic action indicating that he wants to become Svaidāyana's student. This episode from the Brāhmaṇa text may have served as an inspiration for the depiction of Uddālaka Āruṇi in the Upaniṣads. As in the Upaniṣads, Uddālaka Āruṇi does not hesitate to become a student again when he realizes that someone else has superior knowledge. But elsewhere in the *Śatapatha Brāhmaṇa*, Uddālaka Āruṇi is himself depicted as a wise and knowledgeable teacher; he explains all about the *agnihotra* ritual to the student Śauceya Prācīnayogya (11.5.3) and about the mystical connections between the year, the body, the cosmos, meter, and sacrifice to another student, Proti Kauśāmbeya Kausurubindi (12.2.2.13–23).

Gārgī Vācaknavī appears twice in the contest scene in *Bṛhadāraṇyaka Upaniṣad* (3.5 and 3.8). Her first name is a patronym (derivation of a male ancestor's name) and suggests that she is the descendant of the Ṛgvedic sage Garga. Her other name, Vācaknavī, appears to be more of a description; it can be translated as either "eloquent" or "talkative." Gārgī asks Yājñavalkya about the ultimate cause of all things, using the metaphor of weaving. But when she asks him about the cause of *brahman*, he tells her not to "ask beyond," lest her head split apart (*Bṛhadāraṇyaka Upaniṣad* 3.6). At that point, Gārgī falls silent. The problem does not seem to be, however, that she is a woman speaking in male company, but rather that her question goes beyond what is defined as the utmost limit of the knowable in the *Bṛhadāraṇyaka Upaniṣad*, *brahman* itself. Her question is impossible; *brahman* itself is the ultimate cause of all things and cannot therefore have a cause. But a later

Upaniṣad, the *Śvetāśvatara*, does return to Gārgī's impossible question, and even offers an answer: the god Rudra/Śiva is the cause of *brahman*. It seems that Gārgī was merely a few Upaniṣads ahead of her time. When Gārgī rises to challenge the assembly for the second time, however, her challenge is directed at the assembly than at Yājñavalkya, and she accepts that *brahman* is the cause of all things. Intriguingly, Gārgī Vācaknavī is mentioned as a great teacher in the Vedic *Āśvalāyana Gṛhyasūtra* 3.4, but few additional details are provided.

Vidagdha Śākalya is one of Yājñavalkya's many challengers in *Bṛhadāraṇyaka Upaniṣad* 3. The contest scene at Janaka's court in this Upaniṣad is based on a similar scene in the older Vedic text *Śatapatha Brāhmaṇa* (11.6.3ff). In the Brāhmaṇa text, Śākalya is the only challenger to Yājñavalkya, while he is one of many in the Upaniṣad. Śākalya asks Yājñavalkya about the number of deities in the world, which suggests that he is still caught up in a theistic world view and ignorant of the *ātman*. He eventually comes to a gruesome end as his head shatters apart.

Aśvala in another of Yājñavalkya's challengers in *Bṛhadāraṇyaka Upaniṣad* 3.1. The text identifies Aśvala as a *hotṛ*, or a priest of the *Ṛgveda*. Aśvala's questions are about overcoming death and time, but his questions are phrased in a narrow way that is specifically associated with the Vedic sacrifice: "Yājñavalkya," he said, "if everything in this world is caught by death and overwhelmed by death, how can the *yajamāna* [patron of the sacrifice] free himself from the grip of death?" Aśvala then goes on to ask about how the *yajamāna* can free himself from time ("the grip of day and night" and "the grip of the light and dark fortnights"). Although his questions show that he is looking for a higher truth, they also reveal that his thoughts are still preoccupied with old ritual ways of thinking.

Jāratkārava Ārtabhāga in another of Yājñavalkya's interlocutors. In *Bṛhadāraṇyaka Upaniṣad* 3.2, he asks Yājñavalkya what happens to a person after death. In response, Yājñavalkya takes him aside and tells him privately about *karma*. By asking an excellent question, Ārtabhāga shows himself to be worthy of private instruction by Yājñavalkya.

Bhujyu Lāhyāyani is one of Yājñavalkya's challengers in *Bṛhadāraṇyaka Upaniṣad* 3.3. He tells of a past encounter with a girl possessed by a *gandharva* (supernatural spirit). Bhujyu Lāhyāyani and his companions asked the *gandharva* possessing the girl, "Where are the Pārikṣitas?," and now he asks Yājñavalkya the same question. The Pārikṣitas are mythical kings of the Kuru-Pañcāla region. It seems that Bhujyu Lāhyāyani is particularly interested in mythology and cosmology, and Yājñavalkya initially gives him a mythological answer, detailing how the Vedic god Indra led the Pārikṣitas to a particular location associated with the wind after death. But then Yājñavalkya adds, "For both the individual things and the totality of things are just the wind," which conveys the radical identity of all things at heart of Yājñavalkya's teachings to Bhujyu Lāhyāyani.

Maitreyī and **Kātyāyanī**. According to *Bṛhadāraṇyaka Upaniṣad* 2.4.1–5, the wisdom teacher Yājñavalkya has two wives, Maitreyī and Kātyāyanī. He is about to leave home (perhaps for good?) and wants to divide his belongings between his two wives. Maitreyī, however, is not interested in material things and instead asks Yājñavalkya to teach him what he knows instead, so that she may attain immortality. The ensuing dialogue (or rather monologue; Maitreyī does not get to ask a lot of follow-up questions) where Yājñavalkya tells Maitreyī about the *ātman* is included twice in the *Bṛhadāraṇyaka Upaniṣad*. We don't know much about Kātyāyanī, but presumably she, unlike Maitreyī, was satisfied with receiving material wealth and had no questions to ask.

Sayugvān Raikva is an eccentric wisdom teacher in *Chāndogya Upaniṣad* 4.1–3. He is homeless and lives under a cart, but the wealthy **Jānaśruti Pautrāyaṇa** approaches him and wants to be his student. Even when offered great wealth, Raikva does not accept Jānaśruti as his student until Raikva offers him his own daughter. Raikva's initial refusal appears to be part of the common "reluctant teacher" trope in the Upaniṣads, which underscores the importance of students striving for knowledge even in the face of obstacles. The story of a homeless man as a sought-after teacher further suggests that true knowledge may be found in unexpected places in the world of the Upaniṣads.

Satyakāma Jābāla appears both as a student and a teacher in the Upaniṣads. He is the son of a single mother, Jābālā, and his father is unknown. He becomes the student of Hāridrumata Gautama, who is impressed with his honesty in revealing his uncertain ancestry, even if his Brahmanical status is unclear. Satyakāma is taught by Hāridrumata, but also by a series of non-human teachers: a bull, the fire, a water-bird, and a goose. He does, however, return to his Brahman teacher afterward to complete his education. Satyakāma later becomes the teacher of Upakosala but leaves on a journey before the teaching can begin. In his absence, the three household fires become Upakosala's teachers. But even though Satyakāma recognizes that Upakosala has the "glow of a man who knows *brahman*," he still needs to teach Upakosala himself before his education can be complete (*Bṛhadāraṇyaka Upaniṣad* 4.1.6, 6.3.11; *Chāndogya Upaniṣad* 4.4–9, 4.10–15).

Naciketas is the main character in the *Kaṭha Upaniṣad*. When his father, Uśan Vājaśravasa, gives away everything he owns in a large public display of piety, the boy Naciketas asks to whom his father will give him. Annoyed, the father says that he will give him to Yama (the Lord of the Dead). While this seems to be a mere outburst of anger on the father's part, Naciketas obeys his father's command and goes to the realm of the dead to see Yama.

Naciketas is depicted as pious and honest. When Yama offers him three wishes, Naciketas' choices say a lot about his character. His first wish is to be able to return to his father, and for his father no longer to be angry with him. In making this choice, Naciketas reveals himself as an ideal loving son who wishes to reconcile with his father despite the latter's bad temper and hypocritical display of piety. His second wish is to learn about a fire sacrifice that will lead to immortality. As a Brahman boy, Naciketas' desire to gain ritual knowledge is also commendable. But Naciketas' third wish shows that there is more to the boy than being a good son and a good student; he is also ultimately a wisdom seeker who will not be satisfied with anything less than an explanation of what happens to the self after death. When Yama offers him a dazzling array of tempting gifts instead of this final boon, including wealth, a long life, musicians, and dancing girls, Naciketas insists that none of these gifts are comparable to the wisdom that Yama has to offer. Pleased, Yama does agree to teach him. Naciketas has shown himself to be a worthy disciple.

Śāṇḍilya teaches that *ātman* and *brahman* are one. There are two teachers by that name mentioned in the lineage of teachers in *Bṛhadāraṇyaka Upaniṣad* (2.6.1–3 and 4.6), one who is the student of Kauśika and Gautama, and one who is the student of the otherwise unknown teacher Kaiśorya Kāpya. In a different lineage in *Bṛhadāraṇyaka Upaniṣad* 6.5.4, he is listed as the student of Vātsya. Śāṇḍilya is credited with teaching the idea that *ātman* and *brahman* are one in *Chāndogya Upaniṣad* 3.14, although this teaching is not presented in dialogue form, just as a brief statement. Similar teachings are ascribed to Śāṇḍilya in the late Vedic ritual text *Śatapatha Brāhmaṇa* (10.6.3.1–2), where he speaks about meditating on *brahman* and on *ātman*, which is "greater than all existing things." While *ātman* and *brahman* are not explicitly identified in this passage, there is at least a hint that they are the same thing. Intriguingly, the *Śatapatha Brāhmaṇa* invokes both Śāṇḍilya and Yājñavalkya as authority figures in different parts of the text. Śāṇḍilya emerges as the main authority figure in chapters 6–10 of the ritual text, while Yājñavalkya is the primary authority in the other chapters of the text. There is an Upaniṣad, the *Śāṇḍilya Upaniṣad*, named after the sage Śāṇḍilya. This text, which is considerably later than the classical Upaniṣads discussed in this volume, deals with various yogic techniques.

Nārada. According to *Chāndogya Upaniṣad* 7.1, Nārada is learned in the Vedas, but lacks knowledge of *ātman*. Here therefore becomes the student of Sanatkumāra and learns about the importance of happiness (*sukha*).

Sanatkumāra is Nārada's teacher in *Chāndogya Upaniṣad* 7.1. Sanatkumāra's teachings are based on the notion of happiness (*sukha*). From happiness comes actions, from actions creation, from creation faith, from faith thought, from thought knowledge, and from knowledge the truth about *brahman*. Sanatkumāra further identifies happiness with *bhūman* ("fullness"), which is seeing that *ātman* is the entire world (7.24.1). In nineteenth-century Theosophy, Sanat Kumara becomes the name of a mythical enlightened teacher, associated with the planet Venus, but this figure has only the name in common with the Upaniṣadic sage.

Dṛpta Bālāki is presented as a lesser teacher in *Bṛhadāraṇyaka Upaniṣad* 2.1. He believes himself to be knowledgeable and approaches King Ajātaśatru of Kāśi and offers to become his teacher. When asked about *brahman*, Dṛpta Bālāki identifies various persons (*puruṣas*) in the sun, moon, lightning, space, wind, fire, waters, and in the mirror as *brahman*. He does not know, however, that *brahman* is *ātman*. When he discovers that Ajātaśatru knows more about *brahman* than he does, Dṛpta Bālāki asks to become the king's student instead. Dṛpta Bālāki is identified as a Gārgya, or a descendant of the mythical Vedic sage Garga, who is associated with the *Ṛgveda*. "Dṛpta," which means "proud" or "vain," appears to be a nickname describing his character. But Dṛpta Bālāki does swallow his pride when confronted with the king's superior knowledge and asks to become a student instead.

The dialogue between Dṛpta Bālāki and Ajātaśatru is also found in *Kauṣītaki Upaniṣad* 4, but here, Bālāki is simply called Gārgya Bālāki (Bālāki of Garga's lineage) and is not identified by the derogatory epithet "Dṛpta." The *Kauṣītaki Upaniṣad* does present Bālāki in a much better light than the *Bṛhadāraṇyaka Upaniṣad*; although he still becomes the king's student in the *Kauṣītaki Upaniṣad*, he is described as "a learned and well-traveled man" (4.1).

Pippalāda, the mythical founder of one of the recensions of the *Atharvaveda*, is depicted as a kind and paternal wisdom teacher in the *Praṣna Upaniṣad*. He explains to his students the nature of *brahman*. According to Pippalāda, the world is created by Prajāpati, but his narrative of Prajāpati's creation remains quite abstract. The first couple produced is substance (*rayi*) and life breath (*prāṇa*). Life breath comes from the *ātman* itself, and *ātman* is the foundation for all things, including the elements and the senses (4.7–8). Pippalāda identifies the *ātman* with *puruṣa* (9). Interestingly, Pippalāda distinguishes between two forms of *brahman*, a higher and a lower form.

Pippalāda's students. In the *Praśna Upaniṣad*, the sage Pippalāda is approached by six students who ask him six questions. The first question deal with mythological questions such as the creation of the world, but the later questions deal with more abstract and metaphysical matters. Although Pippalāda, like Yājñavalkya, is questioned by multiple men, there is no competition between the characters in the *Praśna Upaniṣad*. The six men approach Pippalāda to learn from him, rather than to challenge him.

Pippalāda's first interlocutor is **Kabandhī Kātyāyana**, who asks him where living beings come from. In response, Pippalāda details the creation of the world by Prajāpati.

It is possible that Kabandhī is the same person as Kabandha Ātharvaṇa, who is mentioned in *Bṛhadaranyaka Upaniṣad* 3.7.1. Since the name Ātharvaṇa signals the character's connection to the *Atharvaveda*, it makes sense that Kabandhī might reappear in the *Praśna Upaniṣad*, which is formally affiliated with the *Atharvaveda*. Kabandha is further a name with old ties to the tradition of the *Atharvaveda*; a Kabandha is said to be the author of *Atharvaveda* 6.75–77. The character Kabandha Ātharvaṇa in the *Bṛhadaranyaka Upaniṣad* is a supernatural being, a *gandharva* possessing a woman, while his counterpart in the *Praśna Upaniṣad* is human. The questions Kabandha and Kabandhī ask in two texts are quite similar, however: in the *Brhadaranyaka Upaniṣad*, Kabandha asks how all living beings are strung together, and in the *Praśna Upaniṣad*, Kabandhī asks where all living beings come from. In response, Pippalāda describes Prajāpati's creation of a primordial couple, substance (*rayi*) and life breath (*prāṇa*). These two abstract principles become part of all aspects of the created world: substance is associated with the moon, with physical form, "the way of the fathers" after death (leading to rebirth, rather than liberation), the dark fortnight of the lunar month, and the night. The life breath, on the other hand, is associated with the sun, the formless, liberation after death, the bright fortnight of the moon, and the day. Through his initial answer to Kabandhī, Pippalāda establishes the superiority of the life breath.

Pippalāda's second interlocutor, **Bhārgava Vaidarbhi**, asks who is supreme among the deities that support a living being. Pippalāda tells him that *prāṇa*, the life breath itself, is the highest deity. Not much else is known about Bhārgava Vaidarbhi. Bhārgava ("descendant of Bhṛgu") is a patronymic name common to many respected teachers in the Upaniṣads and Brāhmaṇas. Bhṛgu is said to be the son of Varuṇa, and as such is mentioned in the *Taittirīya Upaniṣad*, where he receives instructions from his father. "Vaidarbhi" simply indicates that a person comes from the Vidarbha region (present-day Maharashtra).

The third man to question Pippalāda is **Kausalya Āśvalāyana**. He asks where the *prāṇa* comes from and how it enters the body. In response, Pippalāda explains the relationship between *prāṇa* and *ātman* and the doctrine of the five breaths. The name "Kausalya" indicates that this character is from the region of Kosala, and the name "Āśvalāyana" associates him with the family of the priest Aśvala and with the tradition of the *Ṛgveda*. It makes a great deal of sense in a later Vedic context that a person affiliated with the *Ṛgveda* would be particularly interested in deities, since the *hotṛ* priests of the *Ṛgveda* were charged with invoking the gods during Vedic rituals.

The fourth questioner, **Sauryāyaṇī Gārgya**, asks about the agent of actions and the subject of experiences. He asks Pippalāda who it is that goes to sleep inside a person, who stays awake, who experiences dreams and bliss, and on whom all these things are established (4.1). Sauryāyaṇī's name Gārgya suggests that he is one of the descendants of the mythical Ṛgvedic sage Garga. Other members of the Gārgya clan in the Upaniṣads include Dṛpta Bālākī in *Brhadaranyaka Upaniṣad* 2.1 and *Kauṣītakī Upaniṣad* 4, and Gārgī in *Brhadaranyaka Upaniṣad* 3.6.1 and 3.8.1–12. Sauryāyaṇī Gārgya's desire to find out on whom all things are established recalls Gārgī's question about the underlying cause of all things in *Brhadaranyaka Upaniṣad* 3.6.1. Pippalāda explains that it is the breaths that keep a person awake, the mind that experiences dreams, and *ātman* or *puruṣa* (the person) who is really the underlying agent of all actions.

The fifth interlocutor, **Śaibya Satyakāma**, asks about the world a person can attain by meditating on the syllable *oṃ*, which in the *Praśna Upaniṣad* is identified with *brahman* itself. As we have seen, there is also another Satyakāma in the Upaniṣads. Satyakāma Jābāla is mentioned in *Brhadaranyaka Upaniṣad* 6.3 and figures prominently in *Chāndogya Upaniṣad* 4 where he learns the nature of *brahman* from the wild animals. The patronym "Śaibya" ("descendant of Śibi") is only used for Satyakāma in this text. If the two Satyakāmas are meant to be the same character, it is intriguing that Satyakāma is given a patronym in the *Praśna Upaniṣad*. Satyakāma in the *Chāndogya Upaniṣad* did not know who his father was and therefore went by the matronym Jābāla (son of Jabālā) instead. It is possible that the *Praśna Upaniṣad* wants to assure the readers that Satyakāma's paternal lineage has been established and that he is in fact the descendant of the mythical king Śibi. This would make him a *Kṣatriya*, rather than a *brahman*, but there is no further comment on that in the text. The hypothesis that Śaibya Satyakāma in the *Praśna Upaniṣad* is conceived of as the same character as Satyakāma Jābāla is supported by the question Śaibya Satyakāma asks of Pippalāda, which involves (as it turns out) a concept of *brahman* that has four constituent parts.

The final questioner, **Sukeśa Bhāradvāja**, asks Pippalāda about a person consisting of sixteen parts. Sukeśa reveals that he himself was once approached by a prince, Hiraṇyanābha of Kosala, who asked him about the person consisting of sixteen parts. Since Sukeśa had never heard of this doctrine, the prince had to leave without learning what he had sought. This little episode, told secondhand in the *Praśna Upaniṣad*, is reminiscent of the famous dialogue scene between a wisdom teacher and a king in *Bṛhadāraṇyaka Upaniṣad* 3–4. Unlike Yājñavalkya in the *Bṛhadāraṇyaka Upaniṣad*, however, Sukeśa Bhāradvāja does not know the answer to the royal seeker's question. The *Bṛhadāraṇyaka Upaniṣad* also depicts a would-be wisdom teacher, Dṛpta Bālakī, who claims to understand *brahman* and attempts to explain the highest reality to a king, even though his own understanding of *brahman* is flawed. To Sukeśa Bhāradvāja's credit, he does not claim to have more knowledge or understanding than he has, and readily seeks out the wise Pippalāda to find the answer to the question that stumped him.

Pippalāda's answer to Sukeśa Bhāradvāja's question reveals the ultimate truth about the nature of *ātman* and *brahman*. He explains that the sixteenfold person is "right here, within the body" (6.2), and identifies him with the "highest *brahman*, higher than which there is nothing" (6.7). Like the other men approaching Pippalāda, Sukeśa Bhāradvāja bears a name that indicates that he comes from a venerable lineage of scholars. Several Vedic teachers are known by the patronymic name Bhāradvāja ("descendant of Bhāradvāja"). A Bhāradvāja is mentioned in a lineage of teachers and students of the *Yajurveda* in *Bṛhadāraṇyaka Upaniṣad* 2.6.3 and 4.6.3, and an Atharva-teacher Bhāradvāja Satyavāha is mentioned in *Muṇḍaka Upaniṣad* 1.1.2.

The story of the six sages may be more than a literary device to make the Upaniṣad more interesting and lively. The questions in this "Upaniṣad of Questions" (*Praśna Upaniṣad*) are asked by sages whose names are associated with traditional wisdom and good family standing. Since all these sages come to the Atharva-teacher Pippalāda in their quest for the truth, the frame story also serves to legitimize the authority of the Atharvaveda tradition itself. The authority of the *Atharvaveda* is expressed through the respect the learned sages show for the superior wisdom of Pippalāda.

Uṣasta Cākrāyaṇa. We first encounter Uṣasta Cākrāyaṇa in *Bṛhadāraṇyaka Upaniṣad* (3.4), where he appears as one of Yājñavalkya's interlocutors. Uṣasta Cākrāyaṇa asks about "the *brahman* that is clear and not cryptic, the *ātman* within all" (3.4.1), a question that the next challenger, Kahola Kauṣītakeya, repeats verbatim (3.5.1). When Yājñavalkya answers that the self within all "is this self of yours," Uṣasta Cākrāyaṇa pushes further and wants to know what that means. Yājñavalkya then defines the self as the one who breathes within a person, but Uṣasta Cākrāyaṇa does not find this explanation satisfying. Sarcastically, he exclaims, "That's like saying 'This is a cow, and that one is a horse.' Give me a true explanation of the *brahman* that is clear and not cryptic, the *ātman* within all!" In response, Yājñavalkya defines the self as the ultimate agent of action, "the seer who does the seeing," "the hearer who does the hearing," the "thinker who does the thinking," and "the perceiver who does the perceiving." Since Uṣasta Cākrāyaṇa falls silent after this, he is presumably happy with the answer given.

Uṣasta Cākrāyaṇa is also a character in *Chāndogya Upaniṣad* 1.10.1–11 (here called Uṣasti Cākrāyaṇa), where he challenges Brahmans about their knowledge of the High Chant. Uṣasti, who is a Brahman, goes to the court of a king who is about to perform a great sacrifice. He asks questions of the priests who are about the chant and discovers that they do not know the deities the chants are linked to, and he threatens them, saying that if they perform the sacred chants without knowing the deities, their heads will shatter apart. The priests apparently do not know the deities, and they stop singing. Uṣasti himself gets hired as the new priest for the sacrifice, and he correctly identifies the deities linked to the chants as the breath, the sun, and food.

From these two Upaniṣads, Uṣasti/Uṣasta Cākrāyaṇa emerges as a character who is not satisfied with superficial knowledge and wants to know about the ultimate reality. While he is more of a figure of authority in the *Chāndogya Upaniṣad* than in the *Bṛhadāraṇyaka Upaniṣad*, he is nevertheless presented as an earnest wisdom seeker in the *Bṛhadāraṇyaka Upaniṣad*.

Citra Gāṅgyāyani. Citra Gāṅgyāyani is the one who tells Āruṇi and his son Śvetaketu about the path of the soul after death in *Kauṣītaki Upaniṣad* 1.2–4. He appears to be identical to **Jaivali Pravāhaṇa**.

King Janaka of Videha is a prominent character in the *Bṛhadāraṇyaka Upaniṣad*. He hosts a wisdom contest for Brahmans in *Bṛhadāraṇyaka Upaniṣad* 3, and in the fourth chapter of the text, he himself becomes a student of Yājñavalkya. King Janaka is also mentioned in the older Vedic *Śatapatha Brāhmaṇa* (11.6.2.4), where his knowledge is shown to be superior to Yājñavalkya's own. In the *Bṛhadāraṇyaka Upaniṣad*, the king must learn from Yājñavalkya, however. King Janaka is also featured in the later *Rāmāyaṇa* epic, where he hosts a contest for his daughter Sītā's hand and becomes the father-in-law of the hero Rāma.

King Ajātaśatru of Kāśī is himself shown as superior in wisdom to the false wisdom teacher Dṛpta Bālāki, who identifies *brahman* as a person in the sun, the moon, the wind, or the fire. But Ajātaśatru knows that *brahman* is *ātman*. When he understands that Ajātaśatru possesses superior wisdom, Dṛpta Bālāki asks to become the king's student instead. While Ajātaśatru remarks that it seems like a reversal of norms for a Brahman to become the student of a Kṣatriya, he nevertheless agrees to teach the Brahman what he knows. Ajātaśatru's teachings focus on the *ātman* as the "real behind the real" (*Bṛhadāraṇyaka Upaniṣad* 2.1.20). The *ātman* is the basis of all consciousness and perception, and Ajātaśatru wakes a sleeping man to demonstrate that the *ātman* is present even when a person is sleeping.

Jaivali Pravāhaṇa (Pravāhaṇa Jaivali) appears in two different Upaniṣads, the *Bṛhadāraṇyaka* (6.2) and the *Chāndogya* (1.8 and 5.3–10). While he is called a king in *Bṛhadāraṇyaka Upaniṣad* 6.2 and *Chāndogya Upaniṣad* 5.3, his royal status is not mentioned in *Chāndogya Upaniṣad* 1.8, where he is one of three wisdom teachers who explain the High Chant (*udgītha*). While Caikitāyana Dālbhya argues that the foundation of the High Chant is the heavenly world and Śilaka Śālāvatya claims that the foundation is this world, Pravāhaṇa Jaivali correctly points out that the foundation is *ākāśa*, space. In the *Bṛhadāraṇyaka Upaniṣad*, Jaivali Pravāhaṇa is the king of Pañcāla. He quizzes the young Brahman boy Śvetaketu, who has just arrived at his court, about his knowledge of the path of the dead in the afterlife. Śvetaketu is unable to answer and returns home to his father, who has taught him at home, and tells him that the king asked him questions he couldn't answer. Śvetaketu and his father Uddālaka Āruṇi (here called Gautama) go to the king together and ask to become the king's students. Jaivali Pravāhaṇa teaches them about five fires: the fire of the heavenly world, the fire of the raincloud, the fire of the earthly world, the fire of man, and the fire of woman, and about the return of the soul of the dead to a new earthly life. The same story is repeated, with small variations, in *Chāndogya Upaniṣad* 5.3.

Jānaśruti Pautrāyaṇa in *Chāndogya Upaniṣad* (4.1–3) is described as a "man devoted to giving." He is deeply interested in wisdom, and when he learns (from some talking wild geese) that the homeless Raikva who lives under a cart may possess great knowledge, he immediately sends a servant to find him. Jānaśruti Pautrāyaṇa offers Raikva generous gifts in exchange for teaching him what he knows, but the eccentric Raikva merely insults him and refuses to teach him anything until Jānaśruti offers him his own daughter along with the valuable gifts. It is possible, but not certain, that Jānaśruti is a king. His wealth and generosity certainly seem to rival those of King Janaka.

Gods and Demons in the Upaniṣads

Most of the characters we encounter in the Upaniṣads are humans, but there are also a few gods and demons in these texts. The most striking feature of many of the gods that appear as characters in the Upaniṣads is that their divinity is largely irrelevant. Instead, the gods of the old Vedic pantheon, deities like the thunder god Indra, the creator god Prajāpati, and Yama, the Lord of the Dead, take on the roles of wisdom seekers and wisdom teachers, just as humans do.

Intriguingly, demons also appear as wisdom seekers in a few passages of the Upaniṣads. The only named demon is the Upaniṣads, Virocana (*Chāndogya Upaniṣad* 8.7–12), turns out to be an inferior student compared with the god Indra; he accepts a superficial answer to a difficult question much too easily. But in *Bṛhadāraṇyaka Upaniṣad* 5.2, demons, gods, and humans are all the children of the creator god Prajāpati, and each group gets to interpret his teachings for themselves. There is nothing in this text that suggests that demons have less capacity for knowledge and enlightenment than gods or humans.

Indra. Indra is the old Vedic god of thunder, but in the Upaniṣads he often appears as a wisdom seeker and exemplary student. According to *Chāndogya Upaniṣad* 8.7–12, the gods and their enemies the *asuras* are all trying to discover the truth about *ātman*. Prajāpati teaches Indra and the demon Virocana that *ātman* is the body, and Virocana accepts the teaching. Indra, however, comes back to learn more until he is taught that *ātman* is the consciousness and identical with *brahman*. Indra is here a model student, not satisfied with superficial answers and half-truths. The *Kena Upaniṣad* likewise depicts Indra as a wisdom seeker who is trying to understand *brahman.* In *Kauṣītaki Upaniṣad* (3.1–2), Indra is also an enlightened teacher, and he identifies himself with *ātman*, with the life breath *prāṇa*, and with truth. In fact, this text traces Indra's ability to overcome demons not to his superior strength, but to his knowledge of *ātman*:

> When Indra did not understand the self, the demons won over him. But when he knew the self, he smashed the demons, won over them, and attained to lordship over all the gods. (4.20)

Among the many Vedic gods, why does the thunder god Indra in particular become an exemplary wisdom seeker in the Upaniṣads? Although the Vedic Indra is best known for slaying the serpentine monster Vṛtra and destroying enemies with his thunderbolt, Indra is associated with wisdom in the *Ṛgveda* as well: "Splendid are you Indra, intelligent and insightful" (*Ṛgveda* 1.62.12). Although Indra is primarily known for his physical strength, his physical and mental power blend in *Ṛgveda* 6.47.10:

> Be generous, Indra, and lengthen my days.
> Sharpen my thought like a blade of iron.

Here, the sharp iron blade naturally associated with the god of war becomes a metaphor for mental acuity. Moreover, Indra's well-known epithet *śatakratu* ("he of a hundred *kratu*"), used from the *Ṛgveda* onward, may also have inspired the portrayal of Indra as a wisdom seeker in the Upaniṣads. The term *kratu* may either be translated as "sacrificial rite" or as "intelligence." Although Indra is later associated with a hundred sacrifices, the alternative meaning of *kratu* may also resonate in the Upaniṣadic depictions of the wise Indra.

Umā. While we encounter two female wisdom seekers in the Upaniṣads in Gārgī and Maitreyī, Umā in the *Kena Upaniṣad* is the only fully enlightened female wisdom teacher we meet in the

Upaniṣads. In this text, she is the one who explains to Indra the nature of *brahman* itself. In later Hinduism, Umā (also called Pārvatī, "the daughter of the mountain") is the consort of the god Śiva. But in the *Kena Upaniṣad*, Umā is an independent, fully enlightened goddess and wisdom teacher.

Yama. In the *Ṛgveda*, Yama is the first human to die, and he therefore becomes the ruler over the dead. In later Hinduism, he is often perceived as a god, but in the Vedas, he is said to be the son of a water nymph and a *gandharva* (celestial musician). The Vedic Yama also has a twin sister, Yamī, who attempts to seduce him in *Ṛgveda* 10.90, a suggestion that Yama emphatically rejects. In the *Kaṭha Upaniṣad*, Yama functions as the Lord of the Dead, but also as Death personified. Intriguingly, he also becomes a wisdom teacher in this text when a young boy, Naciketas, shows up in his realm and insists on being taught the secrets of life and death. Even though Yama is Death itself, he is still seemingly bound by human-like rules of hospitality, and he panics when it turns out that the boy Naciketas had to wait for him for three days without food or water. To make up for this transgression, Yama offers Naciketas three wishes. Death is a remarkably sympathetic character in this Upaniṣad and a much better father figure for Naciketas than his own temperamental dad. He becomes a wise teacher for the Brahman boy. Although he appears knowledgeable about rituals (especially those that concern immortality), the idea of the eternal *ātman* is at the heart of his teachings.

Prajāpati. In earlier Vedic literature, Prajāpati ("Lord of Creatures") is a creator god, who is often identified with the sacrifice itself. In the *Bṛhadāraṇyaka Upaniṣad*, Prajāpati is identified with the year (1.5.14), and depicted as the creator of the human senses (1.5.21), but in the *Chāndogya Upaniṣad* 8.7–12, Prajāpati is reinterpreted as an Upaniṣadic wisdom teacher, completely unconcerned with ritual. Instead, he is deeply knowledgeable about the nature of *ātman*. Like many Upaniṣadic teachers, he is initially reluctant to teach, and the god Indra and the demon Virocana only get his attention once they have lived as celibate students for thirty-two years (8.7.3). At that point, Prajāpati teaches them that the *ātman* is identical to a person's reflection in water. The demon Virocana interprets that to mean that it is the body that is the *ātman*, and he is content with that. Indra, however, is not satisfied with this answer, and he presses Prajāpati further. After another thirty-two years, Prajāpati explains that the *ātman* is the one who experiences dreams, and after a further thirty-two years that *ātman* can be compared to dreamless sleep. After five more years, Prajāpati divulges to the very patient Indra that the *ātman* is ultimately the agent of all things.

Prajāpati is also featured as a teacher of both gods and demons in *Bṛhadāraṇyaka Upaniṣad* 5.2. In this passage, Prajāpati is said to be the father of both gods, humans, and demons, and he is also their teacher who sees to their Vedic education. After they have all completed their training, each group of children asks him to say something to them. His answer to each group is the same: the single, cryptic syllable *da*. The gods interpret *da* as *dāmyata* ("show restraint"), while the humans assume that *da* is meant to convey *datta* ("give") and the demons understand his message to them to be *dayadhvam* ("be compassionate"). T. S. Eliot famously alludes to this narrative in the fifth part of his poem "The Waste Land," "What the Thunder Said." Why did Prajāpati, of all the Vedic gods, assume the role of a teacher in the Upaniṣads? One of the reasons for this may be that Prajāpati, as a creator, is older than the other gods and functions as a father figure. There is frequent overlap between the roles of father and teacher in the Upaniṣads; several fathers teach their own sons.

Bhṛgu and Varuṇa. Varuṇa, the Vedic guardian of cosmic order (*ṛta*), appears as a character in the *Taittirīya Upaniṣad*. But in this text, Varuṇa is a father and teacher who has little in common with the lofty Vedic god who punishes sinners. Rather, he is focused on teaching his son Bhṛgu about the nature of *brahman* (3.1.1–6). Through practicing austerities and listening to his father's explanations, Bhṛgu attains ever deeper insights into the *brahman*. He goes from identifying *brahman* with food to identifying it with life breath, mind, perception, and finally bliss. Varuṇa defines *brahman* as "that from which these beings are born, through which they live, and into which they enter at death" (3.1.1).

A similar story of Varuṇa instructing his son Bhṛgu is found in an earlier text of the Yajurveda, the *Śatapatha Brāhmaṇa* (11.6.1), but the son's character has changed from the Brāhmaṇa to the Upaniṣad. While Bhṛgu is quite rude and arrogant in the *Śatapatha Brāhmaṇa* and considers himself superior to his father, Bhṛgu in the *Taittirīya Upaniṣad* approaches his father as a reverent student: "Bhṛgu, the son of Varuṇa, went to his father Varuṇa and said: 'Sir, please teach me *brahman*.'" Whereas the Bhṛgu of the *Śatapatha Brāhmaṇa* has bizarre visions of men dismembering and eating each other, which eventually lead him to understand the symbolism of the Vedic *agnihotra* ritual, the Upaniṣadic Bhṛgu practices austerities under his father's wise guidance until he comes to understand the true nature of *brahman*. In the course of his quest for the true understanding of *brahman*, Bhṛgu comes to understand *brahman* as food, *prāṇa* (life breath), *manas* (mind), perception, and joy.

Rudra/Śiva. While other Vedic gods appear as teachers or students in the Upaniṣads, Rudra/Śiva occupies a very different role. In the *Śvetāśvatara Upaniṣad*, the Vedic storm god Rudra is identified with *ātman* itself. In the *Ṛgveda*, Rudra is depicted as a wild and occasionally frightening god who can both bring disease and heal it. The term *śiva* is first applied to Rudra as an adjective in the *Ṛgveda*, with the meaning "kind" or "benevolent." Since the hymns to Rudra often express fear of the deity, it is likely that his epithet *śiva* was meant to implore him to be kind, in spite of the worshipper's fear of his wrath. Over time, Śiva became a personal name attached to Rudra, and eventually the epithet replaced the original name. In the *Śvetāśvatara Upaniṣad*, Rudra/Śiva has evolved beyond his Vedic origins and becomes a benign, all-powerful creator god, identified with the highest *ātman* itself:

> More subtle than the subtle, in the midst of chaos,
> The creator of the universe, with numerous forms,
> The one who encompasses the universe—
> Knowing *Śiva,* one obtains endless peace. (4.14)

Abstract Concepts as Characters

Intriguingly, several abstract concepts also appear as characters in Upaniṣadic narratives and dialogues. Death (*Mṛtyu*) appears as a creator of the world in *Bṛhadāraṇyaka Upaniṣad* 1.2, where he is depicted as a primordial person who desires a mate and copulates with both Speech (*Vāc*) and Hunger (*Aśanā*) to create time in the form of the year. As noted above, Yama in the *Kaṭha Upaniṣad* is also Death personified. Other personifications in the Upaniṣad include Breath (*prāṇa, Bṛhadāraṇyaka Upaniṣad* 1.3.3), Sight (*cakṣus, Bṛhadāraṇyaka Upaniṣad* 1.3.4), Hearing (*śrotra, Bṛhadāraṇyaka Upaniṣad* 1.3.5), Mind (*manas, Bṛhadāraṇyaka Upaniṣad* 1.3.6), and *ātman* itself (*Bṛhadāraṇyaka Upaniṣad* 1.4; *Aitareya Upaniṣad* 1.1–3).

What are we to make of these passages where the Self creates the world, Death longs for love, and Breath couples with Substance? To some extent, the personification of abstract concepts serves to breathe life into the cosmology and philosophy of the Upaniṣads. But on a deeper level, these narratives places human experience at the center of its philosophical universe. The cosmos and its forces are conceived as persons, with human-like desires.

8

The Canonical Status and Reception of the Upaniṣads

The Canonical Status of the Upaniṣads

There are two main categories of sacred Hindu texts: *śruti* and *smṛti*. The first category, *śruti* ("that which is heard"), encompasses the four Vedas (*Ṛgveda*, *Yajurveda*, *Sāmaveda*, *Atharvaveda*), the late Vedic ritual texts called Brāhmaṇas and Āraṇyakas, and the oldest Upaniṣads. The *smṛti* ("remembered") texts include works on the six Vedāṅgas (auxiliary Vedic sciences, i.e., phonetics, prosody, grammar, etymology, rituals, and astrology), the great epic poems of the *Mahābhārata* and the *Rāmāyaṇa*, philosophical texts, legal texts, and the mythological Purāṇas. The *śruti* texts are regarded as the most authoritative ones. The *śruti* texts are generally older than the *smṛti* texts, and they have been transmitted orally with great accuracy. The *smṛti* texts also have a long history of oral transmission before being committed to writing, but these texts contain a great deal more textual variation than the *śruti* texts do. The term *śruti* is often rendered as "revelation" and *smṛti* as "tradition," but these translations are problematic. Hindus believe that the Vedas are eternal, not revealed at one particular time. Moreover, both *śruti* and *smṛti* are "traditional" in all meanings of the word (see Pollock 2011, 44). Pollock has demonstrated that the two terms may have originated in the philosophical tradition of Mīmāṃsā, and that *śruti* and *smṛti* are associated with direct perception and inference. *Śruti* texts like the Vedas can be heard directly during

The Classical Upaniṣads. Signe Cohen, Oxford University Press. © Oxford University Press 2024.
DOI: 10.1093/oso/9780197654156.003.0008

recitation, while *smṛti* texts are no longer heard in recitation, but can be recovered inferentially (Pollock 2011, 46–51).

The classical Upaniṣads are usually regarded as *śruti*, and they were transmitted within schools of Vedic recitation. As such, they are sometimes regarded as the conclusion of the holy Vedas and are therefore occasionally called "Vedānta" ("the end of the Vedas" or "the fulfillment of the Vedas").

The holiness of the *śruti* texts is underscored by the traditional reluctance to write them down; these texts are meant to be heard from the mouth of teachers, not learned through reading. There are numerous manuscripts of the Sanskrit epics and Purāṇas in India, but manuscripts of the Vedas and Upaniṣads are both rare and chronologically late. The oldest surviving manuscripts of the Upaniṣads can be dated to the sixteenth century, about two millennia after the likely date of composition for the oldest of these texts.

The Significance of the Upaniṣads in Hinduism and in Indian Culture

The Indian philosopher Sarvepalli Radhakrishnan referred to the Upaniṣads as "the foundations on which most of the later philosophies of India rest" (Radhakrishnan 1923, 138). Central concepts in the classical Hindu tradition, like *ātman* (the self), *brahman* (the cosmic divine force), *karma*, reincarnation, and salvation through knowledge, are first introduced in the Upaniṣads. While the Vedas are regarded especially as sacred in later Hinduism, especially as a manifestation of sacred sound, the *ideas* of the Upaniṣads have been far more influential on later Hindu thought than those of the Vedas.

The Upaniṣads also contain the seeds of what will later become Sāṃkhya, Yoga, and Vedānta philosophy, three major schools of Hindu thought. The school of Sāṃkhya is codified in Īśvarakṛṣṇa's *Sāṁkhyakārikā* and the school of Yoga in the *Yogasūtras* of

Patañjali. But centuries before the composition of these texts, the earliest traces of Sāṃkhya and Yoga ideas can be found in the Upaniṣads. The Sāṃkhya and Yoga concepts of *puruṣa* (the eternal spirit or consciousness), *prakṛti* ("nature," the primordial physical and mental matter), and the three *guṇas* ("qualities") that make up this primordial nature can all be traced back to the Upaniṣads. The Hindu philosophical tradition of Vedānta, which is perhaps the most significant influence on Hindu thought today, is also based on the Upaniṣads.

The Upaniṣads and Vedānta Philosophy

Although Vedānta is later classified as one of the six classical schools of Hindu philosophy (*ṣad-darśana*) along with Sāṃkhya, Yoga, Nyāya, Vaiśeṣika, and Mīmāṃsā, the term is initially used, as we have seen, to refer to the Upaniṣads. As a philosophical movement, Vedānta has its roots in the Upaniṣads and later develops into a set of related philosophical sub-traditions. All the Vedānta traditions trace their teachings back to the "three sources" (*prasthānatrayī*) of the Upaniṣads, the *Bhagavadgītā*, and the *Brahmasūtra*. Although it forms part of the larger *Mahābhārata* epic, the *Bhagavadgītā*, which consists of a philosophical dialogue between the warrior Arjuna and his divine charioteer Kṛṣṇa on the eve of a cataclysmic battle, contains many parallels in both ideas and language to the older Upaniṣads (see Cohen 2022).

The *Brahmasūtra* (also called the *Vedāntasūtra*) is a fundamental text for all the different sub-schools of Vedānta. This text, which is ascribed to Bādarāyaṇa, was likely compiled over several centuries, and reasonable estimates of its dates of composition range from the second century BCE to the fourth century CE. The *Brahmasūtra* consists of 555 short aphorisms on the nature of *brahman* and systematizes many of the ideas found in the classical Upaniṣads. Although it draws extensively on the *Chāndogya Upaniṣad* in particular, it also quotes the other older Upaniṣads. Although the *sūtras* (aphorisms) are often concise to the point of unintelligibility when read without a commentary, it is clear that the authors of the text regard *brahman* as the absolute highest principle. *Brahman* is the source and origin of the world, and *Brahmasūtra* 2.3.43 states that the self is both different and not different from *brahman*, an idea later associated with Bhedābheda Vedānta philosophy. The text is highly critical of the Sāṃkhya school and its interpretation of the Upaniṣads throughout. The best-known commentaries on the *Brahmasūtra* are composed by Śaṅkara (eighth–ninth century), Bhāskara (eighth–ninth century), Rāmānuja (eleventh–twelfth century), and Madhva (thirteenth century).

These commentaries, along with influential Upaniṣad commentaries by the same authors, created the foundation for the philosophical movement that later came to be known as Vedānta. Another influential early Vedānta text was the sixth-century commentary *Māṇḍūkyakārikā* by Gauḍapāda, which explains the *Māṇḍūkya Upaniṣad*. The *Māṇḍūkyakārikā* is a central text in Advaita Vedānta in particular but also influenced Viśiṣṭādvaita and Dvaita Vedānta (see below). The treatise *Vākyapadīya* by the sixth–seventh-century philosopher of language Bhartṛhari was another significant influence on the early Vedānta schools.

Vedānta split into three main sub-schools: **Advaita** (non-dualist) Vedānta represented by Gauḍapāda and Śaṅkara (788–810? CE), **Viśiṣṭādvaita** (modified non-dualist) Vedānta represented by Rāmānuja (ca. 1077–1157 CE), and **Dvaita** (dualist) Vedānta represented by Madhva (ca. 1199–1278 CE). All these sub-schools grapple with the meaning of the equation between *ātman* and *brahman* in the Upaniṣads.

Śankara and Gauḍapāda's system later came to be called Advaita, although they themselves did not use this term. Śankara called his own philosophy *abheda-darśana* ("theory of non-difference"), pointing to his central tenet of the radical of all things. According to Śaṅkara's non-dualist reading of the Upaniṣads, there is absolutely no difference between *ātman* and *brahman*; they are one and the same. Śaṅkara further sees *brahman* as an impersonal principle, rather than a personal god.

A central notion in Śankara's Advaita is the idea that there is a distinction between that which is ultimately real (*brahman*) and the empirical reality which we can observe around us. For Śankara, the empirical world, with its apparent manifold forms, is less than perfectly real, and he refers to it as *māyā*, which is often translated as "illusion." But *māyā* is not a mere mirage or empty illusion in Advaita thought; Śankara defines it as "neither real nor non-real." The empirical world is not unreal; it is a portion of the reality that is *brahman* that is imperfectly understood. The example often used in Advaita philosophy to explain *māyā* is that of a man seeing a rope at dusk and believing it to be a snake. The snake the man sees in not non-real, but neither is it completely real; it is a reality (rope) misunderstood. In Śankara's philosophy, *māyā* is the superimposition (*abhyāsa*) of that which is not *ātman/brahman* onto the reality of *ātman/brahman*. The manifest phenomenal world that appears to us is therefore a misconception of the one undifferentiated reality by unenlightened self.

This doctrine of *māyā* met with a great deal of criticism from other philosophers, including other Vedāntins. Śaṅkara's critic Bhāskara (himself a proponent of a form of Vedānta often called Bhedābheda, "difference and non-difference," which claims that *ātman* and *brahman* are simultaneously both the same and different) referred to Śaṅkara's teachings disparagingly as *māyā-vāda* ("the doctrine of illusion") and found that Śaṅkara's ideas seemed too much like Buddhism for his taste. The Viśiṣṭādvaita philosopher Rāmānuja also refers to thinkers like Śaṅkara as *prachanna-bauddha* ("crypto-Buddhist," *Śrībhāṣya* 2.2.27).

Other well-known proponents of Advaita Vedānta after Śaṅkara include Maṇḍana Miśra (often identified with Śaṅkara's student Sureśvara), who tried to reconcile Mīmāṃsā and Vedānta philosophy, and the ninth–tenth-century philosopher Vācaspati Miśra, who composed a commentary to Śaṅkara's commentary on the *Brahmasūtra*.

The eleventh–twelfth-century philosopher Rāmānuja is perhaps the most influential Vedānta philosopher after Śaṅkara. His particular form of Vedānta is known as Viśiṣṭādvaita ("non-duality with distinctions"). Unlike Śaṅkara, Rāmānuja did not write commentaries on the Upaniṣads, but he did compose commentaries on the *Brahmasūtra* (the *Śrībhāṣya*) and the *Bhagavadgītā*, and in these commentaries he quotes extensively from the older Upaniṣads. A later philosopher of Rāmānuja's lineage, Raṅgarāmānuja, composed a well-known commentary on the Upaniṣads in the seventeenth century.

Rāmānuja proposes that there is a partial overlap between *ātman* and *brahman*; all *ātmans* are contained within the larger *brahman*, but there is still more to *brahman* than the sum of all *ātmans*. For Rāmānuja, who is a devotee of Viṣṇu, *brahman* is a personal god rather than an impersonal force.

While Śaṅkara had argued that there are two levels of truth, the higher truth that all is *brahman*, and a lower, temporary truth that considers *brahman* as a personal god, Rāmānuja argues that this goes against a reasonable reading of the sacred texts. Rāmānuja rejects the idea of two levels of truth and claims that there is only one truth: *brahman* is the entire world, but also the inner self of all beings, and a personal god, who for Rāmānuja is Viṣṇu, incarnated as Kṛṣṇa in the *Bhagavadgītā*. Rāmānuja rejects the idea of *māyā*, or the phenomenal world that appears as manifold due to our ignorance. For Rāmānuja, both the one and the many are real. The self is different from God, but God is the very essence of the self. The self and the world are both distinct from God, but they are also part of him. Matter and selves are regarded as God's body, but just as there is more to a living being than a body, so there is more to God than matter and *ātman*.

Other Viśiṣṭādvaita philosophers include the thirteenth–fourteenth-century scholars Vedāntadeśika and Piḷḷai Lokācārya, who fused Rāmānuja's theistic reading of the sacred texts with the popular devotion (*bhakti*) to Viṣṇu.

The thirteenth-century South Indian Vaiṣṇava theologian Madhva, founder of Dvaita (dualist) Vedānta, composed commentaries on several Upaniṣads, the *Bhagavadgītā*, and the *Brahmasūtra*. For Madhva, as for Rāmānuja, *brahman* is a personal god, Viṣṇu. Madhva's dualist interpretation of the Upaniṣads is based on the idea that *ātman* and *brahman* are not the same, but rather that *ātman* is dependent on *brahman*. Dvaita Vedānta regards *ātman* and *brahman*/God as different, although God pervades both the *ātman* and the phenomenal world. Dvaita philosophy teaches that there are five fundamental distinctions (*bhedas*): the distinction between God and the self, the distinction between God and matter, the distinction between the self and matter, the distinction between individual selves, and the distinction between different types of matter. This philosophy is quite far removed from the Upaniṣadic identification between *ātman* and *brahman*; for Madhva, there is no unity between the two, but there is a loving encounter. Humans can only be saved through *bhakti*, devotion to God, and liberation only comes from the grace of God, not from knowledge.

Mention must also be made of the Bhedābheda ("difference and non-difference") school of Vedānta, which can be traced back as far as the seventh century. In his commentary on the *Bṛhadāraṇyaka Upaniṣad*, Śaṅkara critiques the ideas of an earlier philosopher by the name of Bhartṛprapañca, who describes the relationship between *ātman* and *brahman* as "both difference and non-difference," an idea later associated with Bhedābheda Vedānta. The philosopher Bhāskara, who appears to have been a younger contemporary of Śaṅkara, defends the Bhedābheda view against Śaṅkara's critique and rejects the idea that the phenomenal world is ultimately not real. In Bhedābheda thought, *ātman* and *brahman* are similar in quality, but different in quantity, like the rays of the sun compared to the sun itself. Bhedābheda ideas influenced many later Indian thinkers and mystics, such as the fifteenth-century Bengali saint Caitanya who inspired the Gauḍīya Vaiṣṇava religious movement, which in turn is the foundation for the International Society for Krishna Consciousness (also known as the Hare Krishna Movement), and the fifteenth–sixteenth-century philosopher-saint Vallabha, who founded a form of Vedānta he called Śuddhādvaita ("Pure non-dualism"), which in spite of its name leans heavily toward Bhedābheda Vedānta.

The Upaniṣads at the Muslim Court

The first known translation of the Upaniṣads from Sanskrit into another language was the Persian version of the Indian prince Dara Shikoh (1615–1659), the great-grandson of Akbar the Great. Like his great-grandfather, Dara Shikoh became a patron of Indo-Persian art and culture. While both men were devout Muslims in their own ways, Dara Shikoh was intrigued by Akbar's notion that all religions contain some truth and that there is a great deal to learn through debate with representatives of other faiths.

As the oldest son of Emperor Shah Jahan, who ruled the Mughal Empire from 1628 to 1658, Dara Shikoh was generally favored to take over the throne after his father. When he was eighteen, the prince was appointed military commander over a portion of his father's army. Over time, he was given greater and greater military responsibilities, and his father eventually confirmed him as his official heir. When Shah Jahan fell ill, however, one of Dara Shikoh's brothers, Shah Shuja, immediately stepped up and declared himself Mughal emperor. The ailing Shah Jahan still supported his oldest son in his claim to the throne, but in the end, another one of Dara Shikoh's brothers emerged victorious in the intense struggle for the Mughal throne that ensued: his younger half-brother Muhi-ud-Din, who later took the name Aurangzeb. In the Battle of Samugarh outside Agra, Aurangzeb's men defeated Dara Shikoh's troops in

1658. Aurangzeb then proceeded to take over Agra and depose his father.

Dara Shikoh was eventually captured by his brother Aurangzeb, and after a brief trial he was declared an apostate from Islam due to his syncretistic views and executed. Although he never became emperor, Dara Shikoh nevertheless left his mark on Indian civilization through his enthusiastic patronage of art, philosophy, and religion.

Dara Shikoh himself was intrigued by the mystical connections between Islam and Hinduism, and he searched for evidence in Muslim and Hindu texts that could confirm his idea that these scriptures contained different articulations of the same eternal truth. In one of his own original poems, Dara Shikoh writes:

> What name should one call the Truth?
> Every name that exists in one of God's names.

As part of his quest for this truth common to all religions, Dara Shikoh translated the Upaniṣads from Sanskrit into Persian, the courtly language of the Mughal Empire, in 1657. This translation of the Upaniṣads was given the title *Sirr-e-Akbar* ("The Great Secret"), although it is occasionally also known as *Sirr al-asrār* ("The Secret of the Secrets"). By giving Muslim readers access to the Hindu Upaniṣads, Dara Shikoh hoped to "help mystics of both faiths."

For Dara Shikoh, there is no conflict between the teachings of the Upaniṣads and those of Islam. In his introduction to his translation, Dara Shikoh even speculates that the Upaniṣads may actually be referred to in the Qur'an, the holy book of Islam. For the Qur'an (56:78) refers to a "hidden book" (*kitab al-maknun*) of mystical wisdom, writes Dara Shikoh, and perhaps this hidden book might be the Upaniṣads themselves.

Dara Shikoh's reading of the passage from the Qur'an is highly idiosyncratic; most Muslim scholars interpret the phrase *kitab al-maknun* simply as a reference to the "well-guarded" (rather than "hidden") Qur'an itself or its eternal heavenly prototype, rather than to a different book. But Dara Shikoh was enamored of the notion that the Upaniṣads might be the secret lost teachings referenced in the Qur'an, and the very name of his translation, *Sirr-i-akbar*, alludes to his understanding of the Upaniṣads as the "Great Secret" of the Qur'an. Intriguingly, the title *Sirr-i-akbar* also has a double meaning hardly lost on Emperor Akbar's great-grandson; the title can mean both "The Great Secret" and "Akbar's Secret." Through this playful pun, Dara Shikoh evokes his ancestor's search for the ultimate truth of all religions and suggests that the secret that Akbar sought might be hidden in the Upaniṣads.

Dara Shikoh's Upaniṣad translation includes fifty texts. In his preface, he states that he does not at all find that these Hindu works undermine the monotheism of Islam. On the contrary; he finds that "the monotheistic verses contained in the four *Vedas* have been collected and elucidated in the *Upanikhat*, which is an ocean of monotheism."

Dara Shikoh writes that he completed his translation with the help of Hindu Pandits from Benares. Some scholars have questioned whether the prince himself actually knew enough Sanskrit to translate the Upaniṣads into Persian. What role did the Pandits play in Dara Shikoh's translation? Did they merely help him with difficult passages, or did they explain the text to him line by line? This is difficult to determine, but Dara Shikoh's own introduction to the text makes clear that he has studied not only Sanskrit, but also Arabic, Syrian, and Hebrew. Given the prince's intelligence and his passionate interest in ancient Hindu texts, it does not seem like too much of a stretch to assume that he had studied Sanskrit, as he claimed.

The Persian translation itself is fluent and accessible. Dara Shikoh's translation of the Sanskrit text is not always precise down to the smallest detail, but it does convey all the main ideas of the Sanskrit texts faithfully in a clear and accessibly manner. Some passages of the original texts are left out altogether, perhaps because

Dara Shikoh did not understand them, or because they did not appeal to him.

The fifty Upaniṣads translated are sorted according to the Vedic text with which they are affiliated, so that the texts associated with the *Ṛgveda* come first. The texts included in the translation (with Persian names in parenthesis) are: *Bṛhadāraṇyaka* (*Brehdarang*), *Chāndogya* (*Tschehandouk*), *Īśāvāsya* (*Eischvasieh*), *Praśna* (*Porsch*), *Māṇḍūkya* (*Mandouk*), *Kena* (*Kin*), *Śvetāśvatara* (*Sataster*), *Kaṭha* (*Kiouni*), *Maitrī* (*Mitri*), *Kauṣītakī* (*Kok'henk*), *Aitareya* (*Sarbsar*, probably a confusion with the late *Sarvasāra Upaniṣad*), *Ānandavallī* (*Anandbli*), *Bṛghuvallī* (*Bharkbli*), *Muṇḍaka* (*Mandek*), *Jābāla* (*Djabal*), *Paiṅgala* (*Pankl*), *Kaivalya* (*Kioul*), *Puruṣasūkta* (*Bark'he soukt*), *Śivasaṃkalpa* (*Schiw sanklap*), *Chāgaleya* (*Tschakli*), *Tadeva* (*Tadiw*), *Mahānārāyaṇa* (*Maha narain*), *Tārasāra* (*Tark*), *Bāṣkala-Mantra* (*Baschkl*), *Sarvasāra* (*Sarb*), *Śaunaka* (*Schavank*), *Yogaśikhā* (*Djog sank'ha*), *Yogatattva* (*Djogtat*), *Mahā* (*Maha*), *Ātmaprabodha* (*Atma pra boudeh*), *Nārāyaṇa* (*Narain*), *Āruṇeya* (*Arank*), *Cūlikā* (*Djourka*), *Atharvaśiras* (*Athrbsar*), *Atharvaśikhā* (*Abrat sak'ha*), *Ātmā* (*Atma*), *Brahmavidyā* (*Brahm badia*), *Amṛtabindu* (*Anbrat bandeh*), *Tejobindu* (*Tidj bandeh*), *Śatarudriya* (*Schat roudri*), *Garbha* (*Karbeh*), *Dhyānabindu* (*Dehian band*), *Mṛtyulāṅgūla* (*Mrat lankoul*), *Haṃsanāda* (*Hensnad*), *Paramahaṃsa* (*Pram hens*), *Amṛtanāda* (*Anbratnad*), *Ārṣeya* (*Ark'hi*), *Prāṇava* (*Pranou*), *Kṣurikā* (*Tschehourka*), and *Nṛsiṃhottaratāpanīya* (*Nersing'heh atma*). Although the Sanskrit names of each Upaniṣad has a lexical meaning, there is no attempt here at translating the titles into Persian. Rather, each title is simply transliterated into Persian, given the approximate pronunciation of the Sanskrit title.

Intriguingly, two of these texts are not Upaniṣads at all. The *Puruṣasūkta* is the famous hymn of the Cosmic Man from *Ṛgveda* 10.90. The *Śatarudriya* is the well-known list of a hundred names of the god Rudra from the *Vājasaneyī Saṃhitā* 16, 1–66 of the Yajurveda. Why are these texts included in Dara Shikoh's Upaniṣad translation? Since the translator does not comment on the inclusion of these texts in his volume, any answer must remain a speculation. It is tempting to assume, however, that the emphasis on cosmic unity in both the *Puruṣasūkta* and the *Śatarudriya* would have been quite appealing to Dara Shikoh in his quest for the unity of religion. The *Puruṣasūkta* describes the entire physical universe as constituting various parts of one universal man (*puruṣa*), while the *Śatarudriya* lists all the various names of the one god Rudra/Śiva. These two texts may have struck Dara Shikoh as perfect illustrations of the Upaniṣadic idea that all reality is one and divine.

Some passages from the original Upaniṣadic texts are missing in the Persian translation, such as the list of teachers in *Bṛhadāraṇyaka Upaniṣad* 2.6, 4.6, and 6.5, large portions of chapters 1, 3, and 4 of the *Chāndogya Upaniṣad* and all of chapter 2, the section 6.33–38 from the *Maitrī Upaniṣad*, 2.4–11 of the *Kauṣītaki Upaniṣad*, and smaller text portions here and there from various Upaniṣads. It is possible that these passages were missing in Dara Shikoh's Sanskrit source texts, although one might also speculate that these particular passages, which are all quite rich in Vedic ritual detail, were simply not quite to Dara Shikoh's taste.

The Upaniṣads in Modern Hindu Thought

The Upaniṣads became particularly important for modern Indian thought during the Hindu Renaissance from ca. 1800 CE onward. Religious and social reform movements such as the Brahmo Samaj, Prarthana Samaj, and Arya Samaj turned to the Upaniṣads to find answers for the modern age.

The Brahmo Samaj ("*brahman* society") was a monotheistic reform movement in Bengal founded by Rammohan Roy (1772–1833) and Dwarkanath Tagore (1794–1846, grandfather of the Nobel Prize–winning poet Rabindranath Tagore) in 1828. The Brahmo Samaj denounced polytheism, image-worship, and the caste system and advocated for a return to the "pure" teachings of the Upaniṣads, which were interpreted as a philosophical and ethical monotheism. According to the teachings of the Brahmo Samaj, there is one divine being, who is limitless and undefinable, present in everyone and everything. But this God should not be worshipped in the form of idols or through formal rituals, but rather recognized as immanent in all things and all beings. The learned Bengali Brahman Rammohan Roy published translations of the Upaniṣads into both Bengali (*Kena*, *Īśā*, *Kaṭha*, *Māṇḍūkya*, and *Muṇḍaka*) and English (*Kena, Īśā, Kaṭha, and Muṇḍaka*).

The Prarthana Samaj ("Prayer Society") was founded by the physician Atmaram Pandurang (1823–1898) in Bombay in 1867, following the visit of Keshub Chandra Sen (1838–1884), a prominent figure in the Brahmo Samaj, who had founded his own breakaway group, the Bharatvarshiya Brahmo Samaj (Indian *brahman* Society). Like the Brahmo Samaj, the Prarthana Samaj embraced a monotheistic theology and advocated for the abolition of child marriage, untouchability, and polygamy. One of the early leaders of the Prarthana Samaj, the Sanskrit scholar Ramakrishna Gopal Bhandarkar, declared that the society was based on four pillars: the Upaniṣads, the *Bhagavadgītā*, Western thought, and the poems of Hindu saints like Namdeo and Tukaram.

The Arya Samaj ("noble society"), founded by Dayananda Sarasvati (1825–1883) in Bombay in 1875, likewise embraced a Hindu monotheism based on the Vedas. Members of the Arya Samaj do not accept any texts as sacred beyond the Vedas, and they reject the *Mahābhārata* and *Rāmāyaṇa* as authoritative texts. They regard the divine as impersonal, eternal, and formless, and they reject all image worship. Although Dayānanda initially embraced a philosophy that included Advaita Vedānta ideas, he later came to reject even the Upaniṣads as sources of truth, accepting only the Vedas as authoritative.

The charismatic Swami Vivekananda (1863–1902) popularized the Upaniṣads both in India and in the West as he introduced

Vedānta philosophy to the world in his famous speech at the World Parliament of Religions in Chicago in 1893. Vivekananda proceeded to give hundreds of lectures in the United States and Europe on Vedānta philosophy, and he founded the Vedanta Societies of New York and San Francisco, which again led to the formation of many more Vedanta Societies throughout the United States and Europe in the years that followed. Vivekananda's theology was a monotheistic one, based on his readings of the classical Upaniṣads and the Vedānta philosophers.

Vivekananda wrote about the Upaniṣads:

> In modern language, the theme of the Upanishads is to find an ultimate unity of things. Knowledge is nothing but finding unity in the midst of diversity. Every science is based upon this; all human knowledge is based upon the finding of unity in the midst of diversity; and if it is the task of small fragments of human knowledge, which we call our sciences, to find unity in the midst of a few different phenomena, the task becomes stupendous when the theme before us is to find unity in the midst of this marvellously diversified universe, where prevail unnumbered differences in name and form, in matter and spirit—each thought differing from every other thought, each form differing from every other form. Yet, to harmonise these many planes and unending Lokas, in the midst of this infinite variety to find unity, is the theme of the Upanishads. (https://vivekavani.com/vedanta-vivekananda/)

For Vivekananda, the Upaniṣads are not merely relevant to the modern age; the "religion of the Upaniṣads" was in fact the only salvation for a spiritually bankrupt world. Vivekananda has been considered "the most influential architect of global Hinduism" (Madaio 2017, 1).

Another influential modern Hindu thinker was Aurobindo Ghose (Sri Aurobindo) (1872–1950), the founder of Integral Yoga. He developed a new form of Vedānta that the philosopher

Haridas Chaudhuri later referred to as Pūrṇādvaita ("integral nondualism"), a term not used by Aurobindo himself. Aurobindo's personal philosophy was "formed first on the study of the Upaniṣads and the Gita" (Aurobindo 2006, 113). He was the author of two important works on the Upaniṣads, *Philosophy of the Upanishads* and *Translating the Upanishads*. He wrote:

> The idea of transcendental Unity, Oneness, and Stability behind all the flux and variety of phenomenal life is the basal idea of the Upanishads: this is the pivot of all Indian metaphysics, the sum and goal of our spiritual experience. (Aurobindo 1972, XII, 1)

The absolute oneness of *brahman* and *ātman* is central to Aurobindo's own philosophy, but his thought differs in some other respects both from the ideas expressed in the Upaniṣads and in later Vedānta philosophy. In Aurobindo's view, the inconceivable *brahman* is one, an absolute, infinite consciousness, but *brahman* chooses to see himself as qualified and produces a shadow of his own being, which Aurobindo calls *parabrahman*. While *brahman* and *parabrahman* are ultimately one and the same reality, *parabrahman* is a mode of the unknowable *brahman* that can be grasped by a yogi and known as *saccidānanda* (being, consciousness, and bliss) (Minor 1978, 24–25). When *brahman* thus sees himself through his own volition as *parabrahman*, the reality which is One is temporarily seen as many. Aurobindo calls this process *māyā*, a Sanskrit term that is often translated as "illusion," but for Aurobindo this "illusion" is not unreality; it is merely a limited way in which *brahman* chooses to perceive itself. Appearances in the world are not illusions, but rather intentional self-representations of *brahman*. From *brahman*'s self-perception come duality and a differentiation between spirit and matter. But the perception of a duality of spirit and matter is ultimately *māyā*; all reality is one, and only *brahman* is real. This absolute *brahman* is identical to the *ātman* within each living being, as taught in the Upaniṣads.

But while the Upaniṣads and Vedānta philosophy are mainly concerned with liberation from the cycle of death and rebirth as a result of seeing the unity between *ātman* and *brahman*, Aurobindo is concerned with a process of perfection that transforms the individual, society at large, and even matter itself. The world, for Aurobindo, is a mode of *brahman* itself, and this *brahman* is evolving back to its original absolute form. Change must begin with the individual striving for perfection through Yoga, but the ultimate goal is the perfection of the world itself. According to Aurobindo, the supreme *brahman* (also known as *puruṣa*, "the person") can descend into the world of matter to transform it and help it evolve. He argued that the *supermind* is an intermediary between the unmanifest *brahman* and the manifest world and that this *supermind* can be realized within each person. Through Yoga, the human consciousness can evolve form the level of the mind, which is characterized by ignorance, to *supermind*, characterized by an infinite knowledge, which has been suppressed by the mind.

The philosopher and statesman Sarvepalli Radhakrishnan (1888–1875), who served as the second president of India, wrote a great deal on the role of Hinduism in the modern world, drawing extensively on his Advaita-inspired reading of the Upaniṣads. He also published an edition and translation of the older Upaniṣads (Radhakrishnan 1953), equipped with explanatory notes that draw parallels to both Buddhist and Christian texts. Radhakrishnan was profoundly influenced by Vivekananda's view of Hinduism as an "eternal religion" (*sanātana dharma*) and saw as the heart of Hinduism the idea that the Absolute is identical to a person's own self. Radhakrishnan wrote his bachelor's degree thesis on "The Ethics of Vedānta and Its Metaphysical Presuppositions" at Madras Christian College, a thesis that is firmly rooted in Śaṅkara's nondualist philosophy. Much like Aurobindo, Radhakrishnan sees the world as *māyā*, not in the sense that it is not real, but as something that is merely to be understood as the objectified thought of *brahman*.

Radhakrishnan taught at the Madras Presidency College, the University of Mysore, and the University of Calcutta, and he held the Spalding Chair of Eastern Religions and Ethics at the University of Oxford from 1936 to 1952. Radhakrishnan's work was instrumental in forming a modern perception of an Upaniṣad-based Vedānta as a cornerstone of "Hinduism" itself. Radhakrishnan also made great contributions to making Indian thought more known in the West. For Radhakrishnan, the Upaniṣads are an essential part of the Indian national character itself: "For us Indians, a study of the Upaniṣads is essential, if we are to preserve our national being and character" (Radhakrishnan 1953, 9). But Radhakrishnan does not see the Upaniṣads only as Indian, but also as universal. In his Upaniṣad translation, Radhakrishnan frequently draws parallels to Plato, the New Testament, and the Buddhist *Dhammapada* to show how universal the ideas of the Upaniṣads are. Radhakrishnan is a prominent representative of a perennialist philosophy that sees all the world's religions as stemming from a single truth.

Vivekananda, Aurobindo, and Radhakrishnan were all important modern interpreters of Hinduism, who to a large extent based their teachings on an Advaita-inflected reading of the Upaniṣads. The term "Neo-Vedānta" was coined by the German Indologist Paul Hacker to describe the teachings of these significant modern thinkers, but Hacker used the term in a pejorative sense to distinguish it from the "traditional" Vedānta of Śaṅkara (Hacker 1995, 227; see critique in Madaio 2017).

Another central figure in modern Hinduism who drew popular attention to the Upaniṣads was Mohandas Karamchand Gandhi (1869–1948), whose nonviolent resistance against the British colonizers played an integral part in India's independence. His well-known epithet, Mahātmā (literally: "the great *ātman*"), itself has Upaniṣadic resonances, and although the *Bhagavadgītā* may have been even closer to Gandhi's heart, the Upaniṣads were also a significant influence on his philosophy.

Gandhi proposed that the first stanza of the *Īśā Upaniṣad* contained "the whole essence of Hinduism." He said: "If all the Upanishads and all the other scriptures happened all of a sudden to be reduced to ashes, and if only the first verse in the Ishopanishad were left in the memory of the Hindus, Hinduism would live forever" (Address in Kotalam, Kerala, January 30, 1937, cited in Easwaran 1987, 205). The first stanza of the *Īśā Upaniṣad* states:

> All this, whatever moves in this moving world,
> is enveloped by the Lord.
> Therefore, find your enjoyment in renunciation,
> and do not covet that which belongs to others.

For Gandhi, the notion that everything and everyone in the world is enveloped by the one Lord implies that all human beings are equal in the eyes of the divine being. In his reading, this stanza speaks out against the caste system of India and establishes all humans as equal. Gandhi further interpreted the last part of the stanza to imply that human beings must surrender themselves completely to God and have faith that he will supply all that they need. Therefore, he concluded, the *Īśā Upaniṣad* encourages renunciation and a simple lifestyle:

> Since he pervades every fiber of my being and of all of you, I derive from it the doctrine of equality of all creatures on earth and it should satisfy the cravings of all philosophical communists. This mantra tells me that I cannot hold as mine anything that belongs to God and that, if my life and that of all who believe in this mantra has to be a life of perfect dedication, it follows that it will have to be a life of continual service of fellow creatures. (Gandhi's speech at Kottayam in 1937, cited from Radhakrishnan 1953, 568)

While Gandhi did describe himself as a follower of Advaita ("non-dualist") philosophy, he understood Advaita very literally as "the essential unity of man and for that matter of all that lives" (Gandhi 1958–1994, 54:165). But for Gandhi, the realization of the unity of *ātman* and *brahman* was not as much a path to personal salvation as a call to social action.

The Upaniṣads in the West

The *Sirr-e-Akbar* was translated into Latin by the Frenchman Abraham Hyacinthe Anquetil-Duperron (1731–1805) under the title *Oupnek'hat, id est Secretum tegendum* ("Oupnek'hat, that is, The Concealed Secret"). *Oupnek'hat* is a distortion of the Persian spelling for Upaniṣad (*upanikhat*), and *Secretum tegendum* ("The Concealed Secret") appears to be a paraphrase of the Persian title *Sirr-i-akbar* ("The Great Secret").

Dara Shikoh's text must have been particularly appealing to Anquetil-Duperron, who as a young man had abandoned his theological studies in order to devote his life to the study of ancient languages. He suspected that many of the questions left unanswered by the Bible might be illuminated by the study of ancient sacred texts from other parts of the world, and he wrote: "[W]ho can say if there were not other historians before Moses, an earlier books?" (App 2010, 364). Anquetil-Duperron was particularly drawn to India because the Vedas were rumored to be of even greater antiquity than the Bible itself. What profound religious secrets could lie hidden in these books? Much like Dara Shikoh himself, Anquetil-Duperron was a mystic at heart, searching for universal answers in ancient religious texts.

Anquetil-Duperron's translation of the Upaniṣads was published in two volumes in 1801 and 1802. A French summary of the translation and commentary was published in Millin's *Magasin Encyclopédique* in 1805. The complete Latin text was eventually translated further into German by Franz Mischel in 1882. After that, direct translations of the Sanskrit texts of the Upaniṣads soon supplanted the need for further translations of Dara Shikoh's text into European languages. But an echo of Dara Shikoh's *The Great Secret* still lingered in the intellectual life of Europe. Anquetil-Duperron' s translation, imperfect as it was, had a profound influence on nineteenth-century European philosophy and contributed to Europe's fascination with Indian religion and culture.

The German Idealist philosopher Georg Wilhelm Friedrich Hegel (1770–1883) studied the traditions of India (as well as those of China) from 1822 onward. At the time, Hegel was a professor of philosophy at the University of Berlin. Influenced by his friend and colleague the Sanskritist Franz Bopp, Hegel read widely in the available literature on Indian philosophy. To Hegel, Indian thought represents an earlier state in the philosophical and historical progress of humankind, a state characterized by a perception of the divine as "pure being" (*das reine Sein*), an undifferentiated abstract unity that does not allow for any self-affirmation of human individuals, who are completely absorbed in this One. The Upaniṣadic notion of *brahman* is mentioned several times in Hegel's own philosophical writings, although Hegel himself is critical of the non-dualist philosophy of the Upaniṣadic, which he sees as anti-individualistic.

Hegel's contemporary and onetime roommate at the University of Tübingen Friedrich Schelling (1775–1854) was also deeply interested in Indian philosophy, and it was due to the influence of his lectures on the topic in Berlin in 1844 that Max Müller, who later became a well-known scholar of Sanskrit, first began to read the Upaniṣads. In his *Philosophie der Mythologie* ("Philosophy of Mythology," published posthumously in 1856–1857), Schelling drew on many ideas from the Upaniṣads, and Max Müller claimed that he had translated several Upaniṣads for Schelling in 1845. Schelling was drawn to the idea of the soul's return to an Absolute "world-soul," an idea that is inspired by the Upaniṣadic concept of *brahman*. In his earlier work *Darstellung meines Systems der Philosophie* ("Presentation of My System of Philosophy," 1801), Schelling talks about the ultimate goal of philosophy as the undivided "absolute identity" (*absolute Identität*), from which everything flows and to which everything eventually returns, an idea that also recalls the notion of *brahman*. Overall, however, Schelling found the Upaniṣads to be "a very unsatisfactory reading" (Schelling 1856–1861, II, 2, 480) because *brahman* was presented in these texts as a completely abstract principle, rather than the God of monotheism, which to Schelling represented the primordial unity (Halbfass 1988, 103). Schelling was fascinated by the Upaniṣads, and he regarded Advaita Vedānta philosophy as the highest form of idealism possible without the revelation of a single God.

The German philosopher Arthur Schopenhauer (1788–1860) was also deeply impressed by the Upaniṣads, which he had read in Anquetil-Duperron' s Latin translation. Schopenhauer wrote in the 1818 foreword to his great philosophical treatise *The World as Will and Representation*: "Access to [the Vedas and Upaniṣads] is in my view the greatest advantage which this still young century has shown over previous ones" (Sedlar 1982, 46). Schopenhauer repeated this sentiment in his very last book, *Parerga and Paralipomena* (1851):

> For how entirely does the Oupnekhat breathe throughout the holy spirit of the Vedas! How is every one who by a diligent study of its Persian Latin has become familiar with that incomparable book, stirred by that spirit to the very depth of his soul! How does every line display its firm, definite, and throughout harmonious meaning! From every sentence deep, original, and sublime thoughts arise, and the whole is pervaded by a high and holy and earnest spirit. Indian air surrounds us, and original thoughts of kindred spirits. . . . In the whole world there is no study, except that of the originals, so beneficial and so elevating as that of the

Oupnekhat. It has been the solace of my life, it will be the solace of my death!" (English translation from Müller 1879, lxi).

What traces of Upaniṣadic thought can we find in Schopenhauer's own philosophy? In *The World as Will and Representation*, Schopenhauer argues that the world we perceive is "representation" (*Vorstellung*), mere shifting phenomena that are not ultimately real. This representation is projected by and supported by the Will (*Wille*), which dwells in everything. This Will is eternal and uncaused, beyond space and time. All the suffering in the world is produced by the desires of the Will, and only by denying this Will through ascetic practice can humans be free of its control. All causation takes place in the phenomenal world of representation; the Will itself is neither cause nor effect. Schopenhauer claims that although we normally only perceive the world of representation, we can know the Will by looking inwards and seeing it in ourselves. The Will is transcendental and universal, but it can be known through introspection since it is only accessible within us.

Schopenhauer's notion of the sensory world as representation appears to owe something to Immanuel Kant's (1724–1804) notion of *das Ding an mich* ("the thing as it appears to me"). While Kant proposed that we can never experience *das Ding an sich* ("the thing in itself," a thing as it truly is apart from our perception of it), Schopenhauer argues that we can experience the ultimate reality as it truly is. Schopenhauer agrees that there is an illusory aspect to the external world ("Vorstellung," or "representation"), but he also claims that our inner will ("Wille") is our connection to the world beyond representation. The notion of an internal faculty in humans that allows us to see the true reality behind the elusive empirical forms can easily be compared to the Upaniṣadic notion of *ātman*. While Schopenhauer himself made a note of the Upaniṣadic concept of *brahman* as a creator ("*Brahma* produces the world through a kind of original sin, but himself remains in it to atone for this until he has redeemed himself from it. This is quite a good idea!"; Schopenhauer 1851, 156), his idea of the Will seems more closely aligned with the creative *ātman* of the Upaniṣads. Just as Schopenhauer's Will and Representation are two aspects of the same reality, so are the Upaniṣadic *ātman* and *brahman* two sides of the same coin. Schopenhauer sees the will as the inner core of all human beings. Similarly, the Upaniṣadic *ātman* is both the inner self of all living beings and that which creates or projects the external reality. As we have seen, several Upaniṣads, such as the *Bṛhadāraṇyaka*, *Chāndogya*, *Aitareya*, and *Taittirīya*, describe the world as created or projected by *ātman*.

Schopenhauer's Will is not rational thought, but rather a subconscious power beyond ordinary worldly experience. It is, like the Upaniṣadic *ātman*, *intellectually* unknowable, and yet it can be experienced through internal contemplation. Schopenhauer called the awareness of the Will "the most direct of all our cognitions" (Schopenhauer 1873, 470–471). Unlike external sensory phenomena, the Will can only be known through a form of direct intuition highly reminiscent of the Upaniṣadic *jñāna*.

The Will, like the *ātman*, is the substrate of all other phenomena. The Will is the only thing that exists; everything else is a secondary manifestation of that Will. In this regard, Schopenhauer's view of external reality as mere manifestation seems to owe something to the Upaniṣadic idea of *māyā*, or illusion. Although Schopenhauer was likely not acquainted with the elaboration of *māyā* in the Advaita Vedānta philosophy of Śaṅkara, as presented in his commentaries on the Upaniṣads, he would have been familiar with the concept of *māyā* as cosmic illusion from *Śvetāśvatara Upaniṣad* 4.9–10. Schopenhauer's diction suggests that he has *māyā* in mind when he writes: "Although no one can recognize the thing-in-itself through the veil of the forms of perceptions, on the other hand everyone carries this within himself, in fact, he himself is it" (Schopenhauer 1958, Vol. 2, 182). Although *māyā* is not yet referred to as a veil in the classical Upaniṣads, this image is foreshadowed by passages in the Upaniṣads referring to *ātman* covering itself with the threads of creation in *Śvetāśvatara Upaniṣad* 6.10, which would have been familiar to Schopenhauer.

We may also note in the passage cited above a distinct echo of the famous Upaniṣadic dictum from the *Chāndogya Upaniṣad* tat *tvam asi* (traditionally translated as "you are it," but see Brereton 1986) in the phrase "he himself is it." This phrase, hinting at a mystical unity between the individual and the highest reality, made a deep impression on Schopenhauer. A note in his handwriting, dated to 1926, says merely: *Tat-twam-asi*. The phrase is mentioned three times in his famous work *The World as Will and Representation*, and he suggests that this phrase can tell a person "about their inner nature" (Schopenhauer 1958, Vol. 1, 220).

Although he was profoundly influenced by the Upaniṣads, Schopenhauer did in later life regard himself as a Buddhist rather than a Hindu. He did, however, see no contradiction between his adopted Buddhist faith and the teachings of the Upaniṣads, and he claimed to recognize many of the most profound thoughts of Buddhism in the *Oupnekhat*.

Schopenhauer's concept of the Will owes a great deal to Upaniṣadic notions of *ātman*: the Will is universal, eternal, uncaused, and accessible through introspection. But simultaneously, the Will embodies striving and desire, which eventually leads to suffering, as these desires are frustrated. Schopenhauer's perception of this Will as a negative influence whose power must be combated through asceticism, however, may perhaps owe more to Buddhist notions that the self is an illusion that must be overcome through mental and physical discipline than to the Upaniṣad's entirely positive view of the *ātman*. Buddhism was not well known in Germany at the time when Schopenhauer wrote *The World as Will and Representation*, however, so it is possible that Schopenhauer's depiction of the *ātman*-like Will as something negative comes from his own philosophical sensibilities, rather than directly from Buddhism, although Schopenhauer seems to have gained a deeper understanding of Buddhism later in life.

Schopenhauer writes a great deal about human suffering, which arises from the strivings of the Will. This suffering can only be overcome through asceticism, which he refers to as "the inner essence of holiness," a denial of the will-to-live prompted by the Will itself. While some scholars have seen this insistence on asceticism as a way to overcome suffering as influenced by Buddhism, it would also be perfectly possible for Schopenhauer to derive such an idea from the Upaniṣads themselves. Through the Latin *Oupnekhat*, Schopenhauer would have been familiar with the *Mahānārāyaṇa Upaniṣad*, a text that advocates penance and asceticism as paths to spiritual liberation.

Schopenhauer's view of aesthetics seems to owe something to the Upaniṣads as well. He describes the aesthetic experience of art or music as a state when one can "no longer separate the perceiver from the perception" (Schopenhauer 1958, Vol. 2, 406), an idea closely related to that found in a famous passage in the *Bṛhadāraṇyaka Upaniṣad*:

> For when there is duality, then one can smell the other, one can see the other, one can hear the other, one can greet the other, one can perceive the other. But when the whole has become one's own *ātman*, then who is there for one to smell and how? Who is there for one to see and how? Who is there for one to hear and how? Who is there for one to greet and how? Who is there for one to think about and how? Who is there for one to perceive and how? (*Bṛhadāraṇyaka Upaniṣad* 2.4.14)

Through an aesthetic experience that collapses the boundaries between the subject and the object, a human being can experience not only momentary relief from life's suffering, but also redemption (*Erlösung*). Schopenhauer's notion of *Erlösung* is quite similar to the Upaniṣadic concept of *mokṣa*, the liberation from the painful cycle of death and rebirth, which likewise can be achieved when there is no longer any distinction between subject and object.

How well did Schopenhauer, who was only familiar with the Upaniṣads through an awkward Latin translation of a Persian translation, actually know the Upaniṣadic texts? From his own writings about the Upaniṣads, we may conclude that he had understood the texts surprisingly well, given the flawed nature of his sources. Even the Sanskrit scholar Max Müller, who had read the Upaniṣads in the original and had few positive things to say about Anquetil-Duperron' s distorted representation of the texts, had good things to say about Schopenhauer's interpretation of the Upaniṣads:

> I must now admit, hat if he had done nothing else but decipher the sense of the Upanishads out of the frightful translation of Anquetil Duperron, this alone would suffice to assure him, even among philosophers, and honorable place as an interpreter. (Max Müller: "Damals und Jetzt," *Deutsche Rundschau*, Vol. XLI 1884, 417, cited in Sedlar 1982, 49)

Oddly, Schopenhauer dismissed the much more accurate translations of the Upaniṣads that became available after Anquetil-Duperron, such as those of Rammohan Roy, because these translations seemed to him to introduce an element of theism that he had not seen in Anquetil-Duperron, a theism Schopenhauer regarded, without much cause, as a later corruption. In an outburst that was simultaneously orientalist and antisemitic, Schopenhauer described Rammohan Roy dismissively as "a Brahman turned Jew" (Schopenhauer 1966, Vol. 5, 341).

Schopenhauer did not borrow Upaniṣadic teachings wholesale, any more than he adopted the complete philosophical systems of Plato and Kant. He did, however, suggest himself that his own philosophy could not have existed without the Upaniṣads: "Moreover, I confess that I do not believe my doctrine could have come about before the Upanishads, Plato and Kant cast their rays simultaneously into the mind of one man" (Schopenhauer 1966, Vol. 1, 422).

Schopenhauer's pessimistic philosophy of the Will as the source of both the representation of external reality and boundless suffering due to its own unfulfilled desires was very much his own and was in no way a mere restatement of the ideas he encountered in the ancient Upaniṣads. His philosophy was, however, deeply inspired by these ancient Indian texts.

The American transcendentalist philosopher and writer Ralph Waldo Emerson (1802–1882) was deeply influenced by Indian philosophy, including the Upaniṣads, the *Bhagavadgītā*, and Vedānta philosophy. The influence of the Upaniṣads on his thought is *particularly* apparent in his 1841 essay "The Over-Soul," inspired by the idea of *ātman* in the Upaniṣads, and his 1857 poem "Brahma," whose opening lines are a variation of *Kaṭha Upaniṣad* 2.19:

> If the red slayer think he slays,
> Or if the slain think he is slain,
> They know not well the subtle ways
> I keep, and pass, and turn again.

The transcendentalist Henry David Thoreau (1817–1862) was also deeply influenced by Indian thought and practiced Yoga, and in his *Walden*, we find echoes of an Upaniṣadic pantheism throughout.

But the Upaniṣads also influenced the thought of prominent scientists in Europe. The Austrian physicist Erwin Schrödinger (1887–1961) was deeply interested in Indian philosophy and turned to the Upaniṣads for answers to questions about the very nature of reality. In his *What Is Life?* (1944), Schrödinger wrote that if the world is created through our acts of observations there should theoretically be as many worlds as there are people, and he asked what would make each person's perceived world synchronize with those of others. His solution to this question was that all minds are one, a thought he had encountered in the Upaniṣads: "There is obviously only one alternative, namely the unification of minds or consciousnesses. Their multiplicity is only apparent, in truth there is only one mind. This is the doctrine of the Upanishads" (Schrödinger 1944).

In one of his letters that was later published in the volume *Mind and Matter*, Schrödinger wrote: "It is the same elements that go to compose my mind and the world. Subject and object are only one. The barrier between them cannot be said to have broken down as a result of recent experience in the physical sciences, for this barrier does not exist. . . . Still, it must be said that to Western thought this doctrine has little appeal, it is unpalatable, it is dubbed fantastic, unscientific. Well, so it is because our science—Greek science—is based on objectivation, whereby it has cut itself off from an adequate understanding of the Subject of Cognizance, of the mind" (Schrödinger 2012, 128–130).

The Serbian-American inventor Nikola Tesla (1856–1953) met Swami Vivekananda at a party hosted by the actress Sarah Bernhardt in 1896, an encounter that sparked Tesla's interest in Indian philosophy. In a 1908 address entitled "Man's Greatest Achievement," (later published in the *New York American*, July 6, 1930), Tesla writes:

> All perceptible matter comes from a primary substance, or tenuity beyond conception, filling all space, the akasha or luminiferous ether, which is acted upon by the life-giving Prana or creative force, calling into existence, in never-ending cycles all things and phenomena. (Pokazanyeva 2016)

Tesla's ideas of *ākāśa* and *prāṇa*, while resonating in interesting ways with the Upaniṣads, are not derived directly from these texts but rather appear to be filtered through the teachings of Vivekananda, who identifies *prāṇa* and *ākāśa* as the two primary universal principles. In his 1896 work *Raja Yoga*, Vivekananda writes:

> By what power is this Akasha manufactured into this universe? By the power of Prana. Just as Akasha is the infinite, omnipresent

> material of this universe, so is this Prana the infinite, omnipresent manifesting power of this universe. At the beginning and at the end of a cycle everything becomes Akasha, and all the forces that are in the universe resolve back into the Prana; in the next cycle, out of this Prana is evolved everything that we call energy, everything that we call force. (Vivekananda 1915, 167)

Both Vivekananda and Tesla regard the Upaniṣadic principles of *prāṇa* ("breath") and *ākāśa* ("ether") as proto-scientific terms for matter and energy. The notion of "Akasha" as energy becomes influential in Theosophy and in Western occult movements. The Theosophy movement introduced the idea of "Akashic records" as an etheric library of human knowledge. The founder of the Theosophical Society, Helena Blavatsky (1831–1891), viewed Akasha as a life force. While she referred to indestructible tablets of astral light preserving human knowledge, she did not use the term "Akashic record," which was introduced in Alfred Percy Sinnett's *Esoteric Buddhism* (1883). The idea of an Akashic Record, preserving all the knowledge of humanity and accessible through occult experiences, was further developed by the Austrian theosophist and occultist Rudolf Steiner (1861–1925), as well as the American self-declared clairvoyant Edgar Cayce (1877–1945). In occultism, the Akashic record is perceived as the compendium of all knowledge from the beginning of time, a record to which all humans are linked, and which humans can access through seances and clairvoyance. This is obviously something very different from the Upaniṣadic notion of *ākāśa* as an elemental ether.

But the concept of Akasha also plays a part in contemporary science; the Hungarian philosopher and systems scientist Ervin László (b. 1932), an advocate of the theory of quantum consciousness, proposed in his 2004 book *Science and the Akashic Field: An Integral Theory of Everything* that there exists an energy field of information (the "Akashic field" or "A-field") that informs all universes past and present.

Editions of the Upaniṣads

The first printed collection of Upaniṣadic texts was Rammohan Roy's editions of four Upaniṣads in Bengali script (*Kaṭha*, *Īśā*, *Kena*, and *Muṇḍaka*; Roy 1818). Other noteworthy editions of collected Upaniṣadic texts are Röer 1850c and 1850d, Harirātmaja 1886, Tatya 1891, Phansîkar 1904 and 1913, Kunhan Raja 1935, Limaye and Vadekar 1958, and Olivelle 1998.

Important editions of single Upaniṣads include Röer's editions of the *Bṛhadāraṇyaka Upaniṣad* and the *Chāndogya Upaniṣad* (Röer 1850a and 1850b), Cowell's 1861 edition of the *Kauṣītaki Upaniṣad* and his 1862 edition of the *Maitrī Upaniṣad* with Rāmatīrtha's commentary, Vidyasagara's editions of the *Bṛhadāraṇyaka Upaniṣad* and the *Chāndogya Upaniṣad* with Śaṅkara's commentary (Vidyasagara 1873 and 1875), Bhāgavata's edition of the *Aitareya Upanishad* (1898), Böhtlingk's editions of the *Bṛhadāraṇyaka Upaniṣad* (1889a) and *Chāndogya Upaniṣad* (1889b) and the *Kaṭha*, *Aitareya*, and *Praśna Upaniṣads* (1890), Gosvāmī's edition of the *Īśā Upaniṣad* (1895), Hertel's edition of the *Muṇḍaka Upaniṣad* (1924), Vidyarnava's edition of the *Maitrī Upaniṣad* (1926), Hauschild's edition of the *Śvetāśvatara Upaniṣad* (1927), Morgenroth's edition of the *Chāndogya Upaniṣad* (1958), van Buitenen's edition of the *Maitrāyaṇīya Upaniṣad* (1962), Frenz's edition of the *Kauṣītaki Upaniṣad* (1968–1969), Maue's edition of the *Bṛhadāraṇyakopaniṣad* (1976), and Pérez Coffie's edition of the second chapter of the *Bṛhadāraṇyakopaniṣad* (1994).

The Sanskrit editions published in the Ānandāśrama Sanskrit Series between 1888 and 1942 in Pune (Poona) are invaluable sources for the study of the Upaniṣads. While the Ānandāśrama Sanskrit Series volumes are not critical editions, they do represent good versions of the received texts of the Upaniṣads. Among the many volumes published in this series are the *Īśā Upaniṣad* with the commentaries of Śaṅkara, Ānandagiri, and Śaṅkarānanda (Āgāśe 1888a), the *Kena Upaniṣad* with Śaṅkara's commentary

(Āgāśe 1888b), the *Kaṭha Upaniṣad* with Śaṅkara's commentary (Rājavāḍe 1889), the *Praśna Upaniṣad* with the commentaries of Śaṅkara, Ānandagiri, and Śaṅkarānanda (Āpṭe 1889a), the *Muṇḍaka Upaniṣad* (Āpṭe 1889b), the *Māṇḍūkya Upaniṣad* with Gauḍapāda's commentary (Kathāvaṭe 1890), the *Aitareya Upaniṣad* with Śaṅkara's commentary (Āpṭe 1889c), the *Taittirīya Upaniṣad* with Śaṅkara's commentary (Islāmpurakara 1889), the *Taittirīya Upaniṣad* with Sureśvara's commentary (Āpṭe 1889d), the *Chāndogya Upaniṣad* with Śaṅkara's commentary (Āgāśe 1890), the *Bṛhadāraṇyaka Upaniṣad* with Śaṅkara's commentary (Āgāśe 1891), the *Bṛhadāraṇyaka Upaniṣad* in three volumes with Śaṅkara's commentary and Ānandagiri's sub-commentary (Āgāśe 1892–1894), the *Śvetāśvatara Upaniṣad* with Śaṅkara's commentary (Āpṭe 1890), a collection of thirty-two Upaniṣads (Āpṭe 1895), the *Bṛhadāraṇyaka Upaniṣad* with Nityānanda's commentary (Āgāśe 1895), another edition of the *Bṛhadāraṇyaka Upaniṣad* (Āpṭe 1902), the *Īśā Upaniṣad* (Āpṭe 1905), the *Kaṭha Upaniṣad* (Āpṭe 1906), the *Kena Upaniṣad* (Āpṭe 1909), a collection of eight Upaniṣads (Āpṭe 1910), the *Chāndogya Upaniṣad* with Rāmānuja's commentary (Gokhale 1910), the *Bṛhadāraṇyaka Upaniṣad* with Raṅgarāmānuja's commentary (Veṇegāvakara 1911), an edition of the *Īśā*, *Kena*, and *Kaṭha Upaniṣads* (Pāṭhaka 1915), the *Chāndogya Upaniṣad* with Nityānanda's commentary (Vaidya 1915), and a collection of ten Upaniṣads (Mārulakara 1937). Most of these texts are today freely available at https://www.sanskritebooks.org/2013/04/anandashram-sanskrit-series-anandashram-samskrita-granthavali/.

The French editions and translations of the Upaniṣads published between 1930 and 1959 are also very useful. This series includes the *Chāndogya-Upaniṣad* (Senart 1930), *Bṛhadāraṇyaka-Upaniṣad* (Senart 1934), *Kaṭha Upaniṣad* (Renou 1943a), *Īśā Upaniṣad* (Renou 1943b), the *Kena Upaniṣad* (Renou 1943c), the *Muṇḍaka Upaniṣad* (Maury 1943), *Māṇḍūkya Upaniṣad* (Lesimple 1944), *Kauṣītaki Upaniṣad* (Renou 1948), *Praśna Upaniṣad* (Bousquet

1948), *Śvetāśvatara Upaniṣad* (Silburn 1948), *Taittirīya Upaniṣad* (Lesimple 1948), *Aitareya Upaniṣad* (Silburn 1950), and *Maitrī Upaniṣad* (Esnoul 1952).

Translations of the Upaniṣads

The Persian *Upaniṣad* translation of Dara Shikoh and the subsequent Latin translation of Anquetil-Duperron (1801–1802) have been mentioned above. Thaddäus A. Rixner's 1808 German translation of the *Chāndogya Upaniṣad* is based on Anquetil-Duperron's Latin text.

The first translation of an Upaniṣad from Sanskrit to English was Sir William Jones's translation of the *Īśā Upaniṣad* (Jones 1799). Henry Thomas Colebrooke translated the *Aitareya Upaniṣad* in 1805. Both the *Kena Upaniṣad* and the *Īśā Upaniṣad* were translated into English by Rammohan Roy (Roy 1816a and 1816b). Rammohan Roy also translated the *Muṇḍaka* and *Kaṭha Upaniṣads* (1819a and 1819b).

Eduard Röer translated a collection of nine Upaniṣads (*Taittirīya, Aitareya, Śvetāśvatara, Kena, Īśā, Kaṭha, Praśna, Muṇḍaka*, and *Māṇḍūkya*) into English in 1853 and the *Bṛhadāraṇyaka Upaniṣad* in 1856. Cowell included translations in his editions of the *Kauṣītaki Upaniṣad* (1861) and the *Maitrī Upaniṣad* (1870). Rajendralala Mitra translated the *Chāndogya Upaniṣad* in 1862. Mention must also be made of the naturalist John Muir's translations of Sanskrit texts, which includes many passages from the Upaniṣads (Muir 1858–1870). Max Müller's translation of the Upaniṣads for the Sacred Books of the East series appeared in two volumes (1879 and 1884) and contained the *Chāndogya, Kena, Aitareya, Kauṣītaki, Īśā, Kaṭha, Muṇḍaka, Taittirīya, Bṛhadāraṇyaka, Śvetāśvatara, Praśna*, and *Maitrī/Maitrāyaṇa* Upaniṣads.

Other noteworthy translation of the Upaniṣads include Deussen's massive German *Sechzig Upanishad's des Veda* (1897), Böhtlink's

German translations included in his editions of the *Bṛhadāraṇyaka* (1889a) and *Chāndogya* Upaniṣads (1889b), Whitney's translation of the *Kaṭha Upaniṣad* (1890), Vasu's 1909 translation of the *Īśā, Kena, Kaṭha, Praśna, Muṇḍaka, Māṇḍūkya* Upaniṣads, his 1910 translation of the *Bṛhadāraṇyaka*, and his 1913–1916 translation of the *Chāndogya*, Hume's *The Thirteen Principal Upanishads* (1921), Charpentier's translation of the *Kaṭha Upaniṣad* (1928–1929), Rudolf Otto's 1936 translation of the *Kaṭha Upaniṣad, Ten Principal Upaniṣads* co-translated by Purohit Swami and William Butler Yeats (1937), Radhakrishnan's 1953 *The Principal Upaniṣads*, and Gambhiranda's *Eight Upaniṣads* (1957–1958). Patrick Olivelle's *Upaniṣads: Translated from the Original Sanskrit* (1996) is an invaluable edition for the modern reader, as is his 1998 *The Early Upaniṣads: Annotated Text and Translation*, which also includes the Sanskrit texts and more comprehensive notes. Valerie Roebuck's *The Upanishads* (2003), published in the Penguin Classics series, is also excellent, as is Vernon Katz and Thomas Egenes's *The Upanishads* (2015).

Glossary of Sanskrit Terms

adhvaryu – a Vedic priest associated with the *Yajurveda*

Advaita Vedānta – a sub-school of the Hindu philosophical school of Vedānta. Advaita Vedānta ("non-dualism") teaches that *ātman* and *brahman* are completely identical to one another.

Āraṇyakas – esoteric ritual texts composed after the Vedas and Brāhmaṇas and before the Upaniṣads

Atharvaveda – "the wisdom of the Atharvan priests," the latest of the four Vedas

ātman – "the self," the eternal soul of a living being

bhakti – "devotion," the love between a human being and a deity

Brahmā – Hindu creator god

brahman – a divine cosmic force

Brahman – priest, the highest social class

Brāhmaṇas – ritual text composed after the Vedas and before the Āraṇyakas and Upaniṣads

Dvaita Vedānta – dualist Vedānta, a Hindu philosophical school founded by Madhva that teaches that *ātman* and *brahman* are not identical

guṇas – the three "qualities" or traits that make up *prakṛti* in Sāṃkhya and Yoga philosophy; the three *guṇas* are *sattva* ("light"), *rajas* ("passion"), and *tamas* ("darkness")

hotṛ – a Vedic priest associated with the *Ṛgveda*

Indra – a Vedic god of thunder and war

Kāṇva – one of the two versions (recensions) of the White *Yajurveda*

karma – "action," the idea that a person's actions will lead to positive or negative results in the future

Kṣatriya – the second of the four social classes mentioned in the Vedas, the social class encompassing warriors and kings

Mādhyaṃdina – one of the two versions (recensions) of the White *Yajurveda*

mantra – a sacred sound in Sanskrit

māyā – illusion, the idea that the external world is not fully real

oṃ – a sacred sound (*mantra*); the word has no lexical meaning

pradhāna – the material substance from which the world is made

prakṛti – in Sāṃkhya and Yoga philosophy, an eternal female principle that encompasses both the material world and parts of the human psyche

prāṇa – life breath

puruṣa – in Sāṃkhya and Yoga philosophy, an eternal male principle that consists of pure consciousness

Ṛgveda – "the wisdom of the verses," the oldest of the four Vedas and the oldest known Hindu text

Rudra – Hindu god. Rudra is a minor storm god in the Vedas, but is later called Śiva and becomes one of the main gods of later Hinduism

śākhā – a school (tradition) of Vedic transmission

Sāmaveda – "the wisdom of the chants," one of the four Vedas

Sāṃkhya – a school of Hindu philosophy that teaches that there are two eternal principles in the world, *puruṣa* and *prakṛti*, and that the path to salvation is to recognize their difference

sandhi – a linguistic phenomenon that occurs in the Sanskrit language. The last sound of one word and the first sound of the following word change to become more phonetically similar to each other.

Śiva – one of the most popular deities in Hinduism, a god who destroys the universe at the end of time

smṛti – "recollection," one of the two categories of sacred Hindu texts, along with *śruti*. The *smṛti* texts include the epics of the *Mahābhārata* and the *Rāmāyaṇa*.

śruti – "that which is heard," one of the two categories of sacred Hindu texts, along with *smṛti*. The *śruti* texts include the Vedas and the Upaniṣads and are the most authoritative Hindu texts.

Śūdra – the lowest of the four social classes mentioned in the Vedas; the servant class

udgātṛ – a Vedic priest associated with the *Sāmaveda*

Vaiśya – the third of the four social classes mentioned in the Vedas. Farmers and merchants are included in this class.

varṇa – a social class within the hierarchical caste system of Hinduism

Vedānta – Hindu philosophical tradition whose teachings are based on the Upaniṣads

Vedas – the four Vedas are the oldest texts of Hinduism

Viśiṣṭādvaita – ("modified non-dualism"), a sub-school of Vedānta philosophy that teaches that *ātman* is contained within *brahman*

Viṣṇu – one of the most popular deities in Hinduism, a god who protects and maintains the universe

Yajurveda – "the wisdom of the sacrificial formulas," one of the four Vedas

Yoga – a school of Hindu philosophy whose teachings are closely aligned with Sāṃkhya, but which also uses meditation, bodily postures, and breathing techniques

Bibliography

Source Texts in Sanskrit

Āgāśe, Bālaśāstrī. 1888a. *Īśāvāsyopaniṣat saṭīkaśāṇkarabhāṣyopetā*. Poona: Ānandāśrama Press.

Āgāśe, Bālaśāstrī. 1888b. *Saṭīkaśāṃkarapadabhāṣyavākyabhāṣyopeta Kenopaniṣat*. Poona: Ānandāśrama Press.

Āgāśe, Kāśīnāthśāstrī. 1890. *Chāndogyopaniṣat*. Ānandāśrama Sanskrit Series, Vol. 14. Poona: Ānandāśrama Press.

Āgāśe, Kāśīnāthśāstrī. 1891. *Bṛhadāraṇyaka-Upaniṣad*. Ānandāśrama Sanskrit Series, Vol. 15. Poona: Ānandāśrama Press [Kāṇva recension]

Āgāśe, Kāśīnāthśāstrī. 1892–1894. *Bṛhadāraṇyaka-Upaniṣad*. 3 vols. Ānandāśrama Sanskrit Series, Vol. 16. Poona: Ānandāśrama Press.

Āgāśe, Kāśīnāthśāstrī. 1895. *Bṛhadāraṇyakopaniṣanmitākṣarā*. Ānandāśrama Sanskrit Series, Vol. 31. Poona: Ānandāśrama Press.

Āpṭe, Hari Nārāyaṇa. 1889a. *Praśnopaniṣat*. Ānandāśrama Sanskrit Series, Vol. 8. Poona: Ānandāśrama Press.

Āpṭe, Hari Nārāyaṇa. 1889b. *Muṇḍakopaniṣat*. Ānandāśrama Sanskrit Series, Vol. 9. Poona: Ānandāśrama Press.

Āpṭe, Hari Nārāyaṇa. 1889c. *Aitareyopaniṣat*. Ānandāśrama Sanskrit Series, Vol. 11. Poona: Ānandāśrama Press.

Āpṭe, Hari Nārāyaṇa. 1889d. *Taittirīyopaniṣat*. Ānandāśrama Sanskrit Series, Vol. 13 Poona: Ānandāśrama Press.

Āpṭe, Hari Nārāyaṇa. 1890. *Śvetāśvataropaniṣad*. Ānandāśrama Sanskrit Series, Vol. 17. Poona: Ānandāśrama Press.

Āpṭe, Hari Nārāyaṇa. 1895. *Śrīnārāyaṇaśaṃkarānandaviracitadīpikāsametānām atharvaśikhādyānāṃ haṃsopaniṣadantānāṃ dvātriṃśanmitānām upaniṣadāṃ samuccayaḥ*. Ānandāśrama Sanskrit Series, Vol. 29. Poona: Ānandāśrama Press. [32 Upaniṣads]

Āpṭe, Hari Nārāyaṇa. 1902. *Bṛhadāraṇyakopaniṣat*. Ānandāśrama Sanskrit Series, Vol. 15. Poona: Ānandāśrama Press.

Āpṭe, Hari Nārāyaṇa. 1905. *Īśāvāsyopniṣat*. Ānandāśrama Sanskrit Series, Vol. 5. Poona: Ānandāśrama Press.

Āpṭe, Hari Nārāyaṇa. 1906. *Kāṭhakopaniṣat*. Ānandāśrama Sanskrit Series, Vol. 7. Poona: Ānandāśrama Press.

Āpṭe, Hari Nārāyaṇa. 1909. *Kenopaniṣat*. Ānandāśrama Sanskrit Series, Vol. 6. Poona: Ānandāśrama Press.

Āpṭe, Hari Nārāyaṇa. 1910. *Īśā kenakaṭhapraśnamuṇḍakamāṇḍūkyā nandavallībhṛgūpaniṣadah*. Ānandāśrama Sanskrit Series, Vol. 62. Poona: Ānandāśrama Press.

Bhāgavata, Rājārāma Rāmakrishna. 1898. *The Aitareya Upanishad*. Bombay: Nirnaya Sagar Press.

Böhtlingk, Otto von. 1889a. *Bṛhadâraṇjakopanishad in der Mâdhjaṁdina Recension*. St. Petersburg: Kaiserliche Akademie der Wissenschaften.

Böhtlingk, Otto von. 1889b. *Khândogjopanishad*. Leipzig: Verlag von H. Haessel.

Böhtlingk, Otto von. 1890. "Drei kritisch gesichtete und übersetze Upanishad mit erklärenden Anmerkungen." *Berichte über die Verhandlungen der königlich sächsischen Gesellschaft der Wissenschaften zu Leipzig, Philologisch-historische Classe* 42: 127–197. [*Kaṭha*, *Aitareya*, and *Praśna* Upaniṣads]

Bousquet, Jacques. 1948. *Praśna Upaniṣad*. Paris: Adrien-Maisonneuve.

Buitenen, J. A. B. [Johannes Adrianus Bernardus] van. 1962. *The Maitrāyaṇīya Upaniṣad: A Critical Essay with Text, Translation, and Commentary*. The Hague: Mouton.

Cowell, Edward Byles 1861. *The Kaushītaki-Brāhmaṇa-Upanishad with the Commentary of Śankarānanda*. Calcutta: Asiatic Society of Bengal.

Cowell, Edward Byles. 1862. *The Maitri, or, Maitrāyanīya Upanishad*. Calcutta: Asiatic Society of Bengal [text with Rāmatīrthi's commentary].

Esnoul, Anne-Marie. 1952. *Maitry Upaniṣad*. Paris: Adrien-Maisonneuve.

Frenz, Albrecht. 1968–1969. "Kauṣītakī Upaniṣad." *Indo-Iranian Journal* 11: 79–129. [Sanskrit text and German translation].

Gokhale, Gaṇeśaśāstrī. 1910. Chāndogyopaniṣad. Ānandāśrama Sanskrit Series, Vol. 63. Poona: Ānandāśrama Press.

Gosvāmī, Śyāmalāla. 1895. *Isa Upanishad with the Bhashyas of Baladeva, Vidyabhushana, Sri Sankaracarya, and the Tika of Anandagiri*. Calcutta: People's Press.

Harirātmaja, Keśavāla 1886. *Śvetāśvataropaniṣatsahitaḥ īśādidaśopaniṣatsaṅgrahaḥ*. Bombay: Nirnaya-Sagara Press.

Hauschild, Richard. 1927. *Die Śvetāśvatara Upaniṣad: Eine kritische Ausgabe mit einer Übersetzung und einer Übersicht über ihre Lehren*. Abhandlungen für die Kunde des Morgenlandes, XVII.3. Leipzig: Brockhaus.

Hertel, Johannes. 1924. *Muṇḍaka Upaniṣad. Kritische Ausgabe mit Rodarneudruck der Erstausgabe (Text und Kommentare) und Einleitung*. Indo-Iranische Quellen und Forschungen, Vol. III. Leipzig: H. Haessel.

Islāmpurakara, Vāmanaśāstrī. 1889. *Taittirīyopaniṣat*. Ānandāśrama Sanskrit Series, Vol. 12. Poona: Ānandāśrama Press.

Kathāvaṭe, Ābājī Viṣṇu. 1890. *Sagauḍapādīyakārikātharvavedīyamāṇḍūkyop aniṣat*. Ānandāśrama Sanskrit Series, Vol. 10. Poona: Ānandāśrama Press.

Kunhan Raja, Chittenjoor. 1935. *Daśopaniṣads*. Adyar: Theosophical Society.

Lesimple, Emile. 1944. *Māṇḍūkya Upaniṣad et Kārikā de Gauḍapāda*. Paris: Adrien-Maisonneuve.

Lesimple, Emile 1948. *Taittirīya Upaniṣad*. Paris: Adrien-Maisonneuve.

Limaye, V. P., and R. D. Vadekar. 1958. *Eighteen Principal Upaniṣads*. Poona: Vaidika Saṃśodhana Maṇḍala.

Mārulakara, Śaṅkaraśāstrī Raṅganātha. 1937. *Daśopaniṣadāḥ*. Ānandāśrama Sanskrit Series, Vol. 106. Poona: Ānandāśrama Press.

Maue, Dieter. 1976. *Bṛhadāraṇyakopaniṣad I: Versuch einer kritischen Ausgabe nach akzentuierten Handschriften der Kānva-Rezension mit einer Einleitung und Anmerkungen*. PhD dissertation, University of Gießen.

Maury, Jacqueline. 1943. *Muṇḍaka Upaniṣad*. Paris: Adrien-Maisonneuve.

Morgenroth, Wolfgang. 1958. *Chāndogya-Upaniṣad. Versuch einer kritischen Ausgabe mit einer Übersetzung und einer Übersicht über ihrer Lehren*. Inaugural-Dissertation, Friedrich-Schiller-Universität Jena.

Olivelle, Patrick. 1996. *Upaniṣads: Translated from the Original Sanskrit*. Oxford: Oxford University Press.

Olivelle, Patrick. 1998. *The Early Upaniṣads: Annotated Text and Translation*. New York: Oxford University Press.

Pāṭhaka, Śrīdharaśāstrī. 1915. *Iśakenakaṭhopaniṣadaḥ*. Ānandāśrama Sanskrit Series, Vol. 76. Poona: Ānandāśrama Press.

Phanśîkar, Vâsudev Laxman Shâstrî. 1904. *The Twenty-Eight Upaniṣads*. Bombay: Nirnaya-Sagara Press.

Phanśîkar, Vâsudev Laxman Shâstrî. 1913. *Īśādyaṣṭottaraśatopaniṣadaḥ* [108 Upaniṣads]. Bombay: Nirṇaya-Sāgara Press.

Pérez Coffie, Carlos A. 1994. *Bṛhadāraṇyakopaniṣad II: Critical Edition of the Second Chapter of the Kāṇva Recension according to Accented Manuscripts with a Critical-Exegetical Commentary*. PhD diss., Harvard University.

Rājavāḍe, Vaijanātha Śarman. 1889. *Saṭīkādvayaśāṃkarabhāṣyopetā Kāṭhakopaniṣat*. Poona: Ānandāśrama Press.

Renou, Louis. 1943a. *Kaṭha Upaniṣad*. Paris: Adrien-Maisonneuve.

Renou, Louis. 1943b. *Īśā Upaniṣad*. Paris: Adrien-Maisonneuve.

Renou, Louis. 1943c. *Kena Upaniṣad*. Paris: Adrien-Maisonneuve.

Renou, Louis. 1948. *Kauṣītaki Upaniṣad*. Paris: Adrien-Maisonneuve.

Röer, Eduard. 1850a. *The Brihad Aranyaka Upanishad with the Commentary of Sankara Acharya and the Gloss of Ananda Giri*. Bibliotheca Indica, Vol. 2. Calcutta: Baptist Mission Press. [Kāṇva recension].

Röer, Eduard. 1850b. *The Chhandogya Upanishad with the Commentary of Sankara Acharya and the Gloss of Ananda Giri*. Bibliotheca Indica, Vol. 3. Calcutta: Baptist Mission Press.

Röer, Eduard. 1850c. The Taittiriya and Aitareya Upanishads with the Commentary of Sankara Acharya, and the Gloss of Ananda Giri, and the Swetaswatara Upanishad with the Commentary of Sankara Acharya. Bibliotheca Indica, Vol. 6. Calcutta: Baptist Mission Press.

Röer, Eduard. 1850d. *The Isa, Kena, Katha, Prasna, Munda, and Mandukya Upanishads with the Commentary of Sankara Acharya, and the Gloss of Ananda Giri.* Bibliotheca Indica, Vol. 7. Calcutta: Baptist Mission Press.

Roy, Rammohun. 1818. *Upanishad.* Calcutta: n.p. [Sanskrit text of *Kaṭha*, *Īśā*, *Kena*, and *Muṇḍaka* in Bengali script].

Rudolf, Otto. 1936. *Die Katha Upanishad.* Berlin: A. Toepelman.

Senart, Émile. 1930. *Chāndogya-Upaniṣad.* Paris: Société d'édition "Les Belles Lettres."

Senart, Émile. 1934. *Bṛhadāraṇyaka-Upaniṣad.* Paris: Société d'édition "Les Belles Lettres."

Silburn, Aliette. 1948. *Śvetāśvatara Upaniṣad.* Paris: Adrien-Maisonneuve.

Silburn, Lilian. 1950. *Aitareya Upaniṣad.* Paris: Adrien-Maisonneuve.

Tatya, Tukaram. 1891. *Twelve Principal Upaniṣads.* Bombay: Bombay Theosophical Publication.

Vaidya, Raṅganāthaśāstrī. 1915. *Chāndogyopaniṣat: Nityānandakṛta mitākṣarāvyākhyāsametā.* Ānandāśrama Sanskrit Series, Vol. 79. Poona: Ānandāśrama Press.

Veṇegāvakara, Śāstrī Śaṃkara. 1911. *Bṛhadāraṇyakopaniṣat.* Ānandāśrama Sanskrit Series, Vol. 64. Poona: Ānandāśrama Press.

Vidyarnava, Srisa Chandra. 1926. *The Maitri Upaniṣat.* Allahabad: Panini Office.

Vidyasagara, Jibananda. 1873. *Chāndogyopaniṣat.* Calcutta: Sucharoo Press.

Vidyasagara, Jibananda. 1875. *The Brihadaranyaka Upanishat.* Calcutta: Beadon Press.

Witzel, Michael. 2004. *Kaṭha Āraṇyaka: Critical Edition with a Translation into German and an Introduction.* Cambridge, MA: Department of Sanskrit and Indian Studies, Harvard University.

Source Texts in Translation

Anquetil-Duperron, Abraham H. 1801–1802. *Oopnek'hat.* Strasbourg: Frères Levault [Latin translation of fifty Upaniṣads.]

Charpentier, Jarl. 1928–1929. "Kāṭhaka Upaniṣad Translated with an Introduction and Notes." *Indian Antiquary* 58: 201–207 and 221–229, and 59: 1–5.

Colebrooke, Henry Thomas. 1805. "On the Védas, or Sacred Writings of the Hindus." In *Asiatic Researches* 8: 369–476. [Includes the *Aitareya Upaniṣad*].

Deussen, Paul. 1897. *Sechzig Upanishad's des Veda.* Leipzig: F. A. Brockhaus. Translated by V. M. Bedekar and Gajanan Balkrishna Palsule as *Sixty Upanishads of the Veda.* 2 vols. Delhi: Motilal Banarsidass, 1980.

Easwaran, Eknath. 1987. *The Upanishads.* Petaluma, CA: Nilgiri Press.

Gambhirananda, Swami. 1957–1958. *Eight Upanisads, with the Commentary of Śaṅkarācārya.* 2 vols. Calcutta: Advaita Ashrama.

Hamm, Frank-Richard. 1968–1969. "Chāndogyopaniṣad VI. Ein erneuter Versuch." *Wiener Zeitschrift für die Kunde Südasiens und Archiv für indische Philosophie* 12–13: 149–159.

Hume, Robert E. 1921. *The Thirteen Principal Upanishads.* Oxford: Oxford University Press.

Jamison, Stephanie W., and Joel P. Brereton. 2014. *The Rigveda: The Earliest Religious Poetry of India.* 3 vols. Oxford: Oxford University Press.

Jones, William. 1799. "Ísávásyam; or, an Upanishad from the Yajur Veda." In *The Works of William Jones*, Vol. VI, 423–425. London: G. G. and J. Robinson.

Katz, Vernon, and Thomas Egenes. 2015. *The Upanishads.* New York: Jeremy P. Tarcher.

Kriyananda Saraswati, Swami. 1975. *Nine Principal Upanishads.* Munger: Bihar School of Yoga.

Limaye, Vishnu Prabhakar, and Ranganath Dattatraya Vadekar. 1958. *Eighteen Principal Upanisads*, vol. I. Poona: Vaidika Saṃśodhana Maṇḍala.

Mitra, Rájendralála. 1862. *The Chhándogya Upanishad of the Sáma Veda.* Calcutta: Baptist Mission Press.

Muir, John. 1858–1870. *Original Sanskrit Texts on The History of the People of India, Their Religion and Institutions.* 5 vols. London: Williams & Norgate.

Müller, Friedrich Max. 1879–1884. *The Upaniṣads.* Oxford: Clarendon Press.

Oberlies, Thomas. 1995. "Die Śvetāśvatara-Upaniṣad: Einleitung—Edition und Übersetzung von Adhyāya I." *Wiener Zeitschrift für die Kunde Südasiens und Archiv für indische Philosophie* 39: 61–102.

Oberlies, Thomas. 1996. "Die Śvetāśvatara-Upaniṣad. Edition und Übersetzung von Adhyāya II–III." *Wiener Zeitschrift für die Kunde Südasiens und Archiv für indische Philosophie* 40: 123ff.

Oberlies, Thomas. 1998. "Die Śvetāśvatara-Upaniṣad. Edition und Übersetzung von Adhyāya IV–VI." *Wiener Zeitschrift für die Kunde Südasiens und Archiv für indische Philosophie* 42: 77ff.

Olivelle, Patrick. 1996. *Upaniṣads: Translated from the Original Sanskrit.* Oxford: Oxford University Press.

Olivelle, Patrick. 1998a. *The Early Upaniṣads: Annotated Text and Translation.* New York: Oxford University Press.

Otto, Rudolf. 1936. *Die Katha-Upanishad, übertragen und erläutert.* Berlin: Alfred Töpelmann.

Purohit Swami, Shree, and William Butler Yeats. 1937. *Ten Principal Upanishads.* London: Faber & Faber.

Radhakrishnan, Sarvepalli. 1953. *The Principal Upaniṣads.* London: G. Allen & Unwin.

Rau, Wilhelm. 1964. "Versuch einer deutschen Übersetzung der Śvetāśvatara-Upaniṣad." *Asiatische Studien* 17: 25–46.

Rau, Wilhelm. 1965. "Versuch einer deutschen Übersetzung der Muṇḍaka-Upaniṣad." *Asiatische Studien* 18–19: 216–226.

Rau, Wilhelm. 1971. "Versuch einer deutschen Übersetzung der Kāṭhaka-Upaniṣad." *Asiatische Studien* 25: 158–174.

Rau, Wilhelm. 1981. "Versuch einer deutschen Übersetzung der *Taittirīya Upaniṣad*." In Peter Herde (ed.): *Festschrift der wissenschäftlichen Gesellschaft an der J. W. Goethe-Universität*, 349–373. Wiesbaden: Steiner.

Rixner, Thaddäus A. 1808. *Versuch einer neuen Darstellung der uralten indischen All-Eins-Lehre*. Nürnberg: Stein.

Roebuck, Valerie. 2003. *The Upanishads*. London: Penguin Books.

Röer, Eduard. 1853. *The Taittaríya, Aitaréya, Śvétáśvatara, Kéna, Íśá, Kaṭha, Praśna, Muṇḍaka and Máṇḍúkya Upanishads*. Calcutta: Bishop's College Press.

Röer, Eduard. 1856. *The Brihad Áranyaka Upanishad*. Calcutta: Baptist Mission Press.

Roy, Rammohun. 1816a. *Translation of the Céna Upanishad, One of the Chapters of the Sáma Véda*. Calcutta: Hindoostanee Press.

Roy, Rammohun. 1816b. *Translation of the Íshopanishad, One of the Chapters of the Yajur Véda*. Calcutta: Hindoostanee Press.

Roy, Rammohun. 1819a. *Translation of the Moonduk-Opunishud of the Uthurvu-Ved*. Calcutta: Times Press.

Roy, Rammohun. 1819b. *Translation of the Kut'h-Opunishud of the Ojoor-Ved*. Calcutta: Times Press.

Vasu, Srisa Chandra. 1909. *Isa, Kena, Kaṭha, Praśna, Muṇḍaka and Mâṇḍūkya*. Allahabad: Panini Office.

Vasu, Srisa Chandra. 1910. *Chhândogya Upanishad*. Allahabad: Panini Office.

Vasu, Srisa Chandra. 1913–1916. *Bṛihadāraṇyaka-Upaniṣad*. Allahabad: Panini Office.

Whitney, William Dwight. 1890. "The Kaṭha-Upaniṣad." *Journal of the Royal Asiatic Society* 21: 88–112.

Secondary Literature

Alsdorf, Ludwig. 1950. "Contributions to the Textual Criticism of the Kaṭhopaniṣad." *Zeitschrift der deutschen morgenländischen Gesellschaft* 100: 621–637.

App, Urs. 2010. *The Birth of Orientalism*. Philadelphia: University of Pennsylvania Press.

Aranjaniyil, Gabriel. 2002. "Transmigration in the Upaniṣads and the Greek Thought." *Journal of Dharma* 27.2: 137–148.

Aurobindo. 1972. *Sri Aurobindo Birth Century Library*. 30 vols. Pondicherry: Shri Aurobindo Ashram.

Aurobindo. 2006. *Autobiographical Notes and Other Writings of Historical Interest (The Complete Works of Sri Aurobindo, Volume 36)*. Pondicherry: Sri Aurobindo Ashram Press.

Beall, Edgar F. 1986. "Syntactical Ambiguity at Taittirīya Upaniṣad 2.1." *Indo-Iranian Journal* 29: 97–102.

Belvalkar, Shripad Krishna, and Ramachandra Dattatray Ranade. 1927. *The History of Indian Philosophy*, Vol. 2: *The Creative Period*. Reprint New Delhi: Oriental Books Reprint Corporation 1974.

Bhat, Govind Keshav. 1973. "Teacher-Pupil Relationship (in the Context of Upaniṣadic Literature)." *Annals of the Bhandarkar Oriental Research Institute, Baroda (ABORI)* 54: 173–178.

Bhatt, Vishnu Prasad. 1973. "On the Meaning of the Title 'Bṛhadāraṇyaka Upaniṣad.'" *Journal of the Oriental Institute, Baroda* 23: 18–26.

Bhatt, Vishnu Prasad. 1975. "Genealogies in the Bṛhadāraṇyaka Upaniṣad." *Journal of the Ganganatha Jha Kendriya Sanskrit Vidyapeetha* 31: 63–70.

Bhattacharya, Dipak. 1978. "The Doctrine of Four in the Early Upaniṣads and Some Connected Problems." *Journal of Indian Philosophy* 6: 1–34.

Bhattacharya, Vidhushekhara. 1925. "The Māṇḍūkya Upaniṣad and the Gauḍapāda Kārikās." *Indian Historical Quarterly* 1: 119–125 and 295–302.

Bhattacharya, Vidhushekhara. 1941. "A Linguistic Note on the Muṇḍaka Upaniṣad." *Indian Historical Quarterly* 17: 89–91.

Biardeau, Madeleine. 1965. "*Ahaṃkāra*: The Ego Principle in the Upaniṣads." *Contributions to Indian Sociology* 8: 62–84.

Black, Brian. 2003. *Dialogue as Discourse: Priests, Kings, and Women in the Early Upaniṣads*. PhD dissertation, School of Oriental and African Studies, University of London.

Black, Brian. 2007. *The Character of the Self in Early India: Priests, Kings, and Women in the Early Upaniṣads*. Albany: State University of New York Press.

Black, Brian. 2011a. "Rethinking the Upaniṣadic *Vaṃśas:* Teacher Lineages as a Literary Genre." *Religions in South Asia* 5: 51–77.

Black, Brian. 2011b. "The Rhetoric of Secrecy in the Upaniṣads." In Steven E. Lindquist (ed.): *Religion and Identity in South Asia and Beyond: Essays in Honor of Patrick Olivelle*, 101–125. London: Anthem.

Black, Brian. 2011c. "Ambhaṭṭa and Śvetaketu: Literary Connections between the Upaniṣads and Early Buddhist Narratives." *Journal of the American Academy of Religion* 79.1: 136–161.

Black, Brian. 2012. "Senses of Self and Non-Self in the Upaniṣads and Nikāyas." In Irina Kuznetsova, Jonardon Ganeri, and Chakravarthi Ram-Prasad (eds.): *Hindu and Buddhist Ideas in Dialogue: Self and No-Self*, 11–27. Burlington: Ashgate.

Black, Brian. 2013. "Ethics in the Upaniṣads." In Vibha Chaturvedi and Pragati Sahni (eds.): *Understanding Ethics*, 69–82. New Delhi: Macmillan India.

Black, Brian. 2018. "The Upaniṣads and the *Mahābhārata*." In Signe Cohen (ed.): *The Upaniṣads: A Complete Guide*, 186–199. London: Routledge.

Black, Brian, and Jonathan Geen. 2011. "The Character of 'Character' in Early South Asian Religious Narratives: An Introductory Essay." *Journal of the American Academy of Religion* 79: 6–32.

Bock-Raming, Andreas. 1996. "Einige Bemerkungen zur Komposition des 6. Prapāṭhaka der Chāndogya-Upaniṣad." *Asiatische Studien* 50: 577–589.

Bodewitz, Hendrik W. 1985. "Yama's Second Boon in the Kaṭha Upaniṣad." *Wiener Zeitschrift für die Kunde Südasiens und Archiv für indische Philosophie* 29: 5–26.

Bodewitz, Hendrik W. 1986. "The Cosmic, Cyclical Dying (*parimara*). *Aitareya Brāhmaṇa* 8.28 and *Kauṣītaki Upaniṣad* 2.11–12." In Wolfgang Morgenroth (ed.): *Sanskrit and World Culture*, 438–443. Berlin: Akademie-Verlag.

Bodewitz, Hendrik W. 1992. "Uddākaka's Experiments with Salt (ChU 6.13)." *Annals of the Bhandarkar Oriental Research Institute* 72–73: 423–436.

Bodewitz, Hendrik W. 1994. "Magic and Ritual: The Second Chapter of the Kauṣītaki Upaniṣad." In Shrikant S. Bahulkar and Sucheta Paranjpe (eds.): *Śruti-cintāmaṇi: Prof. C. G. Kashikar Felicitation Volume*, 51–57. Poona: Tilak Maharashtra Vidyapeeth.

Böhtlingk, Otto von. 1897a. "Bemerkungen zu einigen Upanishaden." *Berichte über die Verhandlungen der königlich sächsischen Gesellschaft der Wissenschaften zu Leipzig, Philologisch-historische Classe* 49: 78–100.

Böhtlingk, Otto von. 1897b. "Kritische Beiträge." *Berichte über die Verhandlungen der königlich sächsischen Gesellschaft der Wissenschaften zu Leipzig, Philologisch-historische Classe* 49: 127–138.

Böhtlingk, Otto von. 1901. "Kritische Beiträge." *Berichte über die Verhandlungen der königlich sächsischen Gesellschaft der Wissenschaften zu Leipzig, Philologisch-historische Classe* 53: 7–17.

Bouy, Christian. 1997. "La Māṇḍūkya Upaniṣad et l'Āgamaśāstra: Concordance externes et citations." *Wiener Zeitschrift für die Kunde des Morganlandes und Archiv für indische Philosophie* 41: 119–158.

Brereton, Joel P. 1986. "'Tat Tvam Asi' in Context." *Zeitschrift der deutschen morgenländischen Gesellschaft* 136: 98–109.

Brereton, Joel P. 1988. "Unsounded Speech: Problems in the Interpretation of BU(M) 1.5.10 = BU(K) 1.5.3." *Indo-Iranian Journal* 31: 1–10.

Brereton, Joel P. 1990. "The Upaniṣads." In William T. de Bary and Irene Bloom (eds.): *Approaches to the Asian Classics*, 115–135. New York: Columbia University.

Brereton, Joel P. 1991. "Cosmographic Images in the *Bṛhadāraṇyaka Upaniṣad*." *Indo-Iranian Journal* 34: 1–17.

Brereton, Joel P. 1996. "Yājñavalkya's Curse." *Studien zur Indologie und Iranistik* 20: 47.

Brereton, Joel P. 1997. "Why Is a Sleeping Dog Like a Vedic Sacrifice? The Structure of an Upaniṣad *bramhodya*." In Michael Witzel (ed.): *Inside the Texts, Beyond the Texts*, 1–14. Columbia, MO: South Asia Books.

Brereton, Joel P. 2006. "The Composition of the Maitreyī Dialogue in the *Bṛhadāraṇyaka Upaniṣad*." *Journal of the American Oriental Society* 126.3: 323–345.

Brereton, Joel P., and Stephanie W. Jamison. 2020. *The Rigveda: A Guide*. Oxford: Oxford University Press.

Brodbeck, Simon. 2018. "The Upaniṣads and the *Bhagavadgītā*." In Signe Cohen (ed.): *The Upaniṣads: A Complete Guide*, 200–218. London: Routledge.

Bronkhorst, Johannes. 1996. "Śvetaketu and the Upanayana." *Asiatische Studien* 50: 592–601.

Bronkhorst, Johannes. 2007. *Greater Magadha: Studies in the Culture of Early India*. Leiden: Brill.

Bryant, Edwin. 2004. *The Quest for the Origins of Vedic Culture*. Oxford: Oxford University Press.

Chand, Tara. 1943. "Dara Shikoh and the Upanishads." *Islamic Culture* 17: 397–413.

Chandra, Pratap. 1971. "Was Early Buddhism Influenced by the Upaniṣads?" *Philosophy East and West* 21: 317–324.

Cohen, Signe. 1998. "The *Śvetāśvatara Upaniṣad* Reconsidered." *Acta Orientalia* 59: 150–178.

Cohen, Signe. 2008. *Text and Authority in the Older Upaniṣads*. Leiden: Brill.

Cohen, Signe. 2018. *The Upaniṣads: A Complete Guide*. London/New York: Routledge.

Cohen, Signe. 2022. "The *Bhagavadgītā* and the Kṛṣṇa Yajurveda Upaniṣads." *International Journal of Hindu Studies* 26: 327–362. https://doi.org/10.1007/s11407-022-09323-0.

Coomaraswamy, Ananda K. 1935. "A Study of the Kaṭha Upaniṣad (IV.1)." *Indian Historical Quarterly* 11: 570–584.

Deshpande, Saroj. 1989. "*Idam* in the Cosmogonical Statements in Early Upaniṣads." *Annals of the Bhandarkar Oriental Research Institute, Baroda* 70: 255–261.

Deussen, Paul. 1919. *The Philosophy of the Upanishads*. Translated by Alfred S. Geden. Edinburgh: T&T Clark.

Distelbarth, Margret. 1989. *Mandukya Upanishad: Die vier Füsse des Bewusstseins*. Gladenbach: Hinder und Deelman.

Ebeling, Florian. 2001. "'Geheimnis' und 'Geheimhaltung' in den Hermetica der Frühen Neuzeit." In Ann-Charlott Trepp and Hartmut Lehmann (eds.): *Antike Weisheit und kulturelle Praxis: Hermetismus in der Frühen Neuzeit*, 63–80. Göttingen: Vandenhoeck & Ruprecht.

Edgerton, Franklin. 1921. "The Upaniṣads: What Do They Seek, and Why?" *Journal of the American Oriental Society* 49.2: 97–121.

Fakirbhai, Dhanjibhai. 1965. *Kristopanishad (Christ-Upanishad)*. Bangalore: Christian Institute for the Study of Religion and Society.

Falk, Harry. 1986. "Vedisch *upaniṣád*." *Zeitschrift der deutschen morgenländischen Gesellschaft* 136.1: 80–97.

Findly, Ellison Banks. 1985. "Gārgī at the King's Court: Women and Philosophic Innovation in Ancient India." In Yvonne Y. Haddad and Ellison Banks Findly (eds.): *Women, Religion, and Social Change*, 37–58. New York: State University of New York Press.

Fišer, Ivo. 1957. "Yājñavalkya in the Śruti Tradition of the Veda." *Acta Orientalia* 10: 55–58.

Fort, Andrew O. 1994. "Going or Knowing? The Development of the Idea of Living Liberation in the Upaniṣads." *Journal of Indian Philosophy* 22: 379–390.

Freedman, Yitzhak. 2012. "Altar of Words: Text and Ritual in *Taittirīya Upaniṣad* 2." *Numen* 59.4: 322–343.

Friš, Oldřich. 1955. "Two Readings of the Kaṭhopaniṣad." *Archiv Orientalní* 23: 6–9.

Fürst, Alfons. 1916. "Der Sprachgebrauch der älteren Upaniṣads verglichen mit dem der früheren vedischen Perioden und dem des klassisschen Sanskrit." *Zeitschrift für vergleichende Sprachforschung auf dem Gebiete der indogermanischen Prachen* 47: 1–82.

Ganeri, Jonardon. 2012. "Dārā Shukoh and the Transmission of the Upanishads to Islam." In William Sweet (ed.): *Migrating Texts and Traditions*, 2nd ed., 177–188. Ottawa: University of Ottawa Press.

Ganeri, Jonardon. 2018. "The Upaniṣadic Episteme." In Signe Cohen (ed.): *The Upaniṣads: A Complete Guide*, 146–152. London: Routledge.

Gandhi, Mohandas K. 1958–1994. *The Collected Works of Mahatma Gandhi*. 90 vols. New Delhi: Publications Division, Government of India.

Goldman, Robert P. 2019. "Creating Context: Ādiśaṅkarācārya's Reading of the Three *Ākhyāyikās* of the *Chāndogya Upaniṣad*." In Lauren M. Bausch (ed.): *Self, Sacrifice, and Cosmos: Vedic Thought, Ritual, and Philosophy. Essays in Honor of Professor Ganesh Umakant Thite's Contribution to Vedic Studies*, 161–181. Delhi: Primus Books.

Goman, Thomas G., and Ronald S. Laura. 1972. "A Logical Treatment of Some Upaniṣadic Puzzles and Changing Perceptions of Sacrifice." *Numen* 19: 52–67.

Gonda, Jan. 1977. "Notes on the Kaṭha Upaniṣad." In Suniti Kumar Chatterji (ed.): *Some Aspects of Indo-Iranian Literary and Cultural Traditions (V. G. Paranjpe Commemoration Volume)*, 60–70. Delhi: Ajanta.

Goto, Toshifumi. 2005. "Yājñavalkya's Characterization of the Ātman and the Four Kinds of Suffering in Early Buddhism." *Electronic Journal of Vedic Studies* 12.2: 70–84.

Gren-Eklund, Gunilla. 1978. *A Study of the Nominal Sentences in the Oldest Upaniṣads*. Uppsala: Almquist & Wiksell.

Gren-Eklund, Gunilla. 1984. "Causality and the Method of Connecting Concepts in the Upaniṣads." *Indologica Taurinensia* 12: 107–118.

Grinshpon, Yohanan. 1998. "The Upaniṣadic Story and the Hidden *Vidyā*: Personality and Possession in the *Bṛhadāraṇyakopaniṣad*." *Journal of Indian Philosophy* 26: 373–385.

Grinshpon, Yohanan. 2003. *Crisis and Knowledge: The Upaniṣadic Experience and Storytelling*. New Delhi: Oxford University Press.

Haas, George C. O. 1922. "Recurrent and Parallel Passages in the Principal Upaniṣads and the Bhagavad Gītā." *Journal of the American Oriental Society* 42: 1–43.

Hacker, Paul. 1995. *Philology and Confrontation*. Albany: State University of New York Press.

Halbfass, Wilhelm. 1988. *India and Europe: An Essay in Understanding*. Albany: State University of New York Press.

Hanefeld, Erhardt. 1976. *Philosophische Haupttexte der älteren Upaniṣaden*. Wiesbaden: Otto Harrassowitz.

Hauer, J. W. 1930. "Die Śvetāśvatara-Upaniṣad." *Zeitschrift der deutschen morgenländischen Gesellschaft* 84: 97–102.

Hauschild, Richard. 1961. "Über altbekannte und neuentdekte metrische Stücke in der Chāndogya-Upaniṣad." *Die Sprache* 7: 32–63.

Helfer, James S. 1968. "The Initiatory Structure of the Kaṭhopaniṣad." *History of Religions* 7: 348–367.

Hillebrandt, Alfred. 1914. "Textkritische Bemerkungen zur Kaṭha- und Praśna-Upaniṣad." *Zeitschrift der deutschen morgenländischen Gesellschaft* 68: 579–582.

Hiltebeitel, Alf. 1984. "Two Kṛṣṇas on One Chariot: Upaniṣadic Imagery and Epic Mythology." *History of Religions* 24.1: 1–26.

Hirst, Jacqueline Suthren. 2018. "*Ātman* and *Brahman* in the Principal Upaniṣads." In Signe Cohen (ed.): *The Upaniṣads: A Complete Guide*, 107–120. London: Routledge.

Hock, Hans H. 2002. "The Yājñavalkya Cycle in the *Bṛhad-Āraṇyaka-Upaniṣad*." *Journal of the American Oriental Society* 122.2: 278–286.

Hopkins, Edward Washburn. 1901. "Notes on the Śvetāśvatara, the Buddhacarita, etc." *Journal of the American Oriental Society* 22: 380–389.

Horsch, Paul. 1968. "Buddhismus und Upaniṣaden." In Jan C. Heesterman, Godard H. Schokker, and Vadasery I. Subramoniam (eds.): *Pratidānam: Indian, Iranian, and Indo-European Studies Presented to Franciscus Bernardus Jacobus Kuiper on his Sixtieth Birthday*, 462–477. The Hague: Mouton.

Insler, Stanley. 1989–1990. "The Shattered Head Split and the Epic Tale of Śakuntalā." *Bulletin d'études indiennes* 7–8: 97–139.

Jacob, George Adophus. 1891. *Upaniṣadvākyakośaḥ: A Concordance to the Principal Upaniṣads and the Bhagavadgītā*. Bombay Sanskrit Series, Vol. 39. Bombay: Government Central Book Depot.

Jayashanmukham, N. 1994. "The Anti-Asceticism of the Īśāvasya Upaniṣad." *Brahmavidya, The Adyar Library Bulletin* 58: 21–40.

Jayashanmukham, N. 1999. "The *Kena* and the Vedic Ideal of Fulfilment." *Journal of Indian Council of Philosophical Research* 11: 93–108.

Ježic, Mislav. 2016. "*Īśā-Upaniṣad:* History of the Text in the Light of the Upaniṣadic Parallels." In Joel P. Brereton (ed.): *The Vedas in Indian Culture and History: Proceedings of the Fourth International Vedic Workshop* (Austin, Texas 2007), 181–203. Florence: Società Editrice Fiorentina.

Johnston, Edward H. 1930. "Some Sāṃkhya and Yoga Conceptions of the Śvetāśvatara Upaniṣad." *Journal of the Royal Asiatic Society* 106: 855–878.

Johnston, Edward H. 1939. "On Some Difficulties of the Kaṭha Upaniṣad." In Sumitra Mangesh Katre and Parashuram Krishna Gode (ed.): *A Volume of Eastern and Indian Studies Presented to Professor F. W. Thomas*, 122–127. Bombay: Karnatak Publishing House.

Jones, Richard H. 1981. "Vidyā and Avidyā in the Īśā Upaniṣad." *Philosophy East and West* 31: 79–87.

Keith, Arthur Berriedale. 1925. *The Religion and Philosophy of the Veda and the Upanishads*. Reprint Delhi: Motilal Banarsidass 1989.

Killingley, Dermot. 1997. "The Paths of the Dead and the Five Fires." In Peter Connolly and Sue Hamilton (eds.): *Indian Insight: Buddhism, Brahmanism, and Bhakti*, 1–20. London: Luzac Oriental.

Killingley, Dermot. 2018a. "The Older Vedas and the Upaniṣads." In Signe Cohen (ed.): *The Upaniṣads: A Complete Guide*, 43–57. London: Routledge.

Killingley, Dermot. 2018b. "*Karma* and Rebirth in the Upaniṣads." In Signe Cohen (ed.): *The Upaniṣads: A Complete Guide*, 121–132. London: Routledge.

Killingley, Dermot. 2018c. "Knowledge and Liberation in the Upaniṣads." In Signe Cohen (ed.): *The Upaniṣads: A Complete Guide*, 133–145. London: Routledge.

Killingley, Dermot. 2018d. "The Upaniṣads and the Emergence of Theism." In Signe Cohen (ed.): *The Upaniṣads: A Complete Guide*, 161–173. London: Routledge.

Killingley, Dermot. 2018e. "The Upaniṣads and Yoga." In Signe Cohen (ed.): *The Upaniṣads: A Complete Guide*, 174–185. London: Routledge.

Killingley, Dermot. 2018f. "The Upaniṣads and Later Hinduism." In Signe Cohen (ed.): *The Upaniṣads: A Complete Guide*, 219–230. London: Routledge.

Killingley, Dermot. 2018g. "The *Bṛhadāraṇyaka Upaniṣad*." In Signe Cohen (ed.): *The Upaniṣads: A Complete Guide*, 247–258. London: Routledge.

Killingley, Dermot. 2018h. "The *Chāndogya Upaniṣad*." In Signe Cohen (ed.): *The Upaniṣads: A Complete Guide*, 259–268. London: Routledge.

Knipe, David M. 1972. "One Fire, Three Fires, Five Fires: Vedic Symbols in Transition." *History of Religions* 12.1: 28–41.

Krishnan, Yuvraj. 1982. "The *Śvetāśvatara-Upaniṣad* and the Doctrine of *Karma* in Indian Philosophy." *Vishveshvaranand Indological Journal* 20: 25–28.

Kuiper, F. B. J. [Franciscus Bernardus Jacobus]. 1960–1961. "The Interpretation of *Chāndogya Upaniṣad* III.2." *Bhāratīya Vidyā* 20–21: 36–39.

Kunst, Arnold. 1968. "Some Notes on the Interpretation of the Śvetāśvatara Upaniṣad." *Bulletin of the School of Oriental and African Studies* 31: 304–314.

Lighthiser, Timothy P. 2002. "Upaniṣads: A Contribution towards Bibliography of Secondary Literature and Reviews." *Journal of Indian Philosophy* 30: 85–101.

Lincoln, Bruce. 2006. "How to Read a Religious Text: Reflections on Some Passages of the *Chāndogya Upaniṣad*." *History of Religions* 46: 127–139.

Lindquist, Steven E. 2004. "Yājñavalkya's Riddle (BĀU 3.9.28K)." In Madhav Deshpande (ed.): *Problems in Sanskrit and Vedic Literature: Felicitation Volume in Honor of G. U Tithe*, 192–211. New Delhi: Indian Book Center.

Lindquist, Steven E. 2008. "Gender at Janaka's Court: Women in the *Bṛhadāraṇyaka Upaniṣad* Reconsidered." *Journal of Indian Philosophy* 36.3: 405–426.

Lindquist, Steven E. 2011a. "Lines of Descent and Dissent: Genealogy, Narrative, and the Upaniṣads." *Religions of South Asia* 5.1/2: 29–49.

Lindquist, Steven E. 2011b. "Literary Lives and a Literal Death: Yājñavalkya, Śākalya, and an Upaniṣadic Death Sentence." *Journal of the American Academy of Religion* 79.1: 33–57.

Lindquist, Steven E. 2011c. "One Yājñavalkya . . . Two? On the (Questionable) Historicity of a Literary Figure." In Steven E. Lindquist (ed.): *Religion and Identity in South Asia and Beyond*, 69–81. New York: Anthem Press.

Lindquist, Steven E. 2017. "The Upaniṣads." In Sarah Johnston (ed.): *Narrating Religion*, 303–316. Farmington Hills, MI: Macmillan Reference.

Lindquist, Steven E. 2018a. "The Social Background: Caste and Gender in the Upaniṣads." In Signe Cohen (ed.): *The Upaniṣads: A Complete Guide*, 81–92. London: Routledge.

Lindquist, Steven E. 2018b. "Prominent Characters in the Upaniṣads." In Signe Cohen (ed.): *The Upaniṣads: A Complete Guide*, 95–106. London: Routledge.

Lipner, Julius J. 1978. "An Analysis of Kaṭha 6.4 and 5, with Some Observations on Upaniṣadic Method." *Journal of Indian Philosophy* 5: 243–253.

Little, Charles Edgar. 1900. *A Grammatical Index to the Chāndogya Upaniṣad*. New York: American Book Co.

Lopez, Carlos. 1997. "Food and Immortality in the Veda: A Gastronomic Theory?" *Electronic Journal of Vedic Studies* 3.2. Online at https://hasp.ub.uni-heidelberg.de/journals/ejvs/article/view/824.

Lowe, Ramesh Kumar. 1985. "A Note on the Construction of the Kaṭha Upaniṣad." *Vishveshvaranand Indological Journal* 23: 31–35.

Luyster, Robert W. 1970. "The Concept of the Self in the Upaniṣads: Its Origins and Symbols." *Philosophy East and West* 20: 51–61.

Madaio, James. 2017. "Rethinking Neo-Vedānta: Swami Vivekananda and the Selective Historiography of Advaita Vedānta." *Religions* 8: 101. doi:10.3390/rel8060101.

Mayeda, Sengaku. 1967. "On Śaṅkara's Authorship of the Kenopaniṣadbhāṣya." *Indo-Iranian Journal* 10: 33–55.

Minor, Robert N. 1978. *Sri Aurobindo: The Perfect and the Good*. Calcutta: Minerva.

Morgenroth, Wolfgang. 1970. "Die Lehre des Uddālaka Āruṇi, Ch. Up. VI. Bemerkungen zur Textkritik und Interpretation." *Archiv Orientálni* 38: 33–44.

Morgenroth, Wolfgang. 1981. "Glossen in der Chāndogya Upaniṣad." *Indologica Tauriensia* 8–9: 283ff.

Myers, Michael. 1993. "*Tat Tvam Asi* as Advaitic Metaphor." *Philosophy East and West* 43: 229–242.

Nakamura, Hajime. 1955. "Upaniṣadic Tradition and the Early School of Vedānta as Noticed in Buddhist Scripture." *Harvard Journal of Asiatic Studies* 18: 74–104.

Nakamura, Hajime. 1967–1968. "Yājñavalkya and Other Upaniṣadic Thinkers in a Jain Tradition." *Adyar Library Bulletin* 31–32: 216–228.

Nakamura, Hajime. 1983. *A History of Early Vedānta Philosophy*. Translated by Trevor Leggett et al. Delhi: Motilal Banarsidass.

Oberlies, Thomas. 1988. "Die Śvetāśvatara Upaniṣad. Eine Studie ihrer Gotteslehre." *Wiener Zeitschrift für die Kunde Südasiens und Archiv für indische Philosophie* 32: 35–62.

Oldenberg, Hermann. 1915. *Die Lehre der Upanishaden und die Anfänge des Buddhismus*. Göttingen: Vandenhoeck & Ruprecht.

Olivelle, Patrick. 1992. *Saṃnyāsa Upaniṣads: Hindu Scriptures on Asceticism and Renunciation*. New York: Oxford University Press.

Olivelle, Patrick. 1996. "*Dharmaskandhāḥ* and *Brahmasaṃsthaḥ*: A Study of Chāndogya Upaniṣad 2.23.1." *Journal of the American Oriental Society* 116: 205–219.

Olivelle, Patrick. 1998b. "Unfaithful Transmitters: Philological Criticism and Critical Editions of the Upaniṣads." *Journal of Indian Philosophy* 26: 173–187.

Olivelle, Patrick. 1999. "Young Śvetaketu: A Literary Study of an Upaniṣadic Story." *Journal of the American Oriental Society* 119.1: 46–70.

Patton, Laurie L. 2004. "Veda and Upaniṣad." In Sushil Mittal and Gene Thursby (eds.): *The Hindu World*. New York: Routledge, 37–51.

Pokazanyeva, Anna. "Mind within Matter: Science, the Occult, and the (Meta) Physics of Ether and Akasha." *Zygon* 51.2 (2016): 318–346.

Pollock, Sheldon. 2011. "The Revelation of Tradition: *śruti*, *smṛti*, and the Sanskrit Discourse of Power." In Federico Squarcini (ed.): *Boundaries, Dynamics and Construction of Traditions in South Asia*, 41–61. London: Anthem Press.

Przyluski, Jean. 1929a. "Le loi de symétrie dans la Chāndogya-upaniṣad." *Bulletin of the School of Oriental and African Studies* 5: 489–497.

Przyluski, Jean. 1929b. "Les influences populaires dans la Chāndogya-upaniṣad." *Bulletin of the School of Oriental and African Studies* 5: 303–306.

Przyluski, Jean, and Etienne Lamotte. 1933. "Bouddhisme et Upaniṣad." *Bulletin de l'École française d'Extrême-Orient* 32: 141–169.

Puligandla, Ramakrishna. 1999. "The Message of the Māṇḍūkya Upaniṣad: A Phenomenological Analysis of Mind and Consciousness." *Indian Philosophical Quarterly* 26: 221–231.

Radhakrishnan, Sarvepalli. 1923. *Indian Philosophy*. 2 vols. London: George Allen & Unwin.

Ranade, Ramachandra Dattatrya. 1926. *A Constructive Survey of Upanishadic Philosophy, Being an Introduction to the Thought of the Upanishads*. Reprint Bombay: Bharatiya Vidya Bhavan, 1986.

Reat, N. Ross. 1977. "Karma and Rebirth in the Upaniṣads and Buddhism." *Numen* 24: 163–185.

Reinvang, Rasmus. 2000. "A Critical Survey of the Dialogue between Yājñavalkya and Maitreyī in the *Bṛhadāraṇyaka Upaniṣad* 2.4 and 4.5." *Acta Orientalia* 61: 145–202.

Renard, Philip. 1995. "Historical Bibliography of Upaniṣads in Translation." *Journal of Indian Philosophy* 23: 223–246.

Renou, Louis. 1948. "Les relations du *Śatapathabrāhmaṇa* avec la *Bṛhadāraṇyakopaniṣad* et la personnalité de Yājñavalkya." *Indian Culture* 14: 75–89.

Renou, Louis. 1953. "Le passage des Brāhmaṇa aux Upaniṣad." *Journal of the American Oriental Society* 73: 138–144.

Renou, Louis. 1955. "Remarques sur la Chāndogya Upaniṣad." *Etudes védiques et pāṇinéennes* 1: 91–102.

Rocher, Ludo. 1973. "Iha ced aśakad boddhum (Kaṭhopaniṣad 6.4)." *Vishveshvaranand Indological Journal* 11: 7–18.

Rocher, Rosane. 1977–1978. "Nathaniel Brassey Halhed on the Upaniṣads (1787)." *Annals of the Bhandarkar Oriental Research Institute* 58–59: 279–289.

Ruben, Walter. 1947. *Die Philosophen der Upaniṣaden*. Bern: A. Francke.

Salomon, Richard. 1981. "A Linguistic Analysis of the Muṇḍaka Upaniṣad." *Wiener Zeitschrift für die Kunde Südasiens* 25: 91–105.

Salomon, Richard. 1986. The *Śvetāśvatara* and the *Nāsadīya*: Vedic Citations in a Śaiva Upaniṣad." *Adyar Library Bulletin* 50: 165–178.

Salomon, Richard. 1991. "A Linguistic Analysis of the Praśna Upaniṣad." *Wiener Zeitschrift für die Kunde Südasiens* 35: 47–74.

Schelling, Friedrich (ed.). 1856–1861. *Friedrich Wilhelm Joseph Schelling's Sämmtliche Werke*. Stuttgart: Cotta.

Schiltz, Elizabeth. 2018. "The *Kaṭha Upaniṣad*." In Signe Cohen (ed.): *The Upaniṣads: A Complete Guide*, 317–325. London: Routledge.

Schneider, Ulrich. 1963. "Die Komposition der Aitareya-Upaniṣad." *Indo-Iranian Journal* 7: 58–69.

Schneider, Ulrich. 1967. "Upaniṣad Philosophie und früher Buddhismus." *Saeculum* 18: 245–263.

Schopenhauer, Arthur. 1873. *Arthur Schopenhauers Sämmtliche Werke*. Vol. 1. Leipzig: F. A. Brockhaus.

Schopenhauer, Arthur. 1958. *The World as Will and Representation*. 2 vols. Translated by E. F. J. Payne. New York: Dover Publications.

Schopenhauer, Arthur. 1966. *Der handschriftlliche Nachlass*. Edited by Arthur Hübscher. 5 vols. Frankfurt am Main: W. Kramer.

Schrader, Otto. 1933. "A Critical Study of Īśopaniṣad." *The Indian Antiquary* 82: 205–212.

Schrödinger, Erwin. 2012. *What Is Life? With Mind and Matter and Autobiographical Sketches*. Cambridge: Cambridge University Press.

Schubring, Walther. 1969. *Isibhāsiyāiṃ: Aussprüche der Weisen*. Hamburg: De Gruyter.

Sedlar, Jean W. 1982. *India in the Mind of Germany: Schelling, Schopenhauer, and Their Times*. Washington, DC: University Press of America.

Sharma, Ashok K. 1928. "The Relation between Buddhism and Upanishads." *The Monist* 38: 443–477.

Sharma, Arvind. 1983. "The Significance of the Epithet Śūdra as Applied to Jānaśruti in Chāndogya Upaniṣad 4.2.5." *Journal of the Asiatic Society (Calcutta)* 25: 31–36.

Sharma, Arvind, and Katherine K. Young. 1990. "The Meaning of *Ātmahano janāḥ* in *Īśā Upaniṣad* 3." *Journal of the American Oriental Society* 110: 595–602.

Sharma, Shubhra. 1985. *Life in the Upanishads*. Delhi: Abhinav Publications.

Slaje, Walter, 2001a. "Water and Salt (I): Yājñavalkya's *saindhava dṛṣṭānta* (BĀU II 4, 12)." *Indo-Iranian Journal* 44: 25–57.

Slaje, Walter. 2001b. "Water and Salt (II): 'Material' Causality and Hylozoic Thought in the Yājñavalkya-Maitreyī Dialogue." *Indo-Iranian Journal* 44: 299–327.

Slaje, Walter. 2002. "Water and Salt (III): An Analysis and New Translation of the Yājñavalkya-Maitreyī Dialogue." *Indo-Iranian Journal* 45: 205–20.

Smith, Caley Charles. 2019. "Adhiyajna: Towards a Performance Grammar of the Vedas." *Religions* 10: 394. doi:10.3390/rel10060394.

Smith, R. Morton. 1952. "Birth of Thought—I: Taittirīya and Aitareya Upaniṣads." *Annals of the Bhandarkar Oriental Research Institute, Poona* 23: 97–113.

Smith, R. Morton. 1965. "Some Notes on the Bṛhadāraṇyakopaniṣad." *Vishveshvaranand Indological Journal* 3.2: 181–191.

Smith, R. Morton. 1975. "Thinking-Class Theism: The Śvetāśvatara Upaniṣad." *Journal of the Oriental Institute, Baroda* 24: 317–337.

Smith, R. Morton. 1976. "The Muṇḍaka Upaniṣad Reconsidered." *Vishveshvaranand Indological Journal* 14: 17–40.

Sogani, Kamal Chand. 1964. "The Concept of Avidyā and the Characteristics of the Converted and Perverted Souls According to the Upaniṣads, the Gītā, and Jainism." *Indian Philosophy and Culture* 9: 33–36.

Söhnen, Renate. 1981. "Die Einleitungsgeschichte der Belehrung des Uddālaka Āruṇi: Ein Vergleich der drei Fassungen Kauṣītaki 1.1, Chāndogya 5.3 und Bṛhadāraṇyaka 6.21–8." *Studien zur Indologie und Iranistik* 7: 177–213.

Söhnen, Renate. 1985. "Zur Metrik der Kaṭha-Upaniṣad." *Münchener Studien zur Sprachwissenschaft* 44: 215–238.

Tesla, Nikola. 1930. "Man's Greatest Achievement." *New York American*, July 6.

Thieme, Paul. 1951–1952. "Der Weg durch den Himmel nach der Kaushitaki-Upanishad." Reprinted in Paul Thieme, *Kleine Schriften*, vol. 1. Wiesbaden: Franz Steiner, 1984: 82–99.

Thieme, Paul. 1965. "*Īśopaniṣad* (=*Vājasaneyi-Saṃhitā* 40) 1–14. *Journal of the American Oriental Society* 85.1: 89–99.

Tola, Fernando, and Carmen Dragonetti. 1987. "Yogic Trance in the Oldest Upaniṣads." *Annals of the Bhandarkar Oriental Research Institute* 68: 377–392.

Tsuchida, Ryutaro. 1985. "Some Remarks on the Text of the Śvetāśvatara-Upaniṣad." *Journal of Indian and Buddhist Studies* 34: 460–468.

Tsuji, Naoshiro. 1955. *Studies in Indology and Buddhology Presented in Honor of Professor Susumu Yamaguchi on the Occasion of His Sixtieth Birthday.* Kyoto: Hazokan Kyoto.

Vanita, Ruth. 2003. "The Self Is Not Gendered: Sulabha's Debate with King Janaka." *National Women's Studies Association Journal* 15.2: 76–93.

Varenne, Jean. 1968. "Notes sur la Śikṣāvallī." In Jean Filliozat (ed.): *Mélanges d'indianisme à la mémoire de Louis Renou*, 733–736. Paris: Éditions de Boccard.

Velankar, Hari Damodar. 1968. "The Ṛgvedic Origin of the Story of Naciketas (ṚV X.135)." In Jean Filliozat (ed.): *Mélanges d'indianisme à la memoire de Louis Renou*, 763–772. Paris: Éditions de Boccard.

Vivekananda, Swami. 1915. *The Complete Works of Swami Vivekananda*. Vol. 1. Calcutta, India: Advaita Ashrama.

Vivekananda, Swami. 1989. *The Complete Works of Swami Vivekananda*. Vol. 5. Calcutta, India: Advaita Ashrama.

Wecker, Otto. 1906. "Der Gebrauch der Kasus in der älteren Upaniṣad-Literatur vergleichen mit der Kasuslehre der indischen Grammatiker." *Beiträge zur Kunde der indogermanischen Sprachen* 30: 1–61 and 177–207.

Welden, Ellwood Austin. 1914. "The Sāṃkhya Teachings in the Maitrī Upaniṣad." *American Journal of Philology* 35: 32–51.

Weller, Friedrich. 1953. *Versuch einer Kritik der Kaṭhopaniṣad*. Berlin: Akademie-Verlag.

Werner, Karel. 1975. "Religious Practice and Yoga in the Time of the Vedas, Upaniṣads and Early Buddhism." *Annals of the Bhandarkar Oriental Research Institute* 56: 179–194.

Wezler, Albrecht. 1982. "Zum Verständnis von Chāndogya-Upaniṣad 5.1.12." *Studien zur Indologie und Iranistik* 8–9: 147–168.

Whitney, William Dwight. 1890. "Böhtlingk's Upanishads." *American Journal of Philology* 11.4: 407–439.

Witzel, Michael. 1987a. "On the Localisation of Vedic Texts and Schools (Materials on Vedic Śākhās, 7)." In Gilbert Pollet (ed.): *India and the Ancient World: History, Trade and Culture before A. D. 650*, 173–213. Leuven: Department Orientalistik.

Witzel, Michael. 1987b. "The Case of the Shattered Head." *Studien zur Indologie und Iranistik* 13–14: 363–415.

Witzel, Michael. 1997. "Macrocosm, Mesocosm, and Microcosm: The Persistent Nature of 'Hindu' Beliefs and Symbolic Forms." *International Journal of Hindu Studies* 1.3: 501–539.

Witzel, Michael. 2003a. "Vedas and Upaniṣads." In Gavin Flood (ed.): *The Blackwell Companion to Hinduism*, 68–101. Oxford: Blackwell.

Witzel, Michael. 2003b. "Yājñavalkya as Ritualist and Philosopher, and His Personal Language." In Siamak Adhami (ed.): *Patimāna: Essays in Iranian, Indo-European, and Indian Studies in Honor of Hanns-Peter Schmidt*, 103–143. Costa Mesa, CA: Mazda Publishers.

Witzel, Michael. 2009. "Female Rishis and Philosophers in the Veda?" *Journal of South Asia Women Studies* 11.1. Online at http://nrs.harvard.edu/urn-3:HUL.InstRepos:9886300.

Wood, Thomas E. 1990. *The Māṇḍūkya Upaniṣad and the Āgama Śāstra: An Investigation into the Meaning of the Vedānta*. Honolulu: University of Hawai'i Press.

Zaehner, Robert Charles. 1969. "Sexual Symbolism in the Śvetāśvatara Upaniṣad." In Joseph Kitagawa et al. (eds.): *Myth and Symbols: Studies in Honor of Mircea Eliade*, 209–215. Chicago: University of Chicago Press.

Zimmermann, Robert. 1915. "Some Remarks on the Chronology of the Upaniṣads." *Indian Antiquary* 44: 130–132 and 177–180.

Subject Index

For the benefit of digital users, indexed terms that span two pages (e.g., 52–53) may, on occasion, appear on only one of those pages.

Brahma Upaniṣad 9
Brahmavidyā Upaniṣad 9, 200
Brahmo Samaj 201–2
Bṛghuvallī Upaniṣad 200
Bṛhadāraṇyaka Upaniṣad 1–3, 4, 8, 33–34, 35, 37, 41, 43, 46, 49–51, 52, 53–55, 56, 57, 61, 62, 63–64, 65–66, 69–71, 72–73, 74, 80, 81–82, 83, 87–88, 94, 96–98, 99–100, 101, 104–6, 108, 110–13, 115–16, 118, 119–22, 123, 124, 125–26, 127, 128–29, 130–31, 134, 136–37, 139, 140, 141–43, 148–50, 153–54, 155, 157–58, 161, 162, 165, 166–67, 168, 169–70, 171–73, 174, 175, 176–78, 179–80, 181, 182–83, 184, 186–87, 189, 196–97, 200, 201, 211–12, 214, 219–22
Bṛhadratha 93, 119–20
Bṛhajjābāla Upaniṣad 9
Buddha 39–42, 43, 44, 49–50
Buddhism 39–40, 41–43, 44, 49–51, 101, 150, 194, 213, 214

Caitanya 196–97
Caṇḍālas 117, 149–50
Caraṇavyūha 3–4, 67
caste 114–16, 117, 118–19, 201–2, 207. See also *varṇa*
Cayce, Edgar 218
Chāgaleya Upaniṣad 200
Chāndogya Brāhmaṇa 53–54, 74–75
Chāndogya Upaniṣad 1–2, 4, 5, 8, 21, 35, 36, 37–38, 41, 46, 49–50, 51, 52, 53, 56, 57, 66, 68–69, 74–78, 94, 96, 97–98, 104–6, 107–10, 111–12, 113, 116, 117, 118–20, 122, 127, 128–29, 130, 134, 137, 143, 144, 149–50, 154, 155–56, 159–60, 161, 162, 163, 165, 168, 169–70, 173–74, 175, 176, 179–80, 181–82, 183–85, 186–87, 192–93, 200, 201, 211–12, 213, 219–22
chariot 22, 26–27, 42–43, 54–55, 56, 84–86, 93, 109–10
Citra Gāṅgyāyani 79, 111, 118, 168, 182
cows 18, 22–23, 25–27, 71, 76–77, 105–6, 109–10, 120, 122, 162, 166–67, 168, 181
Cūlikā Upaniṣad 200

Dakṣiṇāmūrti Upaniṣad 9
Dara Shikoh 96–97, 197–201, 208–9, 221
Darśana Upaniṣad 9
Dāsa 18–19
Dāsyu 18–19
Dattātreya Upaniṣad 9
death 12–13, 30, 34, 36, 38, 40, 42–43, 44, 56, 57, 58, 69–70, 71, 72, 74, 77, 79, 82, 85–86, 102, 105, 108, 109–10, 111, 127, 128–29, 131, 134–35, 140, 141, 143–44, 148–49, 150, 151, 152, 154, 161, 163, 168, 172–73, 174–75, 177–78, 182, 186, 187–88, 189, 205, 214
demon 10–11, 17–18, 27, 74, 78, 109–10, 134, 161, 164, 184–85, 186–87
Devī Upaniṣad 9, 11, 97–98
Dhammapada 42–43
dharma 31, 101, 109, 113, 205
Dharmasūtras 13
Dhyānabindu Upaniṣad 9, 97–98, 200
dice 22–23, 107–8
Dīgha Nikāya 41–42
Dṛpta Bālāki. *See* Bālāki

Ekākṣara Upaniṣad 8–9
Eliot, T. S. 74, 187
Emerson, Ralph Waldo 216

Index of Passages Cited

For the benefit of digital users, indexed terms that span two pages (e.g., 52–53) may, on occasion, appear on only one of those pages.